Indigenous Diplomacy and the Rights of Peoples

Indigenous Diplomacy and the Rights of Peoples

ACHIEVING UN RECOGNITION

James (Sa'ke'j) Youngblood Henderson

Purich Publishing Ltd.
Box 23032, Market Mall Post Office, Saskatoon, SK, Canada, S7J 5H3
Phone: (306) 373-5311 Fax: (306) 373-5315 Email: purich@sasktel.net
Website: www.purichpublishing.com

Library and Archives Canada Cataloguing in Publication

Henderson, James Youngblood, 1944–
Indigenous diplomacy and the rights of peoples : achieving un recognition / James (Sakej) Youngblood Henderson.

Includes index.
ISBN 978-1-895830-35-4

1. Indigenous peoples – Legal status, laws, etc. 2. United Nations. General Assembly. Declaration on the Rights of Indigenous Peoples. 3. Indigenous peoples (International law). I. Title.

K3247.H45 2008 341.4'852 C2008-904858-X

Edited, designed, and typeset by Donald Ward.
Cover design by Duncan Campbell.
Index by Ursula Acton.
Printed and bound in Canada.

Purich Publishing gratefully acknowledges the assistance of the Government of Canada, through the Book Publishing Industry Development Program, and the Government of Saskatchewan, through the Cultural Industries Development Fund, for its publishing program.

This book is printed on 100 per cent post-consumer, recycled, and ancient-forest-friendly paper.

To Helga Lomosits, PhD

our *Austrian sister*
for managing our heart of darkness
by listening, translating, and caring
finding just the right thing to say to make us understand
and letting us know what they really said;
your efforts inspired and stitched together the impossible

Contents

Appendices

1. Foreword

THE GREEN LIGHTS OF THE VOTING SYSTEM in the United Nations General Assembly signaled a new global consensus on September 12, 2007, when member states overwhelmingly endorsed the Declaration on the Rights of Indigenous Peoples (2007).[1] This remarkable vote formally brought to an end the nation-states' history of oppression of Indigenous peoples. One hundred and forty-three countries affirmed the Human Rights Council's recommendation to extend human rights and fundamental freedoms to Indigenous peoples. This new standard in international human rights was consensually established, and its implementation is to be pursued in a spirit of partnership and mutual respect. The signing of the Declaration signaled the nation-states' resolve to accept the UN's systemic obligations toward Indigenous peoples.

Many people educated in the grand narratives of empire and colonialism were surprised by the UN's action, wondering how these poor, defeated, powerless peoples – the vulnerable bottom of global humanity – had found allies in the global assembly, with its complex structures and protocols, and the voice to assert their human rights. How did the Indigenous peoples of the world find the diplomatic skill to defeat colonial ideology through peaceful dialogue? Where did the young, Eurocentrically educated Indigenous peoples who had never experienced traditional civilizations find the desire for cultural restoration and the will to fight for it? How did the elders and the lost or assimilated generations come to join this network? How is it possible that so many diverse peoples came to the knowledge of how to proceed on the Declaration, without leaders, advice, or instruction?

The extension of human rights to Indigenous peoples is difficult to reconcile with the historical legacy of violence and discrimination against them. A shift of consciousness is required to comprehend both the transformational politics involved in the Declaration and the new global consensus. The politics that surrounded the Declaration was a cognitive struggle, a challenge to existing ways of thinking about humanity. It was a manifestation of shared persuasion. The new, emergent consciousness displaces the familiar discriminatory models of imperialism and colonialism, based on racism. Yet it leaves the poverty and vulnerability of Indigenous peoples intact.

Many insights have gone into the creation of the Indigenous diplomacy movement and network. Many perspectives exist, each incomplete. Thousands of Indigenous peoples participated over thirty years in the development of Indigenous diplomacy. They refused to accept the colonial narrative, refused to stand by and watch the destruction of Indigenous legal traditions and knowledge in the structuring of a global order. This book is my attempt to share my insights as a participant, a technical officer, and a legal advisor into these processes for the *Sante Mawio'mi* (Grand Council) of the Mi'kmaw Nation and the Four Directions Council, a non-governmental organization (NGO Status II) of the UN for Indigenous peoples. My perspective is based on events in Canada and North America, with which I am most familiar.

This work is concerned with the rise of Indigenous diplomacy and its international achievements, especially the latest chapter in this unfinished adventure, the Declaration as an achievement of Indigenous peoples in the UN system as self-determining people with human rights. The appendices that contain the relevant UN documents reveal the interrelatedness of the achievements derived from Indigenous diplomacy, which reflect its steady manifestation within the United Nations.

I will attempt to explain, based on my involvement, how Indigenous peoples have achieved the art of the impossible in the realm of the improbable. To place the Declaration in context, it is important to recognize four insights. First, Indigenous peoples reflect diverse humanities, independent of race science and biological concepts, which comprise many overlapping and shifting categories in different knowledge and legal systems.[2] These peoples have shared concerns about the territorial appropriations of their homelands, about cultural and cognitive imperialism, and the exploitation by colonial and decolonized Eurocentric states. The UN system recognizes the key features of Indigenous peoples as a significant historical attachment to territory, an explicit commitment to cultural distinctiveness, and a resolve to preserve both territory and culture as a means of achieving community. Second, Indigenous nations and peoples are never just a product of state ideologies, never just a product of an educational system. They are always able to relate to traditional teachings and Indigenous knowledge, regardless of how state, religious, or educational systems attempt to assimilate them. Third, Indigenous teachings and legal traditions live on in the unconsciousness and the consciousness of the peoples who were oppressed by colonization; they were passed from one generation to another through stories, art, and ceremonies so that each people could restore them at the right time and transform them into the Declaration. Fourth, the Indigenous diplomatic network learned that it could not settle accounts with colonialism in a way that would allow the spirit of colonialism to penetrate our own consciousness, our own activities, and thus our own spirits. We learned that such remedies turn us to revenge, cruelty, and the ideologies of imported colonial strategies rather than giving us the ability to overcome these strategies.

Indigenous peoples have suffered and sacrificed for the Declaration and other UN achievements. We have endured forced assimilation and unjust relationships with the colonizers and their institutions. We have been scorned, persecuted, and jailed. As an Indigenous elder commented about the Declaration, "The text is made up of so many teardrops of the horrible times." These sufferings oblige us to practise justice as healing, not punishment. We have found that liberation from personal anger and misery could occur only in the context of justice and dignity. Those who have really suffered were usually the first to comprehend and share this truth.

Indigenous peoples created the Declaration with their own style of diplomacy with the nation-states and the UN system. This diplomacy is as important as the principles in the Declaration. The tenacity of Indigenous diplomacy and the legal traditions that inform it are the deep structure of the Declaration. It was up to Indigenous peoples to persuade the UN member states of our own worth and dignity. We did not receive any substantial help from the powerful colonial settler states, and thus owe little gratitude to Australia, Canada, New Zealand, or the United States for our human rights. Rather, our gratitude is owed to the postcolonial nations in the General Assembly and their 21st-century sensibilities.

2. The Legacy of Empire

WITH THE TREATY OF WESTPHALIA IN 1648 the monarchs of Western and Central Europe established the primacy of states based on territorial control. This treaty invented not only modern international law but also the natural rights of individuals in national law.[3] The treaty provided the framework for European imperialism and colonialism and the legal and moral struggle to comprehend and resolve the complex issues of Indigenous rights and justice. Thus, international law as it emerged over the centuries was closely connected to a meta-narrative of empire, imperialism, colonialism, and racism.

The European law of nations consists of customary law and the conventional principles that govern the relations and dealings of nations. The tribes, nations, confederacies, and peoples – the "Indigenous others" – struggled to comprehend European ambitions, reconcile them through treaties, and ultimately survive alongside the colonialists. At first, European thought represented the Indigenous societies of America as "ideal societies," which generated new visions of utopia.[4] Their ambitions, however, invoked one of the legacies of imperial Rome – with its idea of *civitas*, barbarians, and conquest – about the justice of enslaving the Indigenous inhabitants of conquered lands. In the great Christian debates about natural law conducted by the conquistador élite in Spain at the beginning of colonization (ca. 1530-50), the Vitorian/de las Casasian idea of "Indians" as human confronted Aristotle's theory of natural slavery with mixed results.[5] The conclusion of this debate was that the Indigenous inhabitants of Central and South America were humans with souls, that they were the true owner of the lands, that they had legal rights requiring protection by discovering powers, but that they were in need of Christian salvation. The enslavement of these peoples was not justified.

In the natural law of Europe, Hugo Grotius, a prominent father of public international law, affirmed Vitoria, rejecting the theory of discovery and colonialist claims that Indigenous territories were empty of humans. For Grotius, all lands inhabited by humans, despite reservations about their cultural and religious inclinations, were not subject to discovery by foreign nations.[6] This principle became part of the customary European law of nations, and led to a more dignified way of dealing with Indigenous nations by means of consensual treaty relationships.[7] These treaties became part of the conventional law of nations, which derives from international agreements and may take any form the contracting parties agree upon.

In 1651, the English philosopher Thomas Hobbes's discussion of Indians in "the state of nature" became the foundation on which the concept of artificial man-sovereignty and empires were built.[8] He established the paradigm that Indigenous peoples were savages who lived in a state of primal anarchy without culture, society, or laws. To justify ancient wrongs and vast privileges, international law and colonialism further characterized the savage as a repository of negative values. Those who were attempting to construct a rational theory of the state began from the notion that the Indigenous inhabitants of the Americas were in an uncivilized state of nature compared to the superior, civilized societies of Europe. This false distinction allowed the colonizers to rationalize their disregard for the moral or human rights of Indigenous peoples. When the missionary and educational efforts toward slavery or assimilation failed, the colonizers saw the Indigenous inhabitants of the lands they had invaded as degenerates stuck in an irreversibly primitive condition. This rationalization projected Indigenous peoples into the past, creating the vanishing race theory, inventing the ideological constructions of racism, and allowing colonial legal systems to ignore the humanity of Indigenous nations. It created the international "otherness" of Indigenous nations and tribes, which became a deadly classification.

At the Congress of Vienna (1814-15), European states and statesmen developed international law governing the rights between a nation or nations and the citizens or subjects of other nations. They rejected natural law, developing instead a Eurocentric, positivist view of international law.

They rejected customs as a valid element of international or public law, and excluded Indigenous nations, their treaties, and peoples as valid subjects of international law.[9] Indigenous nations or peoples were deprived of their customary and conventional rights in public international law. In private international law, which deals with conflicts among persons, natural or juridical, arising out of situations having significant relationship to more than one nation, Indigenous people were deprived of their humanity and rights. In public or private international law, Indigenous people and peoples became non-persons because of European concepts of "race" or "society." Therefore, international law did not then – nor was it required to – impose on European nations any standard of justice or duties with respect to Indigenous treaties, peoples, or individuals. It thus came to regard empire and colonialism as both natural and progressive rather than unjust and oppressive.

The ideological twins of violence and imagination developed the concepts of empire, imperialism, colonialism, and racism in international law; the European nations then applied them around the earth. These twins provide a comprehensive explanation of national and international law, the nation-state, as well as injustice and terrorism toward Indigenous others. They are inverted reflections of one another. Violence controls the physical contexts of genocide and legal authority,[10] while imagination controls the intellectual justification of violence in the context of cognitive and cultural imperialism.[11] The structure of these concepts has deep roots in the development of rational justifications. Justified violence has been the author and consequence of the meta-narratives of "civilization" and "progress" that inform Eurocentric colonization and modernity. At the core of justified aggression is a deep fascination with violence[12] as a means of establishing and maintaining social order. Rule by fear is the method, discourse, and remedy of justified violence. It is an ideology that legitimates the systematic extermination or control of "others."[13] It operates within the legal order and as resistance to that order.

The idea of empire and the colonial state was built on violence toward Indigenous others. It was built on cruelty, destruction, and genocide both in Europe and in the discovered lands. Eurocentrism established its primary elements of individual and subjective interests in the construction of an artificial political and social order regulated by violence and punishment. It established its ideology on the principle that no natural community of common ends exists, and that group life is an artificial creature of individual wills. Thus, individuals and their various desires, values, and interests are locked in a perpetual struggle with one another to create cultures and states that require protection against the ravages of self-interest. The need for protection in conflicts of desire helps explain the importance of general and impersonal legislation as well as the reliance on coërcive enforcement. But the same factors empower a fascination with terror – the systematic use of violence unlimited by law – as a device of political organization. Fear, the rhetoric of exclusion of the other, and punishment displace community. The less ability individuals and groups have to rely on participation in shared needs and communities, the more violence is needed.

The transition to political order and law in the colonial empires grew out of the idea that laws must be capable of coërcive enforcement. Without justified violence against local majorities and their traditions, the notion of a system of law and the development of exclusive state authority in the colonies could not have emerged. These legal systems originated and exist as "thought-objects, products of particular discourses."[14] They are understandable only in terms of colonial discourses, and have never been universally applicable to precolonial or postcolonial societies.[15] The Eurocentric impulse toward centralized state control, racism, and social engineering established the negative framework of the local "other." The adoption of violence as a means of establishing and maintaining empires and social order has broad consequences. Professor Enrico Catellani of the University of Padua noted that international law at the beginning of the 20th century was moving way from the mid-century ideas of justice and equality toward the increasing use of force in the determining the fate of peoples.[16] French international lawyer Charles Solomon wrote that "the history of all colonies begins with violence, injustice and shedding of blood: the result is everywhere the same; the disappearance of the native races (*des races sauvages*) coming into contact with civilized races."[17] Violence was the distinct strategy applied to those who were not Europeans, by Europeans who still acted from a position of superiority toward other peoples; capitulation or puppet regimes, consular jurisdiction, and colonial wars had become banal aspects of the international everyday. Advancing colonial powers had oppressed and impoverished Indigenous peoples to the point of extinction, and accepted this as the inevitable consequence of modernity.

In Eurocentric colonization, as in modernity,[18] the ancient enthrallment with despotic violence as a means of control turned predatory; it became persistent, determined, and aggressive. Modernity was animated by Enlightenment thought, with its emphasis on the individual, empiricism, secularism, rationality, progress, and science. Modernity views society as something to be analyzed and explained in a rational, scientific manner to yield universal laws of human behaviour and knowledge to advance the human condition through social engineering: human societies, like the environment, could be mastered, reconstructed, and improved. Modernity involves the rise of secular forms of government, culminating in the modern nation-state displacing lord, master, priest, king, patriarch, kin, and local communities.

It has been estimated that, from the time of first contact, 80 per cent of the Indigenous others have been annihilated as the result of "developmental" or "utilitarian" genocide by the meta-narratives of modernity and postmodernism.[19] In the 20th century, violence against Indigenous others continued. There has "probably been more genocide, ethnocide, and extinction of tribal or ethnic groups than in any time in history."[20] With the rise of the nation-state and its fascination with violence and power, tens of million of "savage" Indigenous others perished, sixty million others were annihilated in the 20th century, often after nation-states generated projects of social engineering or assimilation.[21] These meta-narratives and their cognitive systems were innovative. They were not based on custom or natural law; rather, they were based on social science and being untraditional. The independent state or individual is free of any attachment – to family, to the environment, to the past, to others – that would characterize "traditional" societies. These meta-narratives reject tradition, but cannot escape its historical roots.[22]

The experiences of Indigenous peoples throughout the long-term violence of imperialism – from exploration to discovery, from the rise of colonies with territorial boundaries to the creation of independent nation-states – has created multi-generational traumas. These traumas have generated the compliance and resistance of the international otherness of peoples to the deceits and unspoken assumptions of the "us-them," as well as the familiar consequences of activities designated as globalism or developmentalism. The colonizers, on the grounds of safety, order, law, and peace have justified these experiences with violence, but usually violence prevents these goals from being achieved. The idea of violence underpins the structures of the legal consciousness of Eurocentrism and empire, relying on the binary opposition of the colonizer and the colonized;[23] each creates the conceptual ideologies of empire, the nation-state, and its geopolitical system.

The violence of colonialism is ancient, but its imaginative component is modern. This modern, cognitive manifestation that began when European societies colonized and enslaved Indigenous peoples has been labelled "Eurocentrism."[24] An extension of Kant's state of nature theory and the Enlightenment, it involved the political and cultural need to categorize and stigmatize. J. M. Blaut argues that Eurocentrism is the colonizers' model of the world.[25] It represents the cognitive forces of European thought about humanity artificially detached from the environment. Europeans and their educational institutions have proclaimed this imaginative component to create a universal civilization. Eurocentrism has evolved, through time, into a generative model, a structured intellectual worldview,[26] and a structure of power that favours Eurocentric perspectives. Eurocentrism does not claim to be a privileged norm. That would be an argument about cultural relativism, which asserts that values arise out of specific cultural contexts.[27] Instead, Eurocentric thought claims to be universal and general.[28] Noël summarizes the function of universalism in colonialism:

> To present himself as the ideal human type, the dominator often invoked irreducible laws sanctioned by Nature, God, or History. In his view, the power he exercised over the oppressed was not so much the result of undue reliance on force as the effect of uncontrollable imperatives, if not a Higher Will. In relation to the universal model that the oppressor seemed to represent, the dominated always appeared to be afflicted with some defect or intrinsic failing.[29]

Eurocentrism is an ultra-theory in modern thought and educational systems. It has many names and manifestations. It is known as epistemological diffusionism,[30] which operates as a general framework for many smaller theories: historical, geographical, psychological, sociological, and philosophical. Blaut argues that diffusionism is based on two axioms: first, that most human communities are uninventive; and second, that a few human communities (or places, or cultures) are inventive and thus remain permanent centres of cultural change or progress. On a global scale, this gives us a model of a humanity with a single, inventive, progressive centre – roughly, European peoples – and a surrounding, uninventive periphery.[31] Diffusionism asserts that European peoples and their descendants are modern, inventive, and progressive, whereas others are historical, stagnant, and unchanging; that the difference between the two races or peoples is intellectual or spiritual, something characteristic of the "European mind," the "European spirit," or "Western Man," which leads to creativity, imagination, invention, innovation, rationality, and a sense of honour or ethics – in other words, "universal values." The lack of these characteristics among Indigenous peoples is the reason for their lack of progress.

The ultra-theory is grounded in the dualism of an inside European identity and an outside international otherness,[32] which has been the intellectual framework of European colonialism. Geo-political maps that show each of the 192-odd nation-states of humanity in a different colour represent the theory. Humanity is viewed as a set of political states, with Europe situated as the centre of the planet. This map does not reveal human or ecological diversity; it reveals only the structural correspondence of the constructed nation-states.

Classic Eurocentric diffusionism asserted the myth of cognitive emptiness for most non-European peoples, and created the legal idea of *terra nullius*, or empty land. The proposition of emptiness rests on four premises, each layered upon the others:

1) A non-European region is empty, or nearly empty, of people, so settlement by Europeans does not displace any – or many – Indigenous peoples;
2) The inhabitants of these regions are mobile, nomadic wanderers; therefore European settlement violates no political sovereignty, since wanderers make no claim to territory;
3) The cultures of these peoples do not possess an understanding of private property, so the region is empty of property rights and claims; hence, colonial occupiers can freely give land to settlers, since no one owns it;

4) the international others are empty of intellectual creativity and spiritual values, sometimes described by Europeans as an absence of "rationality."[33]

Diffusionism asserts, as Blaut emphasizes, that the normal and natural way the international others progress, change for the better, or modernize, is by the cognitive assimilation or diffusion – or spread – of innovative ideas from European peoples, which flow into the Indigenous consciousness as air flows into a vacuum. This flow generally takes the form of ideas or products, through which European values are spread. It asserts that colonialism brings civilization, and is, in fact, the proper way that non-Europeans advance out of cognitive stagnation. Under colonialism, wealth is drawn out of the colonies and enriches the colonizers; European cultures and peoples have traditionally seen this as a normal relationship between European and Indigenous peoples. The Europeans come as bearers of these new, civilizing ideas, and the diffusion of these ideas is compensation for the confiscation of material wealth by Europe from non-Europe, although nothing can fully compensate Europeans for their gift of civilization, since there is always a possibility that ancient, atavistic traits will counter-diffuse back into the civilized core.

Michel Foucault locates at the outset of the colonizing period a shift in the fundamental mode by which knowledge is acquired. The activity of the Eurocentric mind, he writes, will

> no longer consist in *drawing things together,* in setting out on a quest for everything that might reveal some sort of kinship, attraction or secretly shared nature within them, but, on the contrary, in *discriminating,* that is, in establishing their identities. . . . In this sense, discrimination imposes upon comparison the primary and fundamental investigation of difference.[34]

As John Ralston Saul has noted, Eurocentric intellectuals have privileged this approach:

> The renewed and intense concentration on the rational element, which started in the seventeenth century, had an unexpected effect.

> Reason began, abruptly, to separate itself from and to outdistance the other more or less recognized human characteristics – spirit, appetite, faith and emotion, but also intuition, will and, most important, experience. This gradual encroachment on the foreground continues today. It has reached a degree of imbalance so extreme that the mythological importance of reason obscures all else and has driven the other elements into the marginal frontiers of doubtful respectability.[35]

Eurocentric thought and its rational approach established the imaginative strategy of difference and international othering.[36] Through this strategy of difference, European universities created an artificial construct of humanities and racism and spread it throughout humanity. As Albert Memmi explains, "Racism is the generalized and final assigning of values to real or imaginary differences, to the accuser's benefit and at his victim's expense, in order to justify the former's own privileges or aggression."[37] The strategy of racial superiority asserts Eurocentric privileges while discriminating against the international others in a violent and often inhuman way.[38]

Eurocentrism had profound consequences for human psychology, and has left a legacy of trauma, fear, and dread. No ecology, no culture, no people, and no psyche remain untarnished. The technology of social control and oppression is everywhere. The damage inflicted on the international others has been well documented, but it is little understood.[39] The European colonists created new orders, hierarchies, and governments by military or political force, believing in the superiority of Europeans over the colonized, the masculine over the feminine, the adult over the child, the historical over the ahistorical, and the modern or "progressive" over the traditional or "savage."

Eurocentric thinkers took it upon themselves to define human competencies and deviances among international otherness through a strategy of differences, creating political orders defined by polarities: the modern and the primitive, the secular and the non-secular, the scientific and the unscientific, the expert and the amateur, the normal and the abnormal, the developed and the underdeveloped, the vanguard and the led, the liberated and the savable.[40] Blaut tabulated the simplified characteristics of the dualism between the centre and the periphery:[41]

Characteristics of: Eurocentric Centre	International Otherness
Civilized	Savage
Progress	Stagnation
Inventiveness	Imitativeness
Rationality, intellect	Irrationality, emotion, instinct
Abstract thought	Concrete thought
Theoretical reasoning	Empirical, practical
Mind	Body, matter
Discipline	Spontaneity
Adulthood	Childhood
Sanity	Insanity
Science	Sorcery

Eurocentrism created new worldviews that were self-legitimizing. In this new world order, the colonial dominators called upon the colonized to justify their inferiority, and their forceful oppression was masked as progress.[42] Historian Lise Noël has captured the consequences of this cognitive reality for its oppositional dualism:

> Alienation is to the oppressed what self-righteousness is to the oppressor. Each really believes that their unequal relationship is part of the natural order of things or desires by some higher power. The dominator does not feel that he is exercising unjust power, and the dominated do not feel the need to withdraw from his tutelage. The dominator will even believe, in all good faith, that he is looking out for the good of the dominated, while the latter will insist that they want an authority more enlightened than their own to determine their fate.[43]

The cognitive legacy is an integral part of colonization and imperialism, false categories of race and racism, and the oppression of Indigenous peoples. In the actions and beliefs of the colonizing powers, it was considered natural and beneficial. The legacy constructed the general and consistent state actions toward Indigenous others as well as statements of state practices based on the belief in their legality (*opinio juris*).

In the eyes of the colonists, the empire brought European civilization and culture to Indigenous peoples. According to Eurocentrism, all cultures of humanity should throw off their ancient knowledge systems, heritages, customs, teachings, and traditions, and adopt market economies, nation-state governments, laws, and culture.

Many Indigenous nations and peoples challenged this worldview. They wanted to maintain significant aspects of their order, cultures, and traditions, often relying on treaties and agreements with the colonizing nation-state, and they wanted to incorporate their own values into institutions and markets, government and international relations. They challenged the European concept of the artificial nation-state, arguing that the concept may not work for all peoples. The UN decolonization processes adopted the paradigm of the European nation-state, thus blinding themselves to many Indigenous traditions of governance. The Indigenous nations noted that the knowledge systems and languages of the Indigenous peoples were not participating in Eurocentric "nationhood," which is not usually aligned with Indigenous traditions.

New normative declarations and instruments were necessary in international law to rebuke this custom and generate the practices that ought to be followed. Finding ways to generate new normative declarations became the task of the Indigenous diplomacy network within the United Nations system. These declarations had to move from being prescriptive of the violent legacy to normative visions of a new relationship; from acquiescence, beyond apologism, to transformation, to rights and ideal standards of conduct.

The Declaration is a major step toward establishing the normative vision. It seeks to eliminate the human rights violations suffered by Indigenous peoples and the nation-states' justification for their oppression. After centuries of humiliation and suffering, the overwhelming majority of nation-states of the UN General Assembly voted to extend human rights to Indigenous peoples worldwide.[44] The vision and negotiations that led to the Declaration have taken a difficult twenty years.

A brief understanding of the diplomatic struggle for Indigenous rights through the mechanism of the United Nations[45] reveals how urgent the need was for a declaration to replace the legacy of erroneous thought and law about Indigenous peoples. This involved decolonization, the elimination of racial discrimination, and human rights as the remedy for colonialism and racism.

3. The Failure of Decolonization for the Indigenous Others

THE DIPLOMATIC CHALLENGES THAT RESULTED IN the Declaration on the Rights of Indigenous Peoples rose in the public's eye when Indigenous peoples' campaigns for justice were ignored in the decolonization of nation-states, but the Indigenous vision was actually much older. The foundation of the movement resided in the Indigenous legal traditions that had informed the treaties with imperial powers, and the attempts, in the 1920s, of Haudenosaunee/Cayuga chief *Deskaheh* (Levi General), and Maori leader W. T. Ratana to bring the treaty status of Indigenous nations to the attention of the imperial community assembled in the League of Nations. The League had been established "for the purpose of affording mutual guarantees of political independence and territorial integrity to great and small states alike," and article 22 of its Covenant seemed to recognize Indigenous populations, requiring each member-nation to accept a "sacred trust of civilization."[46] This sacred trust was interpreted as a duty to promote the well-being and development of the "Indigenous population" of those "colonies and territories" that remained under their control. The term "Indigenous population" was used to distinguish colonial powers and peoples from peoples who were living under colonial domination.

The Haudenosaunee in 1923 and the Maori in 1925 applied for membership in the League of Nations, on the grounds that they be recognized as part of the sacred trust of civilization. The League categorized their claims as "domestic," and therefore outside its competency.[47]

The League of Nations' avoidance of these treaty issues effectively halted Indigenous diplomatic progress. Over the years, however, there slowly developed an unstructured movement of Indigenous peoples, while the Indigenous nations who had entered into treaties with European nations continued to press for their international status.

The horror of the two world wars, and the holocausts that resulted from and contributed to these global conflicts, revealed to humanity the weakness of international law and national sovereignty, and its reliance on legalized violence. The events of the first half of the 20th century raised profound questions about the validity of the belief that Western Europe represented the highest point of human achievement.

The creation of the United Nations after World War II inspired Indigenous peoples to press their claims in decolonization activities and human rights. The Charter of the UN is the constituting instrument of the UN system.[48] The Charter sets out the rights and obligations of member states, and establishes the UN's organs and procedures. It was based on an innovative concept of peoplehood rather than statehood. It states:

> [W]e the people of the United Nations . . . to reaffirm faith in fundamental human rights, in the dignity and worth of the human person, in the equal rights of men and women and of nations large and small, and to establish conditions under which justice and respect for the obligations arising from treaties and other sources of international law can be maintained . . . united to form a better world.

The declaration regarding non-self-governing territories – article 73 of the Charter, for example – affirmed the peoplehood principle. It refers to the responsibilities of members of the United Nations "for the administration of territories whose peoples have not yet attained a full measure of self-government." Member states recognized the principle that the interests of the inhabitants of these territories were paramount, and accepted as a sacred trust the obligation to promote to the utmost, within the system of international peace and security established by the Charter, the well-being of the inhabitants of these territories. In particular, member states have the responsibility to ensure, with due respect for the culture of the peoples concerned, their political, economic, social, and educational advancement, their just treatment, and their protection against abuse; to develop self-government, to take due account of the political aspirations of the peoples, and to assist them in the progressive development of their free political institutions, according to the circumstances of each territory and its peoples and their varying stages of advancement; and to promote constructive measures of development.[49] The use of the category of "peoples" evidences a shift to a new legal category in international law. The change infers the application of the principle of self-determination to Indigenous peoples within the boundaries of independent or decolonizing states.

The Charter defined the purposes of the United Nations: to maintain international peace and security; to develop friendly relations among nations; to co-operate in solving international economic, social, cultural, and humanitarian problems and in promoting respect for human rights and fundamental freedoms; and to be a centre for harmonizing the actions of nations in attaining these ends.

Among the UN's most pervasive achievements has been the development of a body of international law – conventions, treaties, and standards – that plays a central role in promoting economic and social development, as well as international peace and security. Many of its multilateral treaties and agreements form the basis of the law governing relations among nations. Over 500 treaties and agreements exist that address a broad range of common concerns among states. They are legally binding for the states that ratify them.

In 1949, the General Assembly of the United Nations recommended a study of the conditions of the "Indigenous population and other underdeveloped social groups" of the Americas to promote their integration and development.[50] In the 1950s, the International Labour Organization (ILO) was the first UN agency to undertake a study of the situation of Indigenous workers. The ILO study of a number of Latin American nations revealed a situation of exploitation and forced labour among the miners, most of whom were Indigenous workers. This study led to the adoption in 1957 of ILO Convention No. 107, the Convention Concerning the Protection and Integration of Indigenous and Other Tribal and Semi-Tribal Populations in Independent Countries.[51] This convention was based on an assimilationist approach, and was heavily criticized by Indigenous workers, but at least it provided a means to survive.

The Charter principle of "equal rights and self-determination of peoples," as well as three specific chapters in the Charter[52] devoted to the interests of dependent peoples, established UN decolonization efforts. Decolonization became the principle expression of self-determination. It was the Special Committee on Decolonization, not the Commission on Human Rights, that addressed questions of the self-determination of dependent peoples.

In the Declaration on the Granting of Independence to Colonial Countries and Peoples (1960),[53] the United Nations condemned colonialism and its practices of segregation and discrimination, and solemnly proclaimed the necessity of ending them. Under this Declaration, practically every colony in Asia, Africa, and Oceania availed itself of decolonization and the right of self-determination, opting for political independence.[54] A few colonies chose incorporation or free association with member states. These decisions were mostly the choices of the colonizers' descendents, colonial élites, and some assimilated Indigenous individuals.

Most of the colonized and dependent Indigenous peoples were not recognized as having the right to self-determination in decolonizing efforts.[55] They were seen as "Indigenous populations," and the decolonizing process did not include them, nor was it based on Indigenous treaties with the colonizing state. Decolonization efforts continued to rely on coërcive laws and military force, and reinforced the belief in an artificial and diasporic national culture of the colonizers in its affirmation of decolonialized boundaries and its strategies of acquiring the land and labour of Indigenous populations for the profits of colonial ruling élites and European homelands.

The Commonwealth of Nations, for example, was founded in 1931 on the principle of the self-determination of former British colonies, but many member states – such as Australia, New Zealand, and Canada – denied that right to the Indigenous populations within their borders. The persistent refusal to acknowledge the right of self-determination for Indigenous populations, even those who had entered into treaties with the imperial Crown or colonizing nations, was a surprising manifestation of Eurocentrism in action in law. It had enormous consequences across a range of areas that directly affected the lives and well-being of Indigenous populations, from control over land and resources to community involvement in the planning and delivery of health, welfare, and education services.

The broken promises of decolonization were the basis of Indigenous populations' movement toward human rights.[56] The decolonized states, to maintain control over Indigenous populations, generated new typologies of genocide.[57] Most decolonized states continued the violence against the Indigenous populations within the new borders, usually an affirmation of colonial administration and its divide and rule strategies.[58] Throughout the latter part of the 20th century and the Cold War between capitalism and communism, wars of liberation against European colonizers have witnessed new dimensions and levels of violence involving both decolonized states and colonized populations. Many decolonized nation-states spend more money fighting their own citizens than they do on social and economic programs.

The decolonized nation-state's inability to provide economic opportunities or even basic services to the various ethnic groups and marginalized Indigenous populations within its borders has fuelled violence worldwide. Such marginalized populations are often considered formal citizens, but they are usually excluded from equal participation in the economic, social, political, and justice systems of the nation-state. Instead, they have become part of a political system based not on their own legal traditions but created and defined by Eurocentric traditions.

Indigenous populations struggle to survive. By the end of the 20th century, Indigenous populations were generally characterized by poverty, subsistence holdings, and landlessness, leading to agrarian uprisings and multiple failed experiments with land reforms.[59]

The failure of the development policies pursued by decolonized governments and multilateral organizations during the global "developmental" era stunned government planners and academics. It became apparent that Eurocentric economic theory and policies would not improve the living standards of the poor and the marginalized. While some Indigenous populations were drawn into the modern economic sector through market mechanisms, labour migrations, and expanding infrastructure in terms of communication and transport, they invariably saw the major benefits of growth going to the colonial educated élites.

In 1992, a World Bank study reported that Indigenous populations were, for the most part, poor or extremely poor, and their living standards "abysmal."[60] Beginning in the 1970s, disillusionment with mainstream development strategies motivated the search for alternative or shadow economies.

4. The Convergence of Indigenous Diplomacy

IN THE CONTEXT OF POVERTY AND OPPRESSION, a few Indigenous groups had gained experience in dealing with imposed political systems and social structures. Others had to rely on enforced Eurocentric education in their struggle to survive; they gained university degrees and began to understand the contexts in which they were living. Thus began the Indigenous diplomacy movement.

The Indigenous diplomatic network began as a talking circle at various national and international conferences among the first generation of Indigenous peoples educated in the Eurocentric universities. In Canada, under the leadership of Alex Denny of the Mi'kmaw Nation, Oren Lyons of the Haudenosaunee Confederacy, Ted Moses and Harold Cardinal of the Cree Nation, Marie Smallface Marule of the Blackfoot Confederacy, Dan George of the Salish Nation, and George Manuel of the Shuswap Nation,[61] these talking circles gradually developed rights consciousness and diplomatic strategies. Traditional leaders, along with leaders of newly formed national and provincial organizations, united with the first generation of Eurocentric-educated Indigenous people to reveal what constitutes the Indigenous humanness of human rights.

These talking circles and conferences were searching for a way to rise out of poverty and oppression, to develop a means of talking about our visions for change. We discussed the failure of the United Nations system to decolonize our nations, and the resistance of the colonizing and decolonizing nations to live up to their treaty obligations. We discussed the continuing domestic attempts, through violence or education, to terminate treaty relationships and destroy Aboriginal identity, annihilate or assimilate Indigenous peoples, and the nation-states' failure to extend human rights to our communities.

Elders, traditional leaders, and organizations viewed the Universal Declaration of Human Rights (1948) as an important tool for decolonizing oppressed peoples. One of the major achievements of the UN is the affirmation of a significant body of human rights in international law, found initially in the UN Charter and the Universal Declaration of Human Rights. The Declaration elaborated the references to peoplehood contained in the Charter,[62] but, like all UN declarations, it was not a binding treaty. Along with the Universal Declaration, other declarations have reformed the customary law of the colonial era and generated postcolonial customary law, conventional law, and pre-emptory norms in international law. As well, the General Assembly of the UN, by binding conventions and multilateral treaties, sustained an international consensus that moved the inherent rights of humans into an internationally protected code of human rights, one to which all nations can subscribe and to which all people can aspire. The UN also established educational programs and mechanisms to promote and protect these human rights and to assist governments in carrying out their responsibilities. Many regional systems of human rights have been created, as nation-states have created domestic human rights codes.

As the principles of peace and human rights were declared by the General Assembly, the vision was rekindled among Indigenous peoples. They created the diplomacy network and began to develop a new vision of a just global order based on human rights. With the advent of transnational economies, the line between public and private international law – laws governing the structure and conduct of states, and laws governing cross-border transactions in which different judgements will apply depending on the jurisdiction – has become increasingly uncertain. Many issues of private international law and human rights implicate issues of public international law.

The Indigenous network was impressed with the ideal; the "equal and inalienable right of all members of the human family" was asserted and recognized as the "foundation of freedom, justice and peace in the world."[63] These sentiments of the Declaration were remarkably similar to those embodied in the legal traditions of Indigenous peoples.

In answering the question of where universal rights begin, the chair of the UN Human Rights Commission, Eleanor Roosevelt, stated that universal rights begin in "the places where every man, woman, and child seeks equal justice, equal opportunity, equal dignity without discrimination. Unless these rights have meaning there, they have little meaning anywhere. Without concerned citizen action to uphold them close to home, we shall look in vain for progress in the larger world."[64] In the emerging postcolonial international order, peoples' self-determination, as opposed to national self-determination, is an inalienable,[65] collective human right.[66] As a human right, self-determination is interdependent, indivisible, and interrelated with all other human rights.[67] It is a "prerequisite" for the enjoyment of all other human rights.[68] It is the "oldest aspect of the democratic entitlement."[69] The denial of this right "is essentially incompatible with true democracy."[70]

The initial statement of principles in the Universal Declaration of Human Rights was supplemented by the Declaration on the Elimination of All Forms of Racial Discrimination (1963)[71] and the International Convention on the Elimination of all Forms of Racial Discrimination (1965).[72] Both the Declaration and the Convention affirmed the necessity of eliminating racial discrimination in all its manifestations throughout the member states and of securing an understanding of and respect for the dignity of the human person. They reaffirmed that all human beings are born free and equal in dignity and rights; that all human beings are equal before the law, and are entitled to equal protection against any discrimination or incitement to discrimination. They stated that the existence of racial barriers in any human society are repugnant to the dignity and equality inherent in all human beings. They established that any doctrine of superiority based on racial differentiation is scientifically false, morally condemnable, socially unjust, and dangerous. They affirmed that no justification exists for racial discrimination, in theory or in practice.

The Convention defined the term "racial discrimination" to mean "any distinction, exclusion, restriction or preference based on race, colour, descent, or national or ethnic origin which has the purpose or effect of nullifying or impairing the recognition, enjoyment, or exercise, on an equal footing, of human rights and fundamental freedoms in the political, economic, social, cultural, or any other field of public life."[73] The Convention noted that special measures could be taken for the sole purpose of securing the adequate advancement of certain racial or ethnic groups or individuals requiring such protection as may be necessary in order to ensure such groups or individuals can access equal enjoyment or exercise of human rights and fundamental freedoms, and these were not to be deemed racial discrimination.[74] Under the Convention, these measures are protected only so long as they do not consequently lead to the maintenance of separate rights for different racial groups.[75] These special measures may not be continued after the advancement of the objectives for which they were taken have been achieved.[76]

The Convention's promise of eliminating racial discrimination engaged the Indigenous diplomatic movement. Even though Indigenous peoples were not mentioned, leaders in the diplomatic movement concluded that the promise could lead to the termination of their historical treaty rights. Canada ratified the Convention, for example, and promised to secure the earliest adoption of practical measures to eliminate racial discrimination within its borders. Faced with eliminating racial discrimination in relation to its Aboriginal population, which Canada had viewed as a racially defined category under federal law and separate from the rest of Canadian society, Canada responded with the Statement of the Government of Canada on Indian Policy (1969), the notorious White Paper.[77] The Statement sought to terminate the separate constitutional status of Indians and lands reserved for Indians under federal jurisdiction. The Statement set out to remove many of the distinctive elements that set Indians apart from other Canadians. Included in the policy were plans for ending the treaties, terminating the legal status of Indian peoples in the *Indian Act*, and denying the existence of Aboriginal rights to the land (at the same time, it sought to settle existing land claims). It sought to transfer land reserved to Indians to individual Indians by gradually phasing out federal responsibility for Indians and protection of reserve lands, and eventually repealing the *Indian Act* and dismantling the Department of Indian affairs. In stripping these concepts of their power, the Statement was an attempt to prepare Indians to enter the modern, de-racialized Canadian society. Its goal was the full, free, and non-discriminatory participation of the Indian people in a just Canadian society.

Indians in Canada denounced the Statement and generated a storm of protest. They stated that Indians should not be looked on as a race, but as peoples with distinct heritages and cultures recognized by treaties. Surprised by the massive opposition to this plan of formal equality, the government withdrew its proposal in 1970. However, the misinterpretation of the Convention in the Statement demonstrated the importance of Indigenous diplomacy and the UN declaration and conventions.

The principles of human rights in the Universal Declaration were empowered and transformed into multilateral treaties and an optional protocol, known as the Human Rights Covenants: the International Covenant on Economic, Social, and Cultural Rights (1966),[78] the International Covenant on Civil and Political Rights (1966),[79] and the Optional Protocol to the International Covenant on Civil and Political Rights (1966).[80] This normative declaration and its covenants were a shift in international law from state values to human values. Member states that signed and ratified these agreements agreed to uphold the rights and freedoms defined by the covenants within their own borders. The first article in both covenants asserts, "All peoples have the right of self determination."[81] By virtue of that right, all peoples have the right freely to determine their political status and pursue their economic, social, and cultural development.

Indigenous peoples desired these rights and freedoms, since we were not born free and are not free now. In the 1970s, the elders, organizations leaders, and lawyers forming the diplomacy movement inspired the Human Rights Covenants. Human rights and the pre-eminence of self-determination, human dignity, and integrity became part of our struggle. These rights generated a consciousness that was a remedy both to assimilation and the possibility of armed revolution. But we soon found that the "all" referred to in the covenants was interpreted as not to apply to us.

We attempted to have international and national regimes respond to this interpretation by promoting human rights. Our shared grievances constituted a terrifying list, ranging from genocide, militarization, structural discrimination and exclusion, displacement from ancestral territories, expropriation of lands and resources without consent, extrajudicial killings, illegal arrests, torture, and violence against women to the outright banning of Aboriginal languages, the wearing of traditional dress, and the practise of culture and religions, amounting to ethnocide.

Reluctantly, uncomfortably, but prudently, the United Nations responded to the Indigenous diplomacy questions about the humanity of Indigenous populations – our knowledge, heritage, culture, creativity, identity, and rights. In 1972, the Sub-Commission on the Prevention of Discrimination and Protection of Minorities of the UN Commission on Human Rights appointed a Special Rapporteur to prepare a "study on the problem of discrimination against indigenous populations." In 1977 the International NGO Conference on Discrimination Against Indigenous Populations in the Americas was held in Geneva, where Indigenous peoples participated in the adoption of the Declaration of Principles for the Defence of Indigenous Nations and Peoples of the Western Hemisphere, asserting that Indigenous peoples are subjects of international law. The final report of the Special Rapporteur, which became known as the Martinez-Cobo Study,[82] came out in 1982.

One result of these diplomatic efforts was the development of an organic global network that worked with the UN and its member states to be recognized as Indigenous peoples. The once-fashionable theories of social change, modernization, and nation-building that dominated Eurocentrism were being challenged by the new movements of international others, self-identified as Indigenous peoples. The recognition of the rights of Indigenous peoples was part of the unfinished business of decolonization.

The Indigenous diplomacy movement in the UN was a response to the failures of the member nations – both the colonizer states and the decolonized states – to recognize Indigenous human rights, end racial discrimination, and decolonize Aboriginal peoples. Indigenous leaders began to seek ways to have the UN system recognize their humanity, societies, and traditional civilizations. We moved slowly through the maze of the bureaucratic system. The human rights framework of the UN, rather than the decolonization framework, became the venue for the Indigenous renaissance in contemporary international law.[83]

The network was botanical in structure and operation. It had no artificial bureaucracy, structure, or designated leader. It was practical and tactical, with many engaged and committed participants. It operated by Indigenous concepts of consensus and processes. It had many customs that ensured debate and dialogue, but did not allow for the recording of the debate or the creation of spokespersons. Liberation or freedom was defined, to the extent it was ever defined, as cultural and physical survival.

The diplomatic network was a manifestation of continued resistance to colonization, and it combined the efforts that had been going on in isolation for generations. The idea slowly emerged that Indigenous peoples needed a safe, peaceful place to meet, talk, and grow. We needed to extend our kinship and relationships. We were the unofficially colonized peoples of humanity, the victims of modernization and progress. In every state and educational system, we were under-represented or, more often, ignored. Our poverty and our powerlessness to do anything about it drove us to the ILO, the UN, and UNESCO (UN Educational, Scientific and Cultural Organization), which had a long list of international treaties and covenants that could assist our survival. We sought to understand why the Labour Conventions, the Human Rights Covenants or the Declaration and Conventions of UNESCO had never been used to protect us. In these international systems we found we were invisible; we were neither minorities nor peoples. We were ghost peoples, hidden, like our languages and cultures, by the concept of the nation-state.

Organizing the Indigenous diplomatic network was trying and frustrating. Indigenous peoples have lived, and continue to live, in an intolerant environment of ideologies. We had become accustomed to these ideologies of colonization and racism, and had come to accept them as a fact of life. We had learned to mistrust. We had grown accustomed to saying something different from what we thought and felt to achieve educational success. We lived with the mask of apathy and fatalism. We learned not to believe in our traditions, to ignore or distrust others, to care only for personal survival. If our cultural knowledge and traditions were so powerful, how could we be forced into such wretched conditions? Concepts such as relationship, compassion, humility, honesty, and helping lost their depth and dimension.

Most Indigenous peoples, consciously or unconsciously, had helped or abetted colonization. We yielded to the temptation of vanity, personal ambition, selfishness, and rivalry in our struggle to survive amid colonial and racial ideologies. We had all become responsible, to varying extents, for perpetuating the ideologies that violence can prevail over dignity, deception over truth, and the state over humanity. We were not only victims of colonization, but part of its continuity through our educational achievements, passivity, and nonresistance.

Some understood that it was up to us alone to change this situation. We could not blame the colonialists for every wrong, because doing so hid our own obligation to end colonialism reasonably and as quickly as possible. It would mistake our relationship with the colonialists, to believe in their superiority, to expect a general remedy to come from them alone. It would erase from memory the sources of our redemption. Dignity and self-determination required responsible action and participation from the colonized – from us. We had to comprehend the depth of our oppression, but we also had to imagine the possibilities of transformation by our legal traditions and diplomacy. Once we began to believe in our traditions and our ability, we realized the source of our transformation. Hope and action returned.

5. Communications with the UN Human Rights Committee

AFTER CANADA RATIFIED THE HUMAN RIGHTS COVENANTS IN 1976, and especially during the repatriation of the Constitution of Canada from the United Kingdom in 1977-82, First Nations turned to the covenants for a remedy for the oppression of their legal personality. We began using the Optional Protocol to address the human rights violations occurring in Canada. The Commission on Human Rights of the UN, which defined the rights of humans and established the rights of collective entities to self-determination as peoples, became the initial venue for discussions of self-determination and decolonization. The initial cases brought to the UN Human Rights Committee under the Optional Protocol were *Lovelace* v. *Canada* (1977-1981),[84] *Mikmaq Tribal Society (Denny)* v. *Canada* (1978-1991),[85] and *Lubicon Lake Band (Chief Bernard Ominayak)* v. *Canada* (1984-present).[86] The procedures of the Human Rights Committee were long and slow,[87] but they proved that the Human Rights Covenants did apply to the First Nations of Canada. The Committee affirmed that resource rights are protected under the right of self-determination and cultural rights.[88] We learned, however, that the right of self-determination of Indigenous peoples was a collective right, and therefore beyond the jurisdiction of the Committee, which could not hear complaints committed against peoples, as its competency was limited to violations of individual rights. It disregarded the fact that, under Aboriginal legal traditions and treaties, individual and group rights are neither separate nor in conflict; our individuality depends on our collective heritage and identity.

In 1970, Sandra Nicholas, a Maliseet woman from the Tobique Reserve in New Brunswick, married American airman Bernie Lovelace and moved with him to California. Under the Canadian *Indian Act*, she was deprived of Indian status.[89] When her marriage ended a few years later, Lovelace and her children returned to the Tobique Reserve and found they were denied not only the right to live on the reserve, but housing, education, and health care as well. In 1977, Lovelace took her case to the Human Rights Committee of the UN under the Optional Protocol.[90] Canada responded that it had an obligation to the Indian community to minimize the harm to the Indian family in conformity with article 23 (1) of the Civil and Political Rights Covenant: "the family is the natural and fundamental group unit of society and is entitled to protection by society and the State."[91] In 1981, the UN Committee rejected this argument, finding Canada in breach of art. 27 of the Civil and Political Rights Covenant for violating Lovelace's right to belong to and enjoy her Maliseet culture.[92] In 1985, Canada finally revised the *Indian Act* to allow First Nations women who married non-Indians to retain their status.

In 1980, the UN Human Rights Committee accepted another communication from Alexander Denny, *Jigap'ten* (Grand Captain, Mi'kmaq Grand Council), alleging violations of their right to national self-determination and existing treaties under article 1 of the Political and Civil Rights Covenants in the constitutional discussion about repatriating the Constitution of Canada from the United Kingdom.[93] One month after the Secretary-General served notice on Ottawa, Quebec police launched a raid on the Mi'kmaq Reserve at Listuguj. Shortly afterward, Canada formally replied to the Mi'kmaq submission, challenging the Committee's competence to act on "political matters."[94] It argued that self-determination "cannot affect the national unity and territorial integrity of Canada," and that the Committee cannot lend support to "secessionist movements."[95] With respect to Mi'kmaq claims of pre-existing statehood based on imperial treaties, Canada stated, "these treaties are merely considered to be nothing more than contracts between a sovereign and a group of its subjects."[96] The successful entrenchment of existing Aboriginal and treaty rights in the patriated Constitution of Canada ended the first communication. In January 1986, the Mi'kmaq Nation resubmitted its communication to the Committee, focusing on the political decision by the Prime Minister of Canada to limit consultations on the constitutional conference on implementing the newly enacted s. 35 of the *Canada Act, 1982* to four national Aboriginal organizations, rather than respecting the traditional parties to the treaty rights.[97] The executive officers of the Mi'kmaw Nation argued that this political decision violated their newly affirmed Aboriginal and treaty rights in the Constitution of Canada. Additionally, they argued, this decision violated their rights to self-determination, public participation, and democratic representation under the Political and Civil Rights Covenant. Canada argued that the Human Rights Committee did not have competency to decide this matter under the Optional Protocol. It reasserted that the right to self-determination "cannot be invoked to affect the national unity and territorial integrity of an independent sovereign State, such as Canada." It also denied the peoplehood of the Mi'kmaw, stating that self-determination cannot apply to "a thinly scattered minority dispersed among the majority, like the Mi'kmaqs."[98] As for constitutional conferences, it was simply "not feasible" to consult with each treaty group. In 1990, three years after the constitutional conferences ended, the Committee affirmed its lack of competence to determine claims to self-determination under the Optional Protocol,[99] but affirmed the *Mawio'mi* right to participate in public affairs under article 25 of the Political and Civil Rights Covenant.[100] In 1991, the Committee ruled, as a matter of fact, that the constitutional "interests" of Mi'kmaw peoples did not have the right to choose their own representatives to consult with the national government.[101]

In the *Lubicon Lake* case, the next communication, the Human Rights Committee made a significant procedural decision, reaffirming its incompetency to address the collective right of self-determination. Chief Bernard Ominayak, as an individual, could not claim to be the victim of a violation of the collective right of self-determination, because the Committee was only authorized by the Optional Protocol to determine individual rights conferred upon peoples.[102] The Committee, however, would consider his claims under other provisions of the Covenant. In 1990, the Human Rights Committee delivered its views in the *Lubicon Lake* case. Bernard Ominayak's standing to pursue a representative claim – that the right to natural resources was part of the right to self-determination – on behalf of his band was upheld,[103] and provincial leasing of the band's traditional territory for development purposes without its consent was found to "threaten the way of life and culture of the Lubicon Lake Band" under art. 27 of the Political and Civil Covenant.[104] The Committee disclaimed its competence to determine whether the Lubicon Crees comprise a "people," however. Canada has ignored the Committee's decision, in any case; the land dispute is still unresolved and the case is still before the Human Rights Council.[105]

In 1989, all the members of Whispering Pines Indian Band, a community of the Shuswap Nation in south-central British Columbia, sent a communication to the Human Rights Committee that challenged Canada's Bill C-31, in which certain persons formerly deprived of Indian status on the basis of sex were reinstated based on the *Lovelace* decision, but at the same time, other persons who formerly enjoyed Indian status were deprived of it on the basis of a racial quota and the racial character of "Indian" legal status in Canada under articles 1, 17, 22, 23, 26, 27 of the Civil and Political Rights Covenant.[106] The Committee affirmed that no claim of self-determination may be brought under the Optional Protocol,[107] and rejected the communication for failure to exhaust domestic remedies, as required by the Protocol.[108]

These decisions affirmed that First Nations have specific human rights under the Human Rights Covenants, but those rights could be disregarded by Canada and ignored by the provinces. The covenants gave little protection. We learned that the affirmation of our collective right to self-determination had to be addressed by the UN General Assembly by a declaration, so our attention became focused on generating such a declaration.

The limitations of these decisions concerning self-determination were eventually remedied by the Declaration on the Rights of Indigenous Peoples, in which Indigenous peoples were recognized as having the right of self-determination and their legal personality was distinct from minorities and interest groups. Fortunately, while discussing the declaration in the UN, our effort to have our Aboriginal and treaty rights recognized and affirmed in the Constitution was successful before the courts.[109]

6. The UN Working Group on Indigenous Populations

THESE COMMUNICATIONS PLACED SUFFICIENT PRESSURE on the UN Commission on Human Rights to begin addressing the human rights of Indigenous peoples in its vast bureaucracy. In 1982, in Geneva, the UN created an innovative Working Group on Indigenous Populations.[110] The Working Group was a subgroup of the UN Commission on Human Rights Sub-Commission on Prevention of Discrimination and Protection of Minorities.[111] As a subsidiary organ of the Sub-Commission, the Working Group was located at the lowest level of the hierarchy of UN human rights bodies. Its recommendations have to be considered and accepted first by its superior body, the Sub-Commission, then by the Commission on Human Rights and the Economic and Social Council (ECOSOC) before reaching the General Assembly.

The Working Group had two main tasks: first, to review events relating to the promotion and protection of the human rights and fundamental freedoms of Indigenous peoples, giving particular attention to changes in international standards relating to the human rights of Indigenous peoples. As it was not authorized to examine concrete complaints of alleged human rights violations with the aim of formulating recommendations or adopting decisions on concrete cases or nation-states, its tasks were exercises in international legalism. The Working Group had flexible rules of procedure, enabling all those interested to participate in its deliberations. It received and analyzed oral and written information presented to it by Indigenous peoples, Indigenous organizations, governments, specialized agencies, and other UN organs. Second, it analyzed these statements and information and sent a report to the Sub-Commission on the Promotion and Protection of Human Rights.

Five human rights experts from Africa, Asia, Central and South America, Eastern Europe, and the West lead the Working Group, nominated and elected every four years by the governmental members of the Commission on Human Rights. The members of the group were selected from the 28 representatives of the Sub-commission, who are elected based on their non-partisan expertise in the field of human rights. Dr. Erica-Irene Daes of Greece chaired the Working Group during the development of the Indigenous declaration. The influence of the Working Group has largely been a product of the personality and commitment of Dr. Daes, her ability to listen respectfully and communicate with Indigenous peoples, her personal political stature in the UN system, and the consistent support of her own nation, Greece.

The Working Group in Geneva became a strange passage for Indigenous peoples. We travelled to Europe to articulate our problems with Eurocentric colonization, only to discover cognitive imperialism surviving. We had no wealth to fund our travels, and no means to live in the exorbitant style of Geneva. Yet, we could not continue to live and die in hopelessness. We endured thanks to random acts of kindness and occasional support from organizations. Most participants in the international initiative were forced to live solitary, nomadic lives, yet in our various international ceremonies and diplomacy, we learned to unite by respecting our diversity, comprehending our desperate situation and increasing our capacity for communication and debate. In this way we discovered shared interests, and created a sustainable global voice.

For more than two decades, international human rights experts, states, and Indigenous peoples debated the definition and status of Indigenous peoples in international law and UN law – a legalistic, positivistic, and heartless quibble over categories and terminology. In the Human Rights Covenants, peoples are groups who have an objectively distinct identity of an ethnic, linguistic, national, cultural, or other similar type, and who subjectively perceive themselves as distinct.[112] The pressing question – "Who are Indigenous peoples?" – was a disguised way of questioning our humanity. The need for a definition of Indigenous peoples raised the question of what is human about human rights? and what are the proper legal traditions that inform human rights?

The Special Rapporteur on the rights of persons belonging to ethnic, religious, and linguistic minorities had captured the limitation of Eurocentric positivistic categories: "[P]recise universal definition, while of philosophical interest, would be nearly impossible to attain in the current state of global realities, and would in any event not contribute perceptibly to the practical aspects of defending groups from abuse."[113] These Eurocentric categories were relatively recent, and their meanings had shifted over time, space, and academic disciplines. The challenges of defining Indigenous people begin with the realization that all the world's 6,000 to 10,000 original cultures were Indigenous, but most had been forcibly absorbed by colonialism into the contrived boundaries of nations during the growth of nation-states. Some survive as minorities that are identifiable or who self-identify as culturally distinct groups, but many no longer maintain distinct communities within distinct territories. It is not always clear whether a particular group is a minority or an Indigenous people, and the difference is largely a matter of perspective and degree.

No simple or precise definition of Indigenousness existed that applied equally in all nation-states. Studies by UN legal experts José Martínez Cobo (1984),[114] Dr. Erica-Irene Daes,[115] and Rodolfo Stavenhagen [116] focused on being the first on the land, cultural distinctiveness, self-identification, and oppression.

In the preliminary UN Special Rapporteur study, José Martinez Cobo had offered a cautious analysis:

> Indigenous communities, peoples and nations are those which, having a historical continuity with pre-invasion and precolonial societies that developed on their territories, consider themselves distinct from other sectors of the societies now prevailing in those territories, or parts of them. They form at present non-dominant sectors of society and are determined to preserve, develop and transmit to future generations their ancestral territories, and their ethnic identity, as the basis of their continued existence as peoples, in accordance with their own cultural patterns, social institutions and legal systems.[117]

This definition combines the element of cultural distinctiveness; the experience of colonialism, discrimination, or marginalization; and the desire of Indigenous peoples to continue their cultural integrity into the future.

The chair of the Working Group on Indigenous Populations, Dr. Erica-Irene Daes, has stated that the concept of "Indigenous" is not capable of a precise, inclusive definition that can be applied in the same manner to all regions of the world:

> [T]he international discussion of the concept of "indigenous" evolved, from the late nineteenth century until the establishment of the Working Group in 1982, within the framework of European languages, notably English, Spanish, and German. English and Spanish share a common root in the Latin term *indigenae*, which was used to distinguish between persons who were born in a particular place and those who arrived from elsewhere (*advenae*). The French term *autochthone* has, by comparison, Greek roots and, like the German term "*Ursprung*," suggests that the group to which it refers was the first to exist in the particular location. Hence, the semantic roots of the terms historically used in modern international law share a single conceptual element: priority in time.[118]

In the linguistic framework of European colonization, Daes noted that the term "Indigenous" acquired an implicit element of race.[119] She concluded that

> any inconsistency or imprecision in previous efforts to clarify the concept of "indigenous" was not a result of a lack of adequate scientific or legal analysis, but due to the efforts of some Governments to limit its globality, and of other Governments to build a high conceptual wall between Indigenous and "peoples" and/or "Non-Self-Governing Territories." No one has succeeded in devising a definition of "indigenous" which is precise and internally valid as a philosophical matter, yet satisfies demands to limit its regional application and legal implications. All past attempts to achieve both clarity and restrictiveness in the same definition have in fact resulted in greater ambiguity.[120]

With the assistance of Indigenous and other legal experts, members of the academic family, and modern international organizations, Daes established four factors that inform the concept of "Indigenous peoples":

1) priority in time, with respect to the occupation and use of a specific territory;
2) the voluntary perpetuation of cultural distinctiveness, which may include the aspects of language, social organization, religion, and spiritual values, modes of production, laws and institutions;
3) self-identification, as well as recognition by other groups, or by state authorities, as a distinct collectivity; and
4) an experience of subjugation, marginalization, dispossession, exclusion or discrimination, whether or not these conditions persist.[121]

These factors may be present, to a greater or lesser degree, in different regions and in different national and local contexts. Any definition must be applied in the context of national history and local peoples' aspirations, but taking this into account, these factors do provide general guidance to reasonable decision-making in practice.[122]

Stavenhagen's analysis of the definition of Indigenous peoples emphasized that chronology is not the main point in Indigenous-state relations; the main point, rather, is a type of unjust relationship that creates a situation in which peoples seek to protect their Indigenous heritage in the human rights regime:

> Indigenousness, independently of biological or cultural continuity, frequently is the outcome of governmental policies imposed from above and from the outside. It also quite often is the product of a "constructed discourse" enunciated by the emerging intellectual élites of the indigenous peoples and their sympathizers among other sectors of the population. In any case, the discourse of "indigenousness" leads to a denunciation of injustice (and crimes) committed against the indigenous peoples (genocide, plunder, servitude, discrimination) and to the formulation of specific rights that derived from the injustice suffered. . . .[123]

Since cultural diversity has become the defining characteristic of humanity,[124] no universal, unambiguous definition of the concept of "Indigenous peoples" exists in international law. No single accepted definition captures the diversity of Indigenous heritages, cultures, histories, and current circumstances, or the relationship to the state or states within whose political boundaries the Indigenous community resides. The relationships between Indigenous peoples and dominant or mainstream society vary from country to country. All attempts to define the concept, however, recognize the linkages between people, land, and culture, and they are almost always formulated in the broader context of international efforts to ensure Indigenous peoples' status and rights.

Few nation-states keep detailed or reliable statistics on Indigenous peoples, and the statistics that do exist are based on disparate definitions of "Indigenous." Still, as a starting point for discussion, a conservative estimate of the global population and distribution of Indigenous peoples will number them at about 370 million, or five per cent of the world's population. They embody 80 per cent of the world's cultural diversity, occupy 20 cent of the land surface, and are stewards of 80 per cent of the world's biodiversity. Indigenous peoples inhabit many ecosystems: Arctic regions and deserts, savannahs and forests in both tropical and temperate zones, mountains, tundra, wetlands, and islands. Most have retained social, cultural, economic, and political characteristics distinct from other segments of national populations. They represent over 5,000 languages and cultures in more than 70 nation-states on six continents.

Some 15 percent of the world's undisputed Indigenous peoples live in the Americas. The Pacific Island peoples, Aboriginal Australians, and the Maori of New Zealand clearly satisfy the criteria of aboriginality, cultural distinctiveness, and self-identification. In some nation-states, including Fiji, Tuvalu, and Vanuatu in the Pacific, the Indigenous peoples are the majority and control the state, whereas in Guatemala and Bolivia in South America and the large Arctic regions of Canada, Russia, and Asia, Indigenous peoples are a majority but have historically been deprived of the freedom and resources to govern themselves.

Africa poses problems of definition, because most Africans consider themselves Indigenous people who have achieved decolonization and self-determination. Yet many relatively small, nomadic herding and hunter-gatherer societies – the Tuareg in Niger, the Maasai in Kenya, the Mbuti in Congo, and the San in the Kalahari – have been displaced and oppressed by ethnically unrelated African peoples who have been their neighbours for a millennium or longer.

Perhaps 75 percent of the peoples in South and Southeast Asia and China are Indigenous. Many groups regard themselves as Indigenous, but their status is disputed by the nation-states in which they live. Indigenous peoples in China, such as the Mongolians, are labelled national minorities.

Central and western Asia – Pakistan, Afghanistan, and former Soviet states such as Kazakhstan – pose difficult problems in defining Indigenous peoples, since, in many cases, they contain culturally and linguistically related "tribal" and "non-tribal" groups. The Pathans in Pakistan and the Bedouin of the Arabian peninsula, for example, are sometimes described as Indigenous or tribal peoples. India defines all members of particular ethnic and linguistic groups as "tribal," regardless of where or how they live. By this standard, one-fifth of India's total population is Indigenous.[125]

Most Indigenous peoples face discrimination in terms of access to basic social services, including education and health care. Owing to forced displacement and assimilation, and the fact that many live now in urban and suburban areas, Indigenous peoples have often been disrupted in the transmission of their cultural heritage. Many survive, in precarious and impoverished conditions, on the fringes of society. The continued existence of Indigenous peoples and their communities is closely related to their ability to influence their own fate and preserve and develop their rights, their traditional culture, and their social institutions. They remain deeply committed to the protection and transmission of their heritage and knowledge. Indigenous ways of life, livelihood, spirituality, and culture are inextricably intertwined with traditional environments. Indigenous peoples are particularly vulnerable to the negative impacts of globalization, and see it as vital that international law promote cultural diversity and sustainable development.

At our first talk at the Working Group on Indigenous Populations in the summer of 1982, only two of the 14 Indigenous organizations represented were based outside North America. By the ninth session, more than 70 participated. Two-thirds of them came from Latin America, the Pacific, the Soviet Union, and South and Southeast Asia.[126] By the end of the Working Group's deliberations, more than 2, 500 delegates a year attempted to participate.

Experience did not allow us to trust each other, but we had to learn. It was a time of listening, a time of understanding our teachings and experiences. In the languages of the Indigenous humanities and through translation we discussed our situation and our dreams. Across countless generations, each people was comforted by the survival of Indigenous languages, and the elders and storytellers as they revealed their teachings. At greater length and detail than any one person can hope to grasp in translation, these teachings began to be shared; they converged and give form to an ecological- and compassion-based vision of humanity and human rights.

As the discussions in Geneva progressed, the Indigenous peoples gathered there became people of a shared persuasion. We shared our experiences and ideas, and we used these ideas to persuade others of the good and just road. These paths called on us to face both others and ourselves on pivotal issues. We faced the unresolved and the unknown. We faced Eurocentric thought from the perspective of our own experiences and our visions. From the small meeting rooms where we began to the cavernous rooms of the UN where we ended up, our dialogues were formalized. We found the collective strength to return to our traditional role as the teaching civilization, not the willing learners of modernity. We had to fight the ease of adopting the model of human rights provided by Eurocentric legal traditions, and find our own traditions and empower them.

The Working Group was the first international ceremony of Indigenous peoples, and it became an integral part of Indigenous diplomacy. Each group shared different parts of the new ritual as we struggled to eliminate colonialism and learn the UN legal system. Through the long days in the UN meeting rooms and the uneasy nights in Geneva, we pursued an elusive consensus. Individual loneliness receded as we extended friendships and sympathy to the Indigenous peoples around our mother, the earth. Our extended discussions were an effort to distill our vision of a postcolonial order into words and black ink. As the Lakota holy man Black Elk revealed in an ancient teaching, "A human being who has a vision is not able to use the power of it until after they have realized this vision on earth for people to see." In the alien meeting places of Geneva, which none of us could call home, we pondered the meaning of our humanity and our vision of a just and good society. Through our oral and performance traditions, we explored the unknown territory of our relationships with one another. In many languages and styles, we sought to initiate a creative, transformative vision of human rights to challenge a complacent world order. We probed for agreement on how the existing Human Rights Covenants of the United Nations should be applied to Indigenous peoples.

The Working Group had to produce more than talk and shared visions. If we wanted a better life in an improving world, we had to picture the impossible and translate it into text. We had to explain our dreams to human rights experts and baffled government representatives – and all within the limitations of the six official languages of United Nations law.

From all four directions, Indigenous delegates arrived in Geneva each summer to renew and criticize the drafts prepared by the five human rights experts and their drafting teams of Indigenous lawyers, scholars, and nation-state officials. By the end of the process, several hundred Indigenous peoples' organizations had participated in the Working Group, offering their comments and suggestions.

Indigenous peoples' organizations that work in the UN prefer not to be called non-governmental organizations (NGOs) because they differ widely in who they represent and how they make policy decisions. Unlike typical NGOs that enjoy consultative status at the UN, Indigenous organizations often represent nations, treaty organizations, tribal governments, labour organizations, or political movements. Fewer than 20 Indigenous organizations have acquired permanent consultative status with UN bodies, compared to more than 2,000 non-Indigenous organizations.

The Indigenous peoples' organizations worked collectively through formal and informal Indigenous caucuses, which they created in the Working Group. They came with cultural, ideological, and strategic differences; they were more likely to have shared a common experience of mistreatment than a common culture or economic structure. They were more alike in what they opposed than in what they sought to become. Seeking a fragile unity, they discussed common problems, drew up strategies, and came to consensus on many issues and positions. Faced with a diversity of visions and a complexity of strategies, we sought compromise. Who could choose the "best" among these visions to create a fair and just order? Who could choose which visions could heal our peoples? We talked, we listened, and we learned. And we carried our visions into text.

Animating Indigenous diplomacy in the United Nations meant that we had to be actively engaged in defining our concepts of human rights and responsibilities. The power of Indigenous diplomacy did not reside in military or economic power, but within our heritage, consciousness, and behaviour. Our power was expressed in the development of international dialogue and consensus-building on basic human rights and relationships. If there is to be a peaceful future for humanity, we agreed, international norms and agreements for the actions of nations and peoples must converge. Without the recognition of Indigenous rights in the human rights regime, no solution to a consensually based global order would be complete. We chose the route to consensual action through Indigenous diplomacy because the path was compatible with our own legal traditions of consensus and respect for others and their differences.

The text of the Indigenous declaration was drafted through trans-systemic legalism; it was not the voice of a single tradition, but a voice shared through, across, and beyond many distinct legal traditions. The process demonstrated that the human rights regime was consistent with Indigenous legal traditions and knowledge that predated European colonization. The dialogues surrounding the drafting revealed that many of the protections contained in the American Bill of Rights, which was a key model in producing the Universal Declaration, were based on or borrowed from the Indigenous legal traditions of the eastern confederations, especially the Haudenosaunee and the Five Civilized Nations, and were part of an anti-colonial struggle against monarchy.[127] Europeans had found ways of thinking about society and living together that coalesced in the Enlightenment privileging of the individual and what is now called human rights.[128] As human rights scholar Shelly Wright noted,

> It is difficult to see where concepts such as democratic rule, federal forms of governments, constitutional checks and balances, freedom of expression, thought, consciousness, association and assembly might have come from if some extra-European source cannot be found. These political forms and freedoms did not exist in Europe during the early colonial period and had largely disappeared from smaller

> European nations after their own "colonization" by neighbouring powers. . . . The theoretical foundation of the "rights of Man" in Europe and its colonies are products of the colonial era.[129]

The various legal traditions represented in the United Nations, the structure and style of the Human Rights Covenants, and distinct Indigenous traditions converged in the drafting of the proposed declaration. International human rights experts originally hesitated to endorse the notion that there was a subsisting body of international law or human rights that applied to Indigenous peoples,[130] but 11 years later, in 1993, Indigenous and human rights experts reached a consensus, and drafted for the Working Group the landmark draft declaration on the Rights of Indigenous Peoples, which was eventually ratified by the world's Indigenous peoples and called the Indigenous declaration.[131] The declaration was drafted to confirm the existing international human rights standards that apply to other peoples. Every paragraph was based on known instances of wrongs or violations of the human rights of Indigenous peoples. It crystallized the rights of Indigenous peoples in international law, which have moved from a normative status to a "hardened norm," a legal regime.[132]

Eleven years in consultation, the text was a product of wrongs committed against Indigenous peoples.[133] It was drafted as a dialogue between Indigenous peoples and the independent legal experts of the Working Group; the member states gradually withdrew from the process, or attended in dwindling numbers, owing to frustration with the consultative process. They often criticized the dialogue and the drafted principles as unrealistic or impractical. The drafts did not represent the viewpoint of human rights experts, nation-states, or Indigenous peoples; they were, instead, a unique convergence of these perspectives.

The Indigenous declaration was more a framework of existing rights than a bid to create new ones; it was a document of recognition and interpretation. Indigenous traditions are different from the languages of the United Nations and the Eurocentric systems of law in nation-states. Indigenous legal traditions tell us how we are to conduct ourselves. In Eurocentric systems of law, generally, the state or the Crown tells people what they must not do. These systems, whether the civil law tradition or the legal positivist tradition, were a product of empire, colonization, and imperialism. They had transformed and supplanted the Indigenous legal traditions of Europe, the common law traditions.[134]

Indigenous legal traditions are imbedded in our diverse languages, which in the structure of English grammar would be called verb-based rather than noun-based; they are languages that distinguish not between gender but, rather, between the animate and inanimate. They are beautiful and descriptive languages, steeped in thousands of years of practical observation of nature and the human role in it. They are rich in expression. More importantly, they contain the core values that we are told were given to us by the Life-giver so that we might live our lives in accordance with them. The structure of the languages, more than the words, explains how we should live among each other. It reveals how to treat all life forms with care and respect, and instructs us that our mission is to build relationships among the forces and forms of the environment, and to nurture and care for these communities and relationships. Solemn and sacred undertakings were given to live in peace and harmony as relatives, a further refinement of the basic legal traditions that govern individual behaviour.[135] It was these legal traditions that governed our people in treating with the Indigenous nations as well as the "come from away" nations. They were important to our diplomatic initiatives.

The abstract concepts of the existing Human Rights Covenants were not easy to translate into diverse languages, yet the translation process, based on respect and compassionate comprehension, united Indigenous diplomacy.

Indigenizing the Covenants required us to extend Indigenous legal traditions to comprehend how a self-determining people or individual would behave. This was the implicit spirit and intent of Indigenous legal traditions. The drafting process had to articulate new teachings to help guide peoples whose traditions had been damaged by colonialism, and to help displace their rage. Many experts and state representatives of Eurocentric legal traditions did not comprehend the depth or complexity of the task facing the Working Group. They had little or no understanding of Indigenous legal traditions, and they were not particularly skilled at listening to or consulting with Indigenous people.

As we worked on indigenizing the existing Human Rights Covenants, state representatives challenged our visions and aspirations. They questioned our efforts to change the way the world thought about us. They questioned our motives – were we terrorists? socialists? communists? – never imagining that we had rejected all these categories. They questioned our lifestyles and our sources of funding. When our delegates were persecuted, imprisoned, or killed when they returned home, governments spread rumours and attempted to discredit our efforts to bring tyrants to justice. Ogoni poet and dramatist Ken Saro-Wiwa of Nigeria was a poignant example: the government of Nigeria executed him for treason after he went to the UN to promote the rights of the Ogoni as an Indigenous people.[136]

The arguments and strategies of the nation-states were neither new nor creative; they were oppressively familiar. What was new was that they had to listen to our responses. In the political hierarchy of the nation-states, we were ignored; in the working group, these same governments had to live with our visions and our voices. We forced a debate on their historic denial of our humanity. We were not anti-Eurocentric humanists; we merely questioned our exclusion from the category of human rights. Specifically, we clashed with national leaders over whether Indigenous populations were a "people" or "peoples" under existing UN Human Rights Covenants. This was the famous struggle over the final "s" at the World Conference on Human Rights.[137] The Human Rights Covenants talked about "peoples" who had human rights; in the declaration of the World Conference, however, the states attempted to deny the application of human rights to us through the use of the singular term, Indigenous people. We objected, and resisted. State representatives urged us not to hold fast to our highest visions, labelling them "impossible." They urged us, rather, to reach a consensus at the lowest common denominator. Because the multilateral forum is a maze of competing and conflicting interests, this proposal created distrust among the Indigenous participants. The battle increased the awareness among human rights communities of the tensions nation-states felt about recognizing the human rights of Indigenous peoples.

The Vienna Declaration did not use the concept of "Indigenous peoples," but it did recognize the inherent dignity and the unique contribution of Indigenous people to the development and plurality of society, and strongly reaffirmed the commitment of the international community to their economic, social, and cultural well-being, as well as their enjoyment of the fruits of sustainable development. It urged that states should ensure the full and free participation of Indigenous people in all aspects of society, particularly in matters of concern to them. Considering the importance of the promotion and protection of the rights of Indigenous people, and the contribution of such promotion and protection to the political and social stability of the states in which such people live, it declared that states should, in accordance with international law, take concerted positive steps to ensure respect for all the human rights and fundamental freedoms of Indigenous people, on the basis of equality and non-discrimination, and recognize the value and diversity of their distinct identities, cultures, and social organization. It also recommended the renewal and updating of the Working Group, and urged the Working Group to complete the drafting of a Declaration on the Rights of Indigenous People.

7. Indigenous Diplomacy in other International Forums

INDIGENOUS DIPLOMACY GAINED INDIGENOUS PEOPLES recognition of their legal personality as distinct societies with special collective rights and a distinct role in national and international decision-making. Our organizations demonstrated the ability of oppressed and vulnerable peoples to alter nation-states' positions. There was nothing unique in this. It has happened in almost every movement for positive social change in the past few decades: the black liberation struggle, the women's movement, the Velvet Revolution, the undoing of apartheid. Every one of these was animated by peoples who had been stripped of external power. Powerless peoples moved society and its institutions by drawing on the power of the inner consciousness – a power no one could take from them – in a disciplined and dedicated way. We had to learn to harness the inner power of our humanity, traditions, and spirituality to remake global society.

The Indigenous diplomacy network understood that the processes of creating better environments, governments, and humanity might take a few years or a few generations, but we were resolved to stand firm, with dignity and integrity. Indigenous peoples believed, and still believe, that the 21st century will belong to us. It is a peace movement. It is a redefinition of humanity. Indigenous peoples have survived through caring about our humanity, and we will succeed because we care for each other. Our paths will remain united. We need friends and allies in this struggle, because our discussion is about the future of humanity in United Nations law. Many have joined the struggle, but many more voices need to be heard on this critical issue.

We understood that a meaningful *rapprochement*, a re-establishment of cordial relations, was necessary. The first principle had to be respect. The UN system, including the ILO and UNESCO, as well as academic disciplines and organizations concerned with the humanities, had to respect the humanity of Indigenous peoples. They now understand and honour the fact that our attempts to retain our heritage, our knowledge, our dignity, and our faith in the face of oppression was a manifestation of the enduring strength of the human spirit.

The Indigenous diplomatic network operated on a shared vision of integrated and empowered humanities based in sustainable environments. The network moved opportunistically and tactically for *rapprochement* through the regular sessions of the Commissions, the UN treaty monitoring bodies, and the various declarations and conventions of the UN. The unsatisfactory responses of many nation-states to the violations of Indigenous peoples' human rights has compelled the network to bring their issues to these diverse international forums. The network participated in the Commission on Human Rights, the Commission on Sustainable Development, and the Commission on the Status of Women. Some raised complaints and submitted shadow reports to the treaty bodies of the Human Rights Committee that monitors the implementation of the Human Rights Covenants, and the Committee that monitors the Convention on the Elimination of All Forms of Racial Discrimination. The jurisprudence of these treaty bodies comes from their concluding observations, general comments, or decisions of states in implementing ratification in response to the complaints raised to them. The jurisprudence of these treaty bodies is part of international human rights law.

Other parts of the network became involved in the development of conventions that related to their plight. These processes included other human rights instruments, such as the Convention on the Elimination of All Forms of Discrimination Against Women (1979), the Convention against Torture and other Degrading Treatment or Punishment (1984), the Convention on the Rights of the Child (1989), the International Convention on the Rights of Migrant Workers and Members of their Families (1990), and the Convention on the Rights of Persons with Disabilities (2006). The convention on the rights of the child and the rights of persons with disabilities specifically mention Indigenous children and Indigenous persons with disabilities, respectively.

Often parts of the Indigenous diplomatic network combined, as in the UN Conference on Environment and Development. They participated in the parties and working groups of the Convention on Biological Diversity and the UN Framework Convention on Climate Change. They incorporated Indigenous peoples' rights into conservation, environmental, and development-related instruments and policies.

They also united at other world conferences, including the World Conference on Human Rights (1993), the Fourth World Conference on Women (1995), the International Conference on Population and Development (1994), and the World Summit for Social Development (1995).

To protect their traditional knowledge and heritage, they participated in the World Intellectual Property Organization (WIPO) in the Working Group on Traditional Knowledge, Folklore and Traditional Cultural Expressions. They participated in the UNESCO and WIPO Model Treaty on the Protection of Expressions of Folklore against Illicit Exploitation (1992), and in the UN Development Program study on Indigenous knowledge and intellectual property rights entitled *Conserving Indigenous Knowledge: Integrating Two Systems of Innovation* (1994).

To facilitate the participation of Indigenous representatives in the various forums and processes and to give them seed funds for specific projects, the UN established voluntary funds, including the Voluntary Fund for Indigenous Populations (1984), the Voluntary Fund for the International Decade of the World's Indigenous People (1995), the Voluntary Fund for the Permanent Forum (2002), the Voluntary Fund for Indigenous Peoples of the WIPO (2006), the Voluntary Fund for Indigenous Peoples of the Convention of Biological Diversity (2006), and the Voluntary Fund for the Second Decade of the World's Indigenous People (2005). Indigenous participation in these processes has brought gains in terms of instruments and mechanisms that are now addressing their issues.

The network had to find its voice in these large and often alienating forums by creating their own declarations, in a manner similar to the process of the Indigenous declaration. They also created plans of action to form alliances at these forums, and to provide statements of their own to nation-states, industries, and corporations. As nation-states convened at the World Conference on the Environment at Rio – the Earth Summit of 1992 – Indigenous peoples organized their own summit in the Kari-Oca

Villages of Brazil, resulting in the World Conference of Indigenous Peoples on Territory, Environment and Development.

The drafting of declarations in international forums by Indigenous peoples established a foundation for developing strategies for pursuing cultural and intellectual property rights and human rights, and outlined a relationship between the international forums and Indigenous peoples. These declarations can be seen as the collective voice of Indigenous peoples. In the process, we left many ink trails, or cognitive droppings. Our declarations and statements addressed many topics that concerned us: the Declaration of Continuing Independence of the Red Man in the Western Hemisphere (1974); the World Council of Indigenous Peoples' Declaration (Bogota, 1985); the Manila Declaration on the World Declaration for Cultural Development (Philippines, 1988); the Inuvik Declaration on the Protection of the Arctic Environments (Finland, 1991); the Mataatua Declaration on Cultural and Intellectual Property Rights of Indigenous Peoples (New Zealand, 1993); the Indigenous Peoples of Tropical Forests Charter (Penang, 1993); the Statements of the Coordinating Body of the Indigenous Peoples of the Amazon Basin (1994); the Statements of South Pacific Regional Consultation on Indigenous Peoples' Knowledge and Intellectual Property Rights (1995); the Beijing Declaration of Indigenous Women (1995); the related Declaration of the International Indigenous Women's Forum (New York, 2000); the Declaration of First Indigenous Women's Summit of the Americas (Mexico, 2002); the Baguio Declaration of the Second Asian Indigenous Women's Conference (Philippines, 2004); the Ukupseni Declaration, Kuna Yala on the Human Genome Diversity Project (1997); the Indigenous Peoples Seattle Declaration on Mining (Seattle, 1999); the Taipei Declaration on the Rights of Indigenous Peoples (Taiwan, 1999); the various Declarations on Climate Change (Quito, 2000; France, 2000; Netherlands, 2000; Morocco, 2001; India, 2002; Milan, 2003; Kanien'kehá:ka – Mohawk, 2005); the Indigenous Peoples' Political Declaration at Bali, Indonesia (2002); the Kimberley Declaration and the Indigenous Peoples' Plan of Implementation on Sustainable Development (South Africa, 2002); the Indigenous Peoples' Cancun Declaration on the WTO (2003); the various Indigenous Declarations on Water (2001; Japan, 2003; Mexico, 2006); the Statement of the Indigenous Peoples' Interfaith Dialogue on Globalization and Tourism (Thailand, 2002); the Indigenous

Peoples and Information Society Plan of Action adopted at WSIS (Geneva, 2003); the Indigenous Peoples' Declaration on Extractive Industries (United Kingdom, 2003); the Manukan Declaration of the Indigenous Women's Biodiversity Network (Malaysia, 2004); and the Ayateway Declaration of the Indigenous Peoples' Youth Caucus (Coast Salish Territory, 2006) as part of World Urban Forum III in Vancouver, British Columbia.

The process of building consensus and drafting declarations refined our skills in the complex and often duplicitous world of international diplomacy. Our declarations' impacts were especially profound in those parts of the world where Indigenous peoples traditionally had little contact with outsiders. They generated the useful concepts of Indigenous knowledge, traditional ecological knowledge, Indigenous humanities and science, and began to formulate intercultural, trans-paradigmatic, or trans-systemic understandings of issues and topics of importance to Indigenous peoples.

These experiences created gifted, skilled, articulate spokespeople, including James Anaya of the Apache Nation; Marie Battiste of the Mi'kmaw; Bimal Bhikkhu of the Chakma people of Bangladesh; Larissa Behrendt of the Eualeyai/Kamilaroi nations of New South Wales in Australia; Victoria Tauli-Corpuz of the Kankana-ey Igorot in the Philippines; Kenneth Deer of the Mohawk; Mick Dodson of the Yawuru of West Australia; Marcial Garcia of the Kuna, who live in Panama and Colombia; Debra Harry of the Paiute; Lars Emil Johansen of the Inuit; Ed John of the Tl'azt'en Nation of northern British Columbia; Roger Jones of the Ojibwa; Irja Seurujavi-Kari of the Saami (formerly known as Lapps); Davie Kopenawa of the forest-dwelling Yanomahni people of South America; Winona LaDuke of the Ojibwa; Ron Lameman of the Cree; Debebe Pokh Leanui of Hawaii; Wilton Littlechild of the Cree; Lea Nicholas-MacKenzie of the Maliseet; Art Manuel of the Shuswap; William Means of the Lakota; Mayan Nobel laureate Rigoberta Menchu Tum; John Mohawk of the Seneca; Ted Moses of the Cree; Melissa Nelson of the Ojibwa; Lois O'Donogue of the Torres Strait Islands; Tamati Reedy of the Maori; Mary Simon of the Inuit; Sharon Venne of the Cree; Milo Yellowhair of the Lakota; and many, many others.

Based on consensus, shared vision, and developing skills, the Indigenous diplomacy network united to create new normative standards in UN law, the first being the 1989 International Labour Organization Convention on Indigenous and Tribal Peoples.[138] This Convention defines both "Indigenous peoples" and "tribal peoples." Indigenous peoples are defined in terms of their distinctiveness, as well as their descent from the inhabitants of their territory "at the time of conquest or colonization or the establishment of present state boundaries." Tribal peoples are defined as those "whose social, cultural and economic conditions distinguish them from other sections of the national community, and whose status is regulated wholly or partially by their own customs or traditions or by special laws or regulations." The Convention provides that "self-identification" shall be a fundamental criterion when determining the status of particular groups.

The ILO Convention defined Indigenous self-government in national contexts. It acknowledged Indigenous peoples as distinct polities within states, entitled to negotiate consensually in good faith with state authorities, and sometimes to veto state plans.[139] It acknowledged Indigenous peoples as distinct territorial and political entities over which nation-states have only limited power. Through the Convention, Indigenous diplomacy created the foundation of an ecological order, recognizing Indigenous peoples' collective rights to self-development, cultural and institutional integrity, territory, and environmental security.[140] It referred to Indigenous peoples' rights to the "ownership and possession" of the "total environment" they occupy or use, as well as their right to be protected from environmental degradation, involuntary removal, and unwanted intrusion by outsiders.[141] The ILO Convention has been ratified by enough states to make it part of international law.

The Indigenous diplomacy network also lobbied for self-development, ecological sustainability, and cultural integrity. It attained global consensus on these issues at the 1992 Rio Declaration on the Environment.[142] Principle 22 of the Rio Declaration recognized Indigenous peoples as distinct social partners in achieving sustainable development, emphasizing the unique value and role that Indigenous peoples have "in environmental management and development because of their knowledge and traditional practices."[143] "States should recognize and duly support their identity, culture and interests," the document urged, "and enable their effective participation in the achievement of sustainable development."[144]

The Rio Summit included a chapter for Indigenous peoples' programs in Agenda 21, a comprehensive global and national program of action for achieving sustainable development, which was based on proposals submitted by Indigenous organizations.[145] The inseparability of cultural distinctiveness and territory from the concept of "Indigenous" was noted in Agenda 21, which was adopted by a consensus of member states: "Indigenous people and their communities have a historical relationship with their lands and are generally descendants of the original inhabitants of those lands." The centrality of land tenure systems and ecological knowledge to the knowledge and heritage of Indigenous peoples was reaffirmed, again by consensus, at the International Conference on Population and Development at Cairo (1994).[146]

In 1992, the network lobbied for the recognition and inclusion of "traditional ecological knowledge" in the UN Convention on Biological Diversity, a multilateral treaty to sustain the diversity of life on our planet.[147] We also lobbied the global scientific community to include traditional ecological knowledge in the new commitments for science for the 21st century.[148]

After our resistance in 1992 to the 500th anniversary of the "discovery" of America, the Indigenous diplomacy network lobbied the UN General Assembly for a new partnership, and succeeded in having the General Assembly declare an International Year of the World's Indigenous Peoples in 1993.[149] We also lobbied the General Assembly for an International Decade of the World's Indigenous Peoples to be implemented from 1995 to 2004,[150] a permanent forum on Indigenous Issues,[151] a study on how to protect the heritage of Indigenous people – a postcolonial blueprint for Indigenous humanity[152] – and for a UN study of Indigenous peoples' treaties, lands, and natural resources.[153] At the same time, we lobbied for special recognition and protection of Indigenous peoples in the various meetings that led to the World Conference Against Racism, Racial Discrimination, Xenophobia and Related Intolerances.[154] Combined, these achievements manifested an Indigenous vision of our humanity and human rights in the international forums, and released the power of a vision of an ecological theory of good order and proper relations to the diversities of life.[155]

Agreement on the need to establish a "permanent forum" was perhaps the most important aspect of the UN resolution proclaiming the First Decade. The network recognized that efforts to influence the various UN forums, bodies, and programs needed an institutional body which could discuss and analyze them in a more comprehensive manner and where gains could be used to reinforce previous work in these arenas. The network needed a mechanism that would link the parts of the UN system dealing with Indigenous peoples' issues for better coordination and implementation. In April 2001, after intensive lobbing, the UN announced the establishment of a Permanent Forum on Indigenous Issues.[156] The Forum was established as a subsidiary organ of the Economic and Social Council of the UN New York. It was designed to "serve as an advisory body to the Council with a mandate to discuss Indigenous issues within the mandate of the Council relating to economic and social development, culture and the environment, education and human rights."[157] The Forum was an important venue in which to push for finishing the work of the Indigenous declaration through the UN, and it led the way in creating the Second International Decade for Indigenous Peoples, 2005-2014.[158] It was also an important agency for establishing a better relationship with the UN General Assembly and the various parts of the global order. Since its creation, the Forum has hosted a number of representatives of Indigenous peoples, governments, NGOs, UN bodies, programs and funds, with academia and other multilateral organizations taking part in its annual sessions. The Forum's events have increased to include some 1500 participants annually.

The proclamation of the Second Decade did more than continue the efforts of the first. It reflected an awareness of the injustices that Indigenous peoples continue to endure in many parts of the world. It reaffirmed the urgent need to recognize, promote, and protect more effectively the rights and freedoms of Indigenous peoples.

The achievements and activities of the Indigenous diplomatic network were vital to the emergence of a reoriented body of law that confirms and protects the individual and collective rights of Indigenous peoples. It has moved beyond the original "naming, shaming, and complaining" efforts directed at nation-states. Human rights monitoring has been extended, special procedures have been established, and Special Rapporteurs have been mandated to monitor human rights violations. In the late 1990s the UN system started to integrate human rights into development work, and humanitarian and peace operations. In 2003, UN bodies, agencies, and programs arrived at a "Common Understanding of a Human Rights-Based Approach to Development." This approach integrates the norms, standards, and principles of the international human rights system into the plans, policies, and processes of development. Indigenous peoples had urged this approach, for it approximates their perspective on how development should take place.

The network's thinking and working with human rights NGOs, women's organizations, and labour unions, among others, had generated programs and projects supportive of human rights, and had generated institution building, human rights information, education, and training.

Equally important, the network had introduced into the vast UN system the Indigenous perspective on relationships with the land and peoples. It introduced a nameless, leaderless style of animating humanity. It had been the source of a turning point of this generation of peoples' relationship to the earth – the ecological or green revolution. Indigenous perspectives reveal the quiet hub of true ecological civilization, the ability to live well within the biological constraints of surrounding life, and its various processes. These perspectives carry the teachings and wisdom of generating efforts with sustainable values, revealing the underlying interconnectedness and order of a vulnerable biosphere. It is the knowledge of the deepest spiritual teaching of Indigenous civilizations about the holistic kinship of all life forms, that has survived and taken on new richness in the scientific world of modern ecology. These perspectives assisted in generating the largest cognitive transformation of humanity which declares that every place matters and has value. It has nurtured a cascading global uprising, a movement of ideas, to reclaim basic human rights in relation to the earth. The movement attached to this uprising has overrun Eurocentric ideologies of knowledge and power. In multiple sites, these perspectives have allowed peoples to confront despair, resignation, intolerance, racism, injustice, and power with momentum, conflict, spirit, and heart. It has helped create a global moment that has been called the "blessed unrest."

Still, the network saw it was important to have the UN General Assembly affirm the Indigenous declaration. A shift in global consciousness toward Indigenous peoples and their rights was palpable, but incomplete. The networked decided to refocus on enacting a UN declaration on the rights of Indigenous peoples to make the new frameworks effective.

8. The Indigenous Declaration in the Governments' Working Group

OVER THE YEARS, THE INDIGENOUS DIPLOMATIC NETWORK had documented the gaps in existing international human rights law in relation to the protection of the individual and the collective rights of Indigenous peoples. Our achievements in the UN had not remedied the situation. In our dialogues with experts and nation-states, we became convinced that our human rights should be put down, in black ink, in each of the languages of the UN system. The clarification of our human rights would lead to better comprehension of our vision by member states and the global community, and would generate a better life in a sustainable world. The biggest challenge was how to ensure that Indigenous people could enjoy their individual and collective human rights in their daily lives, in their own communities. This goal would require the adoption of the Indigenous declaration in the Human Rights Committee, where it was labelled the UN Draft Declaration on the Rights of Indigenous Peoples. The adoption of the declaration had been one of the goals of the International Decade of the World's Indigenous People. Indigenous peoples agreed to view and ratify the Indigenous declaration as their first international postcolonial treaty. As Erica-Irene Daes stated,

> It is of particular satisfaction to me that the draft Declaration on the Rights of Indigenous Peoples truly reflects the values, beliefs and aspirations of the peoples concerned. More than that, it has come to be regarded, by indigenous peoples themselves, as their own. . . . The

> members of the Working Group have been inspired by indigenous peoples; they have dared to be visionary, in the true original spirit of the United Nations. . . .[159]

The Indigenous declaration was developed as an interpretive tool for applying the UN Human Rights Covenants to Indigenous peoples. Translating our aspirations and legal traditions into human rights protocols was difficult, a remedial task of converting hope to insight and experience to enactment. The declaration's 45 articles witnessed a new style of collaboration between human right experts and Indigenous peoples.[160] Our fragile Indigenous compromises spoke of honour, caring, and healing; still, they have to be placed in the context of the drafting protocol of UN conventions on human rights and their normative categories. It was a cold and sterile experience; the linguistic protocols camouflaged the bitterness of the debates and the scars of criticism and discord. What emerged for the translating process was the minimal human rights standards necessary for the survival, dignity, and well-being of Indigenous peoples, a "common language of humanity."[161]

The Indigenous declaration goes further than the Convention on Indigenous and Tribal Peoples (1989) as a statement of the aspirations of Indigenous peoples in human rights. It clearly recognizes Indigenous peoples' right to self-determination. It also recognizes the right to self-government within existing states, should Indigenous peoples choose this route. Indigenous peoples' rights to land extend to their traditional territories, not simply the lands they currently occupy, and include surface and subsoil resources. The treaties previously made with Indigenous peoples must be respected according to "their original spirit and intent," and disputes must be submitted to international tribunals. Indigenous peoples would only be subject to laws and institutions of their own choosing, whether they chose to form new, independent states or not.

The Indigenous declaration reasserted the existing right to self-determination: "By virtue of that right they freely determine their political status and freely pursue their economic, social and cultural development."[162] It affirmed that Indigenous peoples are free, and equal to all other individuals and people in dignity and rights,[163] and that they have the right to the full and effective enjoyment of human rights and fundamental freedoms in international human rights law.[164] These rights did not imply, for any state, group, or person, the right to engage in any activity contrary to the UN Charter.[165] The other articles articulated how the right of self-determination operated in the political, economic, social, and cultural development of males and females.[166] They created minimum standards[167] in human rights for our peoples and their children without diminishing or extinguishing any existing or future rights of Indigenous peoples.

The declaration protected our inherent rights,[168] autonomy,[169] social[170] and legal systems,[171] our traditional health practices,[172] treaties,[173] and nationality[174] so that we can enjoy a life that respects our Indigenous humanities and concepts of dignity. It confronted the ideology and broad social and educational forces that produced the influences in colonial society that deprived Indigenous peoples of their wealth, teachings, humanity, and heritage.[175] The declaration also affirmed Indigenous peoples' rights to practise and revitalize our cultural traditions and customs,[176] our spiritual and religious traditions;[177] to revitalize, use, and develop our languages, histories, oral traditions, philosophies, writing systems, and literatures.[178] It affirmed our right to education, to establish and control our educational systems[179] and media,[180] as well as have our traditions reflected in public information and the state educational system.[181] It affirmed our diverse rights regarding lands, territories, and resources essential to the cultural identities of Indigenous peoples,[182] including the protection, restoration, and conservation of their environments.[183]

It provided protection and security in times of armed conflict.[184] It affirmed the right to life, physical security, and liberty,[185] and the right not to be subjected to any act of ethnocide, cultural genocide, or any other act of violence, including the forcible removing of our children.[186] It provided Indigenous peoples with the right to participate in their own affairs, as well as in national and global affairs.[187] It provided us with access to adequate financial and technical assistance to develop and enjoy our rights;[188] it guaranteed prompt decisions for the resolution of conflicts and disputes, and effective remedies;[189] it articulated measures for improving economic and social conditions,[190] for the application of international and national labour laws,[191] and for determining priorities and strategies for development, access to health services, and medical care.[192]

Many nation-states were unsettled by the scope of the declaration. The Sub-Commission on Prevention of Discrimination and Protection of Minority Rights requested a technical review of the draft text by the Secretariat.[193] This involved an examination of the text by the professional staff of the Centre for Human Rights with the aim of flagging internal inconsistencies or conflicts with existing UN instruments. The review committee found the text of the declaration consistent with existing UN human rights. The Sub-Commission passed the Indigenous declaration.[194] Many member states still resisted, and lobbied the Human Rights Committee not to adopt the declaration.

Yielding to pressure, in 1995 the Human Rights Committee created an open-ended intersessional working group of 53 representatives of member states, the Working Group on the Draft Declaration of Indigenous Rights (WGDD), to review the declaration. The ambassador of Peru was elected chair and rapporteur. Indigenous peoples felt they were being exposed to yet another degrading procedure, and our engagement with the nation-states became antagonistic. This was a time of hard, challenging conversations, as each day revealed deep and conflicting interests. It was a time of intrigue, dissent, deceit, and diversity. It brought out the worst – and the best – in all the participants.

Despite international acceptance of the Universal Declaration of Human Rights and the Human Rights Covenants that guaranteed the fundamental rights of all human beings, the nation-states still viewed Indigenous peoples as non-peoples, and not entitled to the same rights as other humans. The necessity of striking the WGDD made it clear that, to influential nation-states, Indigenous humanity remained problematic and threatening. Despite their international rhetoric, nation-states failed to understand the necessity of the equal application of existing human rights to Indigenous peoples. Nation-states rejected the right of Indigenous peoples to self-determination, in particular, since this might lead to unacceptable consequences in terms of their legitimacy and territorial integrity. In effect, they wanted to reserve the right of self-determination to those who are already privileged to exercise it. They ignored the Principles on Friendly Relations Among States in Accordance with the Charter of the United Nations (1970), which granted legitimacy and territorial integrity only to those states that conducted themselves in conformity with the principles of equality and self-determination of all peoples, which would necessarily include Indigenous peoples.[195]

Some nation-states rejected the Indigenous declaration as unrealistic, or too visionary; its provisions went beyond the current practice of most nation-states, in that it called for fundamental changes in the legal structure of many states. But as Dr. Daes reminded them, in the context of 1948, the Universal Declaration of Human Rights was also unrealistic and visionary:

> It was adopted at a time when European empires still spanned the globe, the Cold War was just beginning, and most nations on earth were not free. The drafters of the Universal Declaration were not discouraged by the actual state of affairs in their time. They were not deterred by arguments that they should be more realistic.[196]

The drafters "were concerned with *justice* – and with fixing a proper goal for the work of generations to come."[197] The fact that "the *program* of *justice* set forth in the Universal Declaration is still far from being achieved for all people, in all countries ... does not mean that it was a *mistake* to adopt the Universal Declaration of Human Rights, 47 years ago."[198]

> What a different and unhappy world it would be, today, had Member states of the United Nations *rejected* the Universal Declaration as unrealistic, and dimmed this one, pure, clear light of justice for the hundreds of millions of people who languished under dictatorship and oppression in the decades following the Second World War! ... If we measured the relevance or value of human-rights instruments by the standard of *current practice*, rather than the hopes and dreams of humanity, we should have no choice but to consign them all to the rubbish-heap.[199]

She stressed that "Justice will *always* be an ideal that stands just beyond the reach of humankind,"[200] and that "We are imperfect; ... [b]ut it is the essence of our humanity that we continue to struggle against despair, and towards our vision of justice."[201]

> The United Nations strengthened the struggle of colonized peoples by recognizing their right to be free, long before they were free. It bolstered the struggle of people in authoritarian states for democracy by recognizing the legitimacy of their dreams, decades before the Cold War came to an end. It sustained the long struggle against apartheid, by recognizing the justice of that cause, many years before it finally succeeded. We must remain true to this tradition of giving hope for justice.
>
> We must insist that the draft Declaration on the Rights of Indigenous Peoples be adopted in substantially its present form, without deleting the principles which are central to indigenous peoples' hopes for true justice. I refer, in particular, to the equal right of all peoples, including indigenous peoples, to self-determination.[202]

Most of the nation-states of the WGDD wanted to rewrite the entire text of the declaration to conform to their colonial orthodoxies and their view of Indigenous peoples as minorities. They had no remedies for colonization; they were preoccupied with how to prolong their own privileges. In Eurocentric legal systems, internationally and nationally, the ideal of colonization had taken on a familiar institutional form, making it difficult to represent and discuss alternative civilization or institutions, thus sustaining and developing the privileges of the colonists. The government of the day, often our national legal guardians and fiduciaries, did not want to transform the legal or political structure of their institutions to include or accommodate Indigenous peoples. They did not want to end their national myths. They did not want to expose the injustice that has informed the construction of international law or state institutions and practices. They did not want to create postcolonial states. They did not want to make sustained efforts at institutional reform. They rejected the idea of hybridized states that included Indigenous people in the political or adjudicative realms. They wanted Indigenous people to vanish into sameness, or into replicative or imitative institutions. Their efforts were aimed at concealing the constitutive contradictions of the artificial settler ideologies and the law whose search for an innate order had failed.

In the WGDD, Indigenous people took the position that they would not accept any changes to or censorship of the Indigenous declaration.[203]

The nation-states had no legitimate authority to deny international human rights to Indigenous people or to appropriate their visions or consensus about their human rights. We rooted our support for this uncompromising standard in a sense of justice, based on the abhorrence of the wrongs we had experienced. Our demands were to end colonization and racism. We did not want any more people to have the experience we had endured, rather than achieve a vision of the best life possible. The Indigenous declaration was our expression of our humanity and our international human rights. We refused to have fewer human rights that the colonialists. We felt it would be pointless to accept lower human rights' standards than those accorded to other peoples of the UN.

In this venue, Indigenous peoples continued a creative, if chaotic, dialogue with the nation-states about the wording of the declaration. Ideas derived from colonialism and the failures of liberalism, socialism, and communism in Eurocentric thought confronted the ecological consciousness and order of Indigenous peoples. The intellectual violence of the arguments of the nation-states in the WGDD magnified our daily existence in the nation-states. The disagreement, often heated, was a familiar retaliation to our national assertion of our humanity and rights.

An example of this is the preoccupation of the nation-states with legalism. They devoted painstaking work each year to revising the Indigenous declaration and preparing elaborate counter-proposals, clearly acting as if they believed the resulting document would be legally binding, and a single poorly-chosen word or phrase could lead to national tragedy. They worried about the implications of Indigenous rights, refusing to acknowledge the privileges they had appropriated for themselves. Legalism dominated the daily discussions, mostly affirming that the UN Human Rights Covenants protected only the colonizers, while denying the colonized the same rights. In the context of human rights, the antidote for colonization, the nation-states sought an implausible legal sanctification of colonization in the declaration. Only Canada had stated that Indigenous peoples have a right to self-determination. Nevertheless, even Canada requested a more comfortable wording to limit Indigenous peoples' right to unilateral succession. In many ways, the resisting state representatives had lost their faith in the ideal of self-determination.

The chair of the Working Group on Indigenous Populations, Dr. Daes, for the Sub-Commission on Prevention of Discrimination and Protection of Minorities, described our position accurately when she stated that the declaration was "belated state-building." Indigenous peoples know that the nation-states are strong and that we are vulnerable and poor. The discussion over Indigenous human rights confirmed this imbalance, making compromise difficult. Gradually, an innovative and transformative dialogue emerged. In an awkward way, this dialogue was forging the future of the environment and humanity.

To counteract the nation-states, Indigenous representatives had to demonstrate the validity of their teachings. In such a reactionary environment, our behaviour was tested. We had to be decent, just, humble, responsible, courageous, comprehending, and honest, as our traditions had taught us. We had to act in harmony with our vision, rather than become tactical and authoritative, imitating the techniques of the colonizers. This may not have been the most practical strategy, and maintaining civility, trust, and openness was difficult, but in the process we discovered that Eurocentric expertise that is not grounded in or did not converge with Indigenous traditions and responsibilities cannot make us more human. Self-determination is more than a paper right, it is a state of being, and it is a difficult and complex duty.

By 2004, the final year of the First Decade, consensus had been reached on only two of the 45 articles. The future looked bleak. At the centre of the discussion was the right to self-determination. For the Indigenous delegates at the Working Group, the right of self-determination was fundamental. If it was not accepted as formulated in the declaration, identical with the existing wording of the Human Rights Covenants, many of the remaining articles would be meaningless. Self-determination is a prerequisite for the exercise of spiritual, territorial, social, cultural, economic, and political rights, as well as for practical survival. Most states, led by Australia, Canada, and New Zealand, wanted the self-determination of Indigenous peoples to be qualified. We responded that they should then attempt to qualify the existing right of self-determination for all peoples in the Human Rights Covenants, which is a basic principle of international law and the foundation of the international human rights system. We argued that it would be unacceptable and discriminatory to qualify or restrict Indigenous peoples' right of self-determination. Without the non-discriminatory application of international standards, the fundamental integrity of the UN's standard-setting on the rights of Indigenous peoples would be seriously compromised.

Many states had suggested alternative strategies. Norway suggested, for example, that the right of self-determination should be addressed in the Preamble to reflect the language of the Declaration on Friendly Relations (1970) as it currently exists in international law. The problem of articulating specific qualified rights could therefore be avoided, leaving article 3 identical to the other Covenants.[204]

We had few allies. Humanity's academics, universities, and their professional organizations were uncommitted to our struggle to define our humanity and protect our heritage. They chose not to aid us as we attempted to remedy the toxic legacies of colonization. We have never experienced the beneficial force of international solidarity.

Only a few scholars have affirmed our humanity and our declaration. Most academics, either in law or the humanities, have not supported the Indigenous quest for equal human rights. Like their nation-states, most Eurocentric academics were struggling with the challenges of our request for transformation. Most have offered little explanation for their position in these crucial discussions. They were engaged in the International Year of Indigenous Peoples, and in the International Decade of Indigenous Peoples, but they were not a force in the discourses of the WGDD. I am not sure why most of them stood aloof from these complex issues about our humanity and human rights. Some Indigenous thinkers have offered explanations for this apathy. Perhaps most important is the apprehension that Eurocentrism's legacy in the humanities was being challenged. Yet there were some exceptions, notably the Humanities Research Unit at the University of Saskatchewan, led by Dr. Len Findlay.[205]

In the 2004 debates on the creation of the Second International Decade of the World's Indigenous Peoples, the UN General Assembly and Secretary General subtly responded to the lack of progress in the WGDD. The General Assembly took note of the Commission on Human Rights' resolution expressing its concern about the precarious economic and social situation Indigenous people continued to endure in comparison to the overall population, and the persistence of grave violations of their human rights; it reaffirmed the urgent need to recognize, promote, and protect more effectively their rights and freedoms.[206] It recalled that, in creating the First International Decade, the General Assembly had put on record its expectation of achieving the adoption of a declaration on Indigenous rights as a major objective.[207] It noted that the declaration had not been achieved in the first Decade. It reaffirmed that nation-states should, in accordance with international law, take concerted, positive steps to ensure respect for the human rights and fundamental freedoms of Indigenous peoples, on the basis of equality and non-discrimination, recognizing the value and diversity of their distinctive identities, cultures, and social organization.[208] It urged all parties to the process to do their utmost to carry out the mandate of the WGDD and to present for adoption as soon as possible a final draft of the declaration on the rights of Indigenous peoples.[209]

UN Secretary General Kofi Annan also responded to the perplexing situation in the WGDD:

> For far too long the hopes and aspirations of indigenous peoples have been ignored; their lands have been taken; their cultures denigrated or directly attacked; their languages and customs suppressed; their wisdom and traditional knowledge overlooked; and their sustainable ways of developing natural resources dismissed. Some have even faced the threat of extinction. . . . The answer to these grave threats must be to confront them without delay.[210]

Under this pressure, after 11 years of negotiation and sometimes vitriolic debate, the governments' working group reached a consensus on the Declaration in 2006.[211] The WGDD adopted most of the principles and wording of the Indigenous declaration, with only minor changes in the wording.

9. The UN Declaration on the Rights of Indigenous Peoples

IN THE UN HUMAN RIGHTS COUNCIL, which in March 2006 had replaced the discredited Human Rights Commission, the draft Declaration was affirmed by 30 votes of the 47-member council.[212] Only Canada and Russia voted against the proposal, although 12 nation-states abstained or were absent. Following a request for a vote by Australia, New Zealand, and the United States in the UN General Assembly in 2007, the Declaration was affirmed by 143 recorded votes, with 11 abstentions[213] and 36 absent.[214] Only four nation-states voted against it: Australia, Canada, New Zealand, and the United States.[215]

Canada and the Aboriginal political organizations and NGOs were active participants in the 20-year movement toward the Declaration and its affirmation of Indigenous "peoplehood." For two decades, Canada was a reluctant ally of the project,[216] yet it was one of the first governments to accept the principles of the Indigenous declaration.[217] Under a new minority Conservative government, however, Canada's position on the Declaration was reversed. Canada explained its position by claiming it was representing the interests of the United States, Australia, and New Zealand, rather than Canadians or Aboriginal peoples. When pressed, Canada said that some of its provisions were incompatible with Canadian law and wanted two more years of discussions. Human rights experts and Indigenous peoples' organizations pointed out that the Declaration would not override any domestic laws or existing human rights obligations. International law existed as a separate legal system from national legal systems. In addition, the

Declaration contains specific assurances, introduced by Canada, that its provisions must be interpreted in a fair and balanced manner that respects basic principles of human rights, democratic society, and good government.[218] Canada remained defiant.

The Declaration is not a perfect document; it is a negotiated compromise among Indigenous peoples and the nation-states of the United Nations General Assembly. But it is a just document, one that expresses minimum standards of human rights. As such, it leaves room for future changes at the international, national, and local levels. This allows the document to accommodate a great deal of cultural and institutional variation, and to leave a large space for dialogue and democratic decision-making. Neither the Declaration nor the existing Human Rights Covenants tells peoples everything we need to know about human rights or humanity; these documents only reveal the existing global consensus.

The Declaration is interrelated with the multilateral treaties on human rights among nation-states and is an integral part of the Human Rights Covenants that owe their existence to the consensual ratification of a multilateral treaty of the UN that regulates nation-states' actions, and related declarations. It is an interpretative document that explains how existing human rights are applied to Indigenous peoples and their contexts. It is a restatement of principles for postcolonial self-determination and human rights. In Indigenous legal traditions, it embodies some of our teachings about human rights and being human in a complex world.

The Declaration clearly affirms that Indigenous peoples are peoples whom nation-states cannot arbitrarily deny the right of self-determination. It affirms the collective and individual dignity of Indigenous peoples – our rights to be considered as full human beings, and to construct lives, societies, and civilizations that transcend the vulnerabilities and uncertainties imposed by colonization and empire. The human rights of Indigenous peoples and the responsibilities of the UN and the nation-states contained in the Declaration constitute minimum standards for the survival, dignity, and well-being of Indigenous peoples.[219] They are the beginning of the teachings that fair consensus could be reached with Indigenous peoples and the states. They are not the entire teachings.

The human rights and freedoms acknowledged in the Declaration are guaranteed equally to males and females,[220] to elders, children, and youth,[221] and to people with disabilities.[222] These rights and freedoms "shall be interpreted in accordance with the principles of justice, democracy, respect for human rights, equality, non-discrimination, good government, and good faith."[223]

"Indigenous peoples have the right to the full enjoyment, as a collective or as individuals, of all human rights and fundamental freedoms as recognized in the Charter of the United Nations, the Universal Declaration of Human Rights and international human rights law" is the deep agreement with which the intricate Declaration begins.[224] Indigenous peoples and individuals are free and equal to all other peoples and individuals and have the right to be free from any kind of discrimination in the exercise of their rights, in particular those rights that are based on their Indigenous origin or identity.[225] Every Indigenous person has the right to a nationality.[226] Indigenous peoples and individuals have the right to belong to an Indigenous community or nation, in accordance with the traditions and customs of the community or nation concerned.[227] No discrimination of any kind may arise from the exercise of such a right.[228]

Indigenous peoples have the right to maintain and strengthen their distinct political, legal, economic, social, and cultural institutions, while retaining the right to participate fully, if they choose, in the political, economic, social, and cultural life of the state.[229] They have the right to promote, develop, and maintain their institutional structures and their distinctive customs, spirituality, traditions, procedures, practices and, where they exist, juridical systems or customs, in accordance with international human rights standards.[230] They have the right to maintain and develop their political, economic, and social systems or institutions, be secure in the enjoyment of their own means of subsistence and development, and engage freely in all their traditional and other economic activities.[231]

The Declaration reasserted the existing right to self-determination. The General Assembly agreed that "Indigenous peoples have the right to self-determination. By virtue of that right they freely determine their political status and freely pursue their economic, social and cultural development."[232] Indigenous peoples, in exercising their right to self-determination, have the right to autonomy or self-government in matters relating to their internal and local affairs, as well as ways and means of financing their autonomous functions.[233] They have the right to participate in decision-making in matters that would affect their rights, through representatives chosen by themselves in accordance with their own procedures, as well as to maintain and develop their own Indigenous decision-making institutions;[234] to determine their own identity or membership in accordance with their customs and traditions, without impairing the right of Indigenous individuals to obtain citizenship of the states in which they live;[235] to determine the structures and select the membership of their institutions in accordance with their own procedures;[236] and to determine the responsibilities of individuals to their communities.[237] Indigenous peoples, in particular those divided by international borders, have the right to maintain and develop contacts, relations, and co-operation, including activities for spiritual, cultural, political, economic, and social purposes, with their own members as well as with other peoples across borders.[238]

Indigenous peoples have the right to the recognition, observance, and enforcement of treaties, agreements, and other constructive arrangements concluded with states or their successors and to have states honour and respect such treaties, agreements, and other constructive arrangements.[239] Nothing in the Declaration is to be interpreted as diminishing or eliminating the rights of Indigenous peoples contained in treaties, agreements, and other constructive arrangements[240] or to be construed as diminishing or extinguishing the rights Indigenous peoples now enjoy or may acquire in the future.[241]

In terms of development, which is necessary for self-determination, the General Assembly declared and affirmed that Indigenous peoples have the right to determine and develop priorities and strategies for exercising their right to development.[242] In particular, Indigenous peoples have the right to be actively involved in developing and determining health, housing, and other economic and social programs affecting them and, as far as possible, to administer such programs through their own institutions.[243] They have the right to enjoy fully all rights established under applicable international and domestic labour law.[244] They have the right, without discrimination, to the improvement of their economic and social conditions, including education, employment, vocational training and retraining, housing, sanitation, health, and social security.[245] The right to development involves adequate standards of living and economic well-being.

In terms of the right to cultural integrity and development, the General Assembly declared the global consensus that Indigenous peoples have the right to practise and revitalize their cultural traditions and customs. This includes the right to maintain, protect, and develop the past, present, and future manifestations of their cultures, such as archaeological and historical sites, artefacts, designs, ceremonies, technologies, and visual and performing arts and literature.[246] Indigenous peoples have the right to:

- manifest, practise, develop, and teach their spiritual and religious traditions, customs, and ceremonies;
- maintain, protect, and have access in privacy to their religious and cultural sites;
- the use and control of their ceremonial objects, and the right to the repatriation of their human remains;[247]
- revitalize, use, develop, and transmit to future generations their histories, languages, oral traditions, philosophies, writing systems, and literatures;
- designate and retain their own names for communities, places, and persons;[248]
- establish and control their educational systems and institutions, providing education in their own languages, in a manner appropriate to their cultural methods of teaching and learning;[249]
- the dignity and diversity of their cultures, traditions, histories, and aspirations which shall be appropriately reflected in educational and public information;[250]
- establish their own media in their own languages and have access to all forms of non-Indigenous media without discrimination;[251]
- maintain, control, protect, and develop their cultural heritage, traditional knowledge and cultural expressions, as well as the manifestations of their sciences, technologies, and cultures, including human and genetic resources, seeds, medicines, knowledge of the properties of fauna and flora, oral traditions, literatures, designs, sports and traditional games, and visual and performing arts;[252] and
- maintain, control, protect, and develop their intellectual property over such cultural heritage, traditional knowledge, and traditional cultural expressions.[253]

In terms of the right to personal integrity, the General Assembly declared the global consensus that Indigenous peoples have the collective right to live in freedom, peace, and security as distinct peoples, and shall not be subject to any act of genocide or other violence, including forcibly removing children of the group to another group.[254] Indigenous peoples and individuals have the right not to be subjected to forced assimilation or the destruction of their culture.[255]

In terms of the right to personal integrity and health, the General Assembly declared the global consensus that Indigenous peoples have the right to traditional medicines and to maintain their health practices, including the conservation of vital medicinal plants, animals, and minerals.[256] Additionally, Indigenous individuals have the right to access, without discrimination, all social and health services.[257] They have an equal right to the enjoyment of the highest attainable standard of physical and mental health.[258] Indigenous individuals have the rights to life, physical and mental integrity, liberty, and security of the person.[259] These rights, especially the right to life, are connected to the right to development and self-determination; together they generate the conditions of economic livelihood.

In terms of territorial rights, the General Assembly declared the global consensus that Indigenous peoples have the right to maintain and strengthen their distinctive spiritual relationship with their traditionally owned or otherwise occupied and used lands, territories, waters, and coastal seas and other resources, and to uphold their responsibilities to future generations in this regard.[260] They have the right to the lands, territories, and resources they have traditionally owned, occupied, or otherwise used or acquired.[261] They have the right to own, use, develop, and control the lands, territories, and resources they possess by reason of traditional ownership or other traditional occupation or use, as well as those they have otherwise acquired.[262] They have the right to determine and develop priorities in the use of their lands or territories and other resources.[263] They have the right to the conservation and protection of the environment and the productive capacity of their lands or territories and resources.[264] These territorial rights are significant, as there are no formal guarantees over the rights to land in other international human rights declarations or documents. They are connected to the right to development and economic security.

In terms of legal rights and state remedies, the General Assembly declared the global consensus that Indigenous peoples have the rights to participate in a fair, independent, impartial, open, and transparent process established by the states, with Indigenous participation, to recognize and adjudicate the rights of Indigenous peoples pertaining to their lands, territories, and resources.[265] Indigenous peoples have the right to redress, by means that can include restitution or, where this is not possible, just, fair, and equitable compensation for the lands, territories, and resources they have traditionally owned or otherwise occupied or used, and which have been confiscated, taken, occupied, used, or damaged without their prior and informed consent.[266] Unless otherwise freely agreed on by all concerned, compensation shall take the form of lands, territories, and resources equal in quality, size, and legal status or of monetary compensation or other appropriate redress.[267]

The General Assembly declared that Indigenous peoples shall not be forcibly removed from their lands or territories. No relocation shall take place without the prior and informed consent of the peoples concerned and after agreement on just and fair compensation and, where possible, with the option of return.[268] Indigenous peoples deprived of their means of subsistence and development are entitled to just and fair redress.[269]

The Declaration is a tipping point in international law and history. It is viewed as essential to promote harmonious relations and mutual respect among Indigenous peoples and nation-states, since it affirms the collective right to live in freedom, peace, and security as distinct peoples and their right to participate in decision-making.

As Indigenous peoples enter the 21st century as self-determining people, the need is great for humanity to embrace a consciousness that enables all peoples to enrich their character and dignity. This consciousness should allow the once-powerless voices of Indigenous peoples to emerge, and these voices should be welcomed as positive contributions to human and cultural diversity. To be heard in this way is one of the fundamental rights Indigenous peoples seek, but it is a right that is countered by structural marginalization and contested sites of struggle.

For Indigenous peoples to emerge from these contested sites with the justice, harmony, and dignity envisioned in the Declaration, they are required to reach deep into their legal traditions. The Human Rights Covenants do not specifically refer to the protection of the territorial integrity of the nation-states; however, article 46(1) of the Declaration does:

> Nothing in this Declaration may be interpreted as implying for any State, people, group, or person any right to engage in any activity or to perform any act contrary to the Charter of the United Nations or construed as authorizing or encouraging any action which would dismember or impair, totally or in part, the territorial integrity or political unity of sovereign and independent States.[270]

This passage is consistent with the law of relations among states in international law,[271] and with the Indigenous legal traditions and teachings that underlie our ancestors' intent in the treaties. Most civil and political rights in the Human Rights Covenants are not absolute – they are, in some cases, overridden by other considerations and rightly set aside. For example, article 4 of the Civil and Political Rights Covenant permits rights to be suspended during times "of public emergency which threatens the life of the nation."[272]

Also consistent with Indigenous legal traditions is the provision that, in the exercise of the rights in the Declaration, "the human rights and fundamental freedoms of all shall be respected."[273] The exercise of these rights will be "subject only to such limitations as are determined by law, and in accordance with international human rights obligations."[274] These limitations shall be "non-discriminatory and strictly necessary solely for the purpose of securing due recognition and respect for the rights and freedom of others and for meeting the just and most compelling requirements of a democratic society."[275]

The Declaration affirms that the organs and specialized agencies of the UN system and other intergovernmental organizations shall contribute to the full realization of the provisions through the mobilization, *inter alia*, of financial co-operation and technical assistance.[276] The UN system is required to establish ways and means of ensuring the participation of Indigenous peoples on issues affecting them.[277] Indigenous peoples have the right of access to financial and technical assistance through international co-operation, for the enjoyment of the rights contained in the Declaration.[278]

These rights and duties in the Declaration are not new to most nation-states. Rather, they are declaratory of existing duties. The most basic tenet of international human rights is to regulate the behaviour of governments toward humans. All member states of the United Nations are legally bound to uphold at all times the purposes and principles of the UN Charter. They have a duty to guarantee respect for human rights.[279] Their obligations include "promoting and encouraging respect for human rights and for fundamental freedoms for all without distinction as to race, sex, language, or religion."[280] Under international human rights covenants[281] and other instruments,[282] Canada and other states have a duty to "promote the realization of a right of self-determination" and to "respect that right, in conformity with the provisions of the Charter of the United Nations."[283] They have guaranteed to respect human rights.[284]

The full realization of the human rights of Indigenous peoples in the Declaration is intimately tied to the implementation of the existing international human rights covenants that many states have ratified.[285] It is guided by the purposes and principles of the UN Charter, and good faith in the fulfilment of the obligations is assumed by states in accordance with the Charter. It expressly acknowledges its relationship to the International Human Rights Covenants as well as the Vienna Declaration and Program of Action. However, states with more legalistic cultures may pay more attention to a convention, such as the covenants that are multilateral treaties, than a declaration. In the strict legal sense of the United Natrions, the rights in the Declaration, without the Human Rights Covenants, are not directly binding[286] on nation-states, because the UN system operates by consensual, rather than forced, relations. As a global consensus, however, these rights have a certain intellectual force and political weight. Promotional activity, censure, and publicity are the principal diplomatic forces of human rights advocacy, and they are equally available whether the rights are in a convention, a multilateral treaty, or a declaration.

The usual interpretation of a declaration as a non-binding instrument on nation-states is challenged in the Declaration by its relations to the Human Rights Covenants, its long history of legalistic negotiations, the wording of the text, and its institutional or systematic commitments. In general, the text of the Declaration enacted by the General Assembly encourages states to comply with and effectively implement their obligations as they apply to Indigenous peoples under international instruments, in particular those related to human rights, in consultation and co-operation with the peoples concerned.[287]

The Assembly declared that states:

- shall take effective measures to ensure that these international human rights are protected and also to ensure that Indigenous peoples can understand and be understood in political, legal, and administrative proceedings, where necessary through the provision of interpretation or by other appropriate means;[288]
- shall promote respect for and full application of the provisions of the Declaration and follow up the effectiveness of the Declaration;[289]
- shall pay particular attention to the rights and special needs of elders, women, youth, children, and persons with disabilities in the implementation of the Declaration;[290]
- provide Indigenous peoples access to financial and technical assistance for the enjoyment of the rights contained in the Declaration;[291]
- in consultation and co-operation with Indigenous peoples,[292] shall take appropriate measures, including legislative measures, to achieve the ends of the Declaration;[293] and
- shall consult and co-operate in good faith with the Indigenous peoples concerned through their own representative institutions in order to obtain their free, prior, and informed consent before adopting and implementing legislative or administrative measures that may affect them.[294]

Specifically, the General Assembly provided in the Declaration that states shall:

- take effective measures, in consultation and co-operation with the Indigenous peoples concerned, to combat prejudice and eliminate discrimination, and to promote tolerance, understanding, and good relations among Indigenous peoples and all other segments of society;[295]

- take measures, in conjunction with Indigenous peoples, to ensure Indigenous women and children enjoy the full protection and guarantees against all forms of violence and discrimination;[296]
- not discriminate against Indigenous individuals, particularly children, in any level or form of education;[297]
- in conjunction with Indigenous peoples, take effective measures in order for Indigenous individuals, particularly children, including those living outside their communities, to have access, when possible, to an education in their own culture and provided in their own language;[298]
- in consultation and co-operation with Indigenous peoples, take measures to protect Indigenous children from economic exploitation and from performing any work that is likely to be hazardous or interfere with the child's education, or be harmful to the child's health or physical, mental, spiritual, moral, or social development, taking into account their special vulnerability and the importance of education for their empowerment;[299]
- take effective measures and, where appropriate, special measures to ensure the continuing improvement of Indigenous peoples' economic and social conditions, paying particular attention to the rights and special needs of elders, women, youth, children, and persons with disabilities;[300]
- take the necessary steps with a view to achieving progressively the full realization of the highest attainable standard of physical and mental health.[301]
- take effective measures to ensure, as needed, that programs for monitoring, maintaining, and restoring the health of Indigenous peoples are implemented;[302] and
- take effective measures to ensure that state-owned media duly reflect Indigenous cultural diversity and, without prejudice to

ensuring full freedom of expression, should encourage privately owned media to adequately reflect Indigenous cultural diversity.[303]

To create justice and remedy conflicts, the Assembly declared that states shall:

- create just and fair procedures for the resolution of conflicts and disputes with Indigenous peoples or other parties, as well as effective remedies for infringements of their individual and collective rights;[304]
- give due consideration to the customs, traditions, rules, and legal systems of the Indigenous peoples concerned and international human rights in such decisions;[305]
- provide Indigenous peoples and individuals with effective mechanisms for the prevention of, and redress for:
    - any action which has the aim or effect of depriving them of their integrity as distinct peoples, their cultural values, or ethnic identities;
    - any action which has the aim or effect of dispossessing them of their lands, territories, or resources;
    - any form of forced population transfer which has the aim or effect of violating or undermining any of their rights;
    - Any form of forced assimilation or integration;
    - Any form of propaganda designed to promote or incite racial or ethnic discrimination against them.[306]

The Assembly declared that states must give legal recognition and protection to traditional lands, territories, and resources with due respect to the customs, traditions, and land tenure systems of the Indigenous peoples concerned.[307] The states shall:

- establish and implement assistance programs for Indigenous peoples for the conservation and protection of their traditional lands, without discrimination.[308]
- establish and implement, in conjunction with the Indigenous peoples concerned, a fair, independent, impartial, open, and transparent process, giving due recognition to Indigenous peoples' laws, traditions, customs, and land tenure systems, to recognize and adjudicate the rights of Indigenous peoples pertaining to their lands, territories, and resources, including those that were traditionally owned or otherwise occupied or used (Indigenous peoples shall have the right to participate in this process);[309]
- consult and co-operate in good faith with the Indigenous peoples concerned through their own representative institutions in order to obtain their free and informed consent prior to the approval of any project affecting their lands or territories and other resources, particularly in connection with the development, utilization, or exploitation of mineral, water, or other resources;[310]
- provide effective mechanisms for just and fair redress for any such activities, and take appropriate measures to mitigate adverse environmental, economic, social, cultural, or spiritual impacts;[311]
- in consultation and co-operation with Indigenous peoples, take effective measures to facilitate the exercise and ensure the implementation of the right of Indigenous peoples to maintain and develop contacts, relations, and co-operation across international borders, especially when they are divided by them;[312]
- undertake effective consultations with the Indigenous peoples concerned, through appropriate procedures and through their representative institutions, prior to using their lands or territories for military activities;[313]
- take effective measures to ensure that no storage or disposal of hazardous materials shall take place in the lands or territories of

> Indigenous peoples without their free, prior, and informed consent, and ensure that the peoples affected by hazardous material in the past are involved in programs for monitoring, maintaining and restoring their health.[314]

The General Assembly declared that states, in conjunction with Indigenous peoples, must take effective measures to recognize and protect the exercise of Indigenous rights to cultural heritage, traditional knowledge, and traditional cultural expressions, as well as the manifestations of their sciences, technologies, and cultures.[315] States shall:

- provide redress through effective mechanisms, which may include restitution, developed in conjunction with Indigenous peoples, with respect to their cultural, intellectual, religious, and spiritual property taken without their free, prior, and informed consent or in violation of their laws, traditions, and customs.[316]
- seek to enable the access and/or repatriation of ceremonial objects and human remains in their possession through fair, transparent, and effective mechanisms developed in conjunction with Indigenous peoples concerned.[317]

As the passage of these rights and freedoms in the Declaration illustrates, human consciousness and sensitivities are changing so rapidly that none of the existing theory or familiar indicators are adequate to define or describe them. Humanity stands today in a situation of extraordinary challenge and openness. This is part of the belated consequence of decolonization,[318] which began some 60 years ago, and the processes of civilizational transformation that make the old international order problematic and point toward a new, more equitable, productive order. General respect for peoples and human rights, authentic legal and political pluralism, and deep democracy are growing. The solidarity of humanity is expanding to include Indigenous humanity. The redemption of the ecology lies in human consciousness, the human capacity to reflect, and the power to sustain relationships. Human responsibilities coupled with modesty of the unfolding consciousness of the blessed unrest are the genuine core of re-oriented humanity. Without these attributes, ecology and politics will not change, and a breakdown will be unavoidable.

The rise of self-determination and human rights has created a persuasive model of development, which is displacing colonialism that operated under the camouflage of development. No matter what kind of qualifier one chooses to add before the word "development," and no matter how pernicious one may find the identification of development as "simple" economic development, the idea as embraced and admired by Eurocentrism has been and remains part and parcel of the colonial synthesis that Europe succeeded in forging over a period of centuries. Consisting of ideas, values, and practices based on rationalism, individualism, the belief in science, progress, and materialism, the colonial synthesis of Eurocentrism offered humanity one certain guide to human survival and prosperity.

This model no longer commands admiration and allegiance. The ideas and values that formed its backbone and its engine are losing relevance and validity. It is becoming increasingly clear that modernization, the movement against tradition in Western civilization, is drawing to a close. The Eurocentric model can no longer provide answers to the burning questions of human survival and prosperity, questions concerning the environment, social justice, the individual and the community, and issues regarding the objectives of a self-determining life. It is increasingly clear that environmental damage, economic polarization, disease, poverty, and stagnation are owing not to an accidental configuration of factors, but to a growing tension and contradiction within and among the ideas and values that reside at the core of colonialism. A growing sense of crisis has been evident for a number of years, a sense that the ideals and ideas that had seemed self-evident to certain parts of humanity for generations are increasingly irrelevant, even counter-productive. The ideologies and assumptions on which modern society was built are incapable of addressing many of the central problems facing humanity now: racism, environmental degradation, inequalities among individuals and nations, the dehumanization of work, and the consequent deprivation of purpose and meaning in life.

The arrogance that assumed the universality and inevitability of the Eurocentric model of development prevented Indigenous peoples from seeing that the model is embedded in racism, colonialism, and imperialism. Postcolonial development cannot be properly understood without recourse to self-determination and human rights. This points to a process of civilizational transformation, as the spirit of self-determining peoples overruns the imposed scripts of nation-states.

10. Implementation Quandaries

THE SUPREME COURT OF CANADA, like most national courts, seldom has an opportunity to discuss international law or treaties, as it has no jurisdiction over nation-states. When it had the opportunity, however, it stated in the *Patriation Reference*[319] and reaffirmed in the *Quebec Secession Reference*[320] that the Constitution of Canada includes the global system of rules and principles which govern the exercise of constitutional authority in the whole and in every part of the Canadian state. In the *Quebec Secession Reference*, the Court noted that, while international law generally regulates the conduct of nation-states, it does recognize the right of a *people* to self-determination.[321] It affirmed that the existence of the right of a people to self-determination "is now so widely recognized in international conventions that the principle has acquired a status beyond 'convention' and is considered a general principle of international law."[322] The Court noted that international law grants the right to self-determination to "peoples" and, as the right has "developed by virtue of a combination of international agreements and conventions, coupled with state practice, with little formal elaboration of the definition of 'peoples,' the result has been that the precise meaning of the term 'people' remains somewhat uncertain."[323] However, it determined:

> It is clear that "a people" may include only a portion of the population of an existing state. The right to self-determination has developed largely as a human right, and is generally used in documents that simultaneously contain references to "nation" and "state." The juxtaposition of these terms is indicative that the reference to "people" does

> not necessarily mean the entirety of a state's population. To restrict the definition of the term to the population of existing states would render the granting of a right to self-determination largely duplicative, given the parallel emphasis within the majority of the source documents on the need to protect the territorial integrity of existing states, and would frustrate its remedial purpose.[324]

In international law, the Declaration on the Rights of Indigenous Peoples has affirmed the legal personality of Indigenous peoples and their entitlement to self-determination.

Under the Human Rights Covenants, which are binding multilateral treaties, Canada and other states have a duty to "promote the realization of a right of self-determination" and "respect that right, in conformity with the provisions of the Charter of the United Nations."[325] Under the Optional Protocol,[326] the UN Human Rights Committee has explicitly confirmed that First Nations in Canada possess human rights under Canada's accession to the Civil and Political Rights Covenant.[327] In 1996, the Royal Commission on Aboriginal Peoples concluded that "the Aboriginal peoples of Canada possess the right of self-determination."[328]

In 1996, the government of Canada formally declared before the Commission on Human Rights that it is legally and morally committed to the non-discriminatory application of the right of self-determination to Indigenous and non-Indigenous Peoples. The right of self-determination

> is fundamental to the international community, and its inclusion in the UN Charter, and in the International Covenant on Civil and Political Rights, and the International Covenant on Economic, Social and Cultural Rights bears witness to the important role that it plays in the protection of human rights of all peoples. . . . Canada is therefore legally and morally committed to the observance and protection of this right. We recognize that this right applies equally to all collectivities, indigenous and non-indigenous, which qualify as peoples under international law.[329]

In 2005, in the First Nations/Federal Crown Political Accord on the Recognition and Implementation of First Nation Governments, both parties agreed that policy development would be "informed by discussions and agreements at the international level involving Canada with respect to the rights of indigenous peoples including the right to self-determination."[330] Both First Nations and Canada agreed that they were committed to respecting human rights and applicable international human rights instruments.[331]

Even if Canadian courts were to rule that the right of self-determination under the Human Rights Covenants has not been incorporated into Canadian law by enactment,[332] they could still find that the right of self-determination and the rights in the Human Rights Covenants and the Declaration are an essential aspect of the interpretation and exercise of the rights of Aboriginal peoples under the Constitution of Canada.[333] In addition, human rights are considered general principles of customary international law, if not also a peremptory norm,[334] which means that the right to self-determination would likely be considered a part of Canadian constitutional law without legislative enactment.[335] This was the position of the Attorney General of Canada in the *Quebec Secession Reference*:

> [T]he principles of customary law relating to the right of self-determination are applicable in the present case, because they do not conflict with the applicable Canadian domestic law. Since these principles of customary law can be "incorporated" into domestic law by Canadian courts, it is respectfully submitted that Canadian courts unquestionably have jurisdiction to apply them.[336]

The courts are not the answer to the realization of the human rights of Indigenous peoples. As our elders teach, the Declaration, like our Aboriginal and treaty rights, is but one wing of Indigenous diplomacy. The other wing is political action and strategy. As with eagles and condors, both wings are necessary for flight, and these two wings are necessary for us to move toward our dignity and responsibilities. The legal documents and the courts play a limited role, but the ultimate answer is political. The courts cannot do the political work of self-determining peoples.

Indigenous peoples must understand that the implementation of our human rights and fundamental freedoms is the art of politics.[337] Politics is the principle diplomatic force of human rights advocacy and implementation. Political inspiration is vision; it is also struggle, contests, and compromise. Implementation and politics are tightly related. In a sense, almost every transformation in contemporary society is political, even if it wears another label, such as fate and law, to avoid detection.[338] To become fully empowered to displace our poverty will take new political talents and competencies. In Canada, we have already learned the basics of these skills in negotiating the Declaration as well as in constitutional reform. However, these skills are often considered legal rather than political – another camouflage. Indigenous peoples must extend diplomacy and politics under the Declaration to the UN system and the nation-states. We cannot wait for governments, political parties, or courts to act. We are self-determining peoples. We have the authority to act for the implementation of our rights in every venue. This action is not designed to embarrass the state, but to provide a decent and dignified future for our children and grandchildren.

We should not allow the significance of the Declaration to be minimized in any way by the United Nations, the nation-states, or the rich and powerful, as that will continue the legacy of discrimination that we seek to displace. Our path will be fraught with challenges, but we have a shared vision in the Declaration. We must develop strategies about the next steps in implementing this vision, without wondering about the scope of the changes or the limits of the possible. The possibilities are in the next steps, in our learning from experience and action.

In the UN Permanent Forum for Indigenous Issues, article 42 of the Declaration, which promises that the UN and its agencies will promote respect for and full application of the provisions of the Declaration, will become the foundation and framework for implementing its mandates. It is a guide for knowledge exchange and transmission, for raising awareness in our rights-based development. Existing and future standards in international law will have to be reconciled with the Declaration. The Declaration will reimagine the whole world, emphasizing transformative opportunities. It is consistent with the recent critiques by legal philosophers who assert that nation-states and their ideal of a legal system, both internationally and nationally, are in decline with the emergence of the new regime based on the rights of peoples.[339] The Declaration helps in creating new standards for evaluating the legitimacy of government action toward peoples by international agencies and those who apply national law.

In 2007, the UN Human Rights Council adopted by consensus a resolution to establish the Expert Mechanism on the Rights of Indigenous Peoples to replace the Working Group on Indigenous Populations.[340] The expert mechanism will report directly to the Council as a subsidiary body that will "assist the Human Rights Council in the implementation of its mandate." The body will consist of five independent experts, selected according to UN criteria. The expert mechanism resolution "strongly recommends" the inclusion of Indigenous experts. Members of the group will provide thematic expertise and make proposals and recommendations directly to the Council regarding the rights of Indigenous peoples.

Also in 2008, the UN Human Rights Council appointed the first Indigenous person, international law scholar James Anaya, as UN Special Rapporteur on the situation of human rights and fundamental freedom of Indigenous peoples, to investigate human rights violations as they pertain to Indigenous peoples and make recommendation and find remedies for these violations to the UN and governments under the Declaration.

The "fulfilment" of human rights remains a vague idea in most nation-states. No nation-state fully satisfies human rights; all have significant human rights problems. Many still rely on prolonging the ideology of empire that gave birth to their nation. They also continue to rely on the stagnant idea of legal positivism and justified coërcion behind their legal systems rather than conflict avoidance, reconciliation, and maintaining the peace. The positivistic idea of law, developed during colonization as primary rules of obligation and secondary rules of recognition,[341] has become controversial because it identifies with the formal operation of the secondary rules and prevents an analysis of the content of the law.[342] Its attention is directed exclusively inward, rather than outward, because the state legal system is viewed as supreme within its territory and independent of other legal systems. Under the closed idea of formal positivism, courts require obedience to legislation or regulation; they cannot distinguish between a just or an unjust law, bad or an evil law, a corrupt or a rapacious law.[343] That British law allowed one to identify law without regard to its content is unique in humanity and law, which typically unites substance with procedures, morality and law.[344] The decline of the independent concept of legal systems within a state's territory and the rise of consensual international law and legal traditions are "rooted in a particular way of understanding the world that refuses to recognize the reasons for their existence; their actual existence is increasingly challenged; where they would exist, they deny their own normativity."[345] These legal systems ignored human rights for legislative supremacy.

The development of human rights are reactions against positive law, its concept of rule of rules, and its theory and justification of legal systems. Human rights have been developed to provide protection against state power and paper laws. The concept of international human rights empowers substance, not formality. It acknowledges a particular way of life based on consent rather than borders. It is about consensual principles that a state has promised to engage, respect, and implement as its membership in the constitution of the earth.

In the perplexing context of settler states and their concept of legal systems, the implementation of human rights and fundamental freedoms will not come easily. Human rights are easy to agree to, but difficult to implement. The enforcement machinery of international human rights is extremely weak.[346] Unless nation-states that have made a commitment to international human rights enact appropriate domestic legislation, they can ignore their commitment with impunity – at least regarding their own citizens. Canada, for example, was one of only four states to oppose the Declaration. The minority government of the Conservatives has since claimed that the Declaration is not applicable in Canada. However, on April 8, 2008, the House of Commons passed a motion in favour of implementing the Declaration: "That the government endorse the United Nations declaration on the rights of indigenous peoples as adopted by the United Nations General Assembly on 13th September, 2007, and that Parliament and the Government of Canada fully implement the standards contained therein."[347] The resolution was passed by 148 to 113, the members of the New Democratic Party, Liberals, and Bloc Québécois voting in favour and the Conservatives against. This resolution expresses the will of the House and of Canadians, and should override the executive decision of the government to reject the Declaration.

The resolution did not resolve the need for continued political action on implementing the Declaration, but is a part of the political implementation strategy. It is supported by the strong argument for domestic implementation of the Declaration that exists under current Human Rights Covenants and by the constitutional supremacy that protects the rights of Aboriginal peoples. This is especially valid when the Aboriginal peoples of Canada also ratify the Declaration under their existing Aboriginal and treaty rights.

The affirmation of the concept of territorial integrity in the Declaration is integral both to Indigenous mobilization and the state's implementation of our collective rights.[348] The Supreme Court of Canada has already noted that the Human Rights Covenants define the realm of the right to self-determination – a peoples' pursuit of its political, economic, social, and cultural development – in terms that are normally attainable within the framework of an existing state.[349] It emphasized that the self-determination of peoples is consistent with the maintenance of the territorial integrity of those states.[350] It determined that there is no necessary incompatibility between the maintenance of the territorial integrity of existing states and the right of a "people" to achieve a full measure of self-determination.[351] It affirmed that the territorial integrity of any sovereign state will be entitled to protection under international law only if its government represents the whole of the people or peoples resident within its territory, equally and without discrimination, and respects the principles of self-determination in its own internal arrangements.[352]

The territorial integrity provision obligates every state to promote the Declaration. The affirmation of internal self-determination in the concept of territorial integrity requires that the state recognize Indigenous peoples for the self-determining agents we are. It requires that the state respect the inherent rights and treaty rights of Indigenous peoples, recognize their self-determination and their institutions, and displace colonial legislation with the rights affirmed in the Declaration. It requires every state to represent all the people within its borders without discrimination, establish new collaborative and co-operative relations, and reaffirm that the assimilation or exploitation of any people constitutes a violation of their human rights.

The Aboriginal and treaty rights of Aboriginal peoples in Canada are protected in s. 35 of the *Constitution Act, 1982*,[353] as human rights.[354] As Irvin Cotler states, in listing the various categories of human rights, "A ninth category . . . increasingly recognized in international human rights law – is the category of aboriginal rights."[355] Like the rights articulated in the Declaration and other international human rights instruments, Aboriginal peoples' rights are of a political, economic, social, cultural, and spiritual nature, and they are predominantly collective.[356] Thus, reliance on the Declaration and other international concepts in understanding these constitutional rights is highly appropriate. As underlined by Chief Justice Beverley McLachlin of the Supreme Court of Canada, emerging international norms guide both governments and the courts and cannot be ignored:

> Aboriginal rights from the beginning have been shaped by international concepts. . . . More recently, emerging international norms have guided governments and courts grappling with aboriginal issues. Canada, as a respected member of the international community, cannot ignore these new international norms any more than it could sidestep the colonial norms of the past. Whether we like it or not, aboriginal rights are an international matter.[357]

Additionally, each treaty contains rights that are human rights. Treaties are consensual manifestations of the right of self-determination. In general or specific terms, Aboriginal peoples' treaties constitute an elaboration of arrangements relating to the political, economic, social, cultural, or spiritual rights and jurisdictions of the Indigenous peoples concerned. These treaties were specifically affirmed by the General Assembly in the Declaration. The Supreme Court of Canada has acknowledged that Indigenous treaties are sacred.[358] Failure to respect the status and significance of treaties would be inconsistent with the Crown's constitutional fiduciary obligations – as well as with the principles of good faith, honour of the Crown, and trust that are associated with such obligations and with the process of treaty making itself.[359] Indigenous treaties serve as a benchmark for measuring fairness and justice.

The constitutional rights of the Aboriginal peoples of Canada, a special form of human rights, are protected by ss. 35 and 52 of the *Constitution Act, 1982*, from government power and personal rights. Both the 1996 Royal Commission on Aboriginal Peoples and the courts have confirmed that the right of self-determination is an existing right under section 35.[360] The constitutional wording of "peoples" would reinforce the relationship with the Human Rights Covenants and the Declaration and the application of the right of self-determination to Aboriginal peoples. This interpretation is consistent with the Court decision in the *Quebec Secession Reference*, where it applied the "living tree" doctrine to the underlying principles in Canada's Constitution, which include the protection of the rights of Aboriginal people separate from other rights and powers.[361]

This flexible doctrine would enable Aboriginal peoples' rights under the Constitution to be interpreted in a manner consistent with their right to self-determination and its general principles under international law. This would apply to Aboriginal peoples and include cultural, social, and economic rights. It is worth noting that the existing Human Rights Covenants can be interpreted as enunciating the "rights" of Aboriginal peoples under the wording of ss. 25-27 of the *Charter of Rights and Freedoms*.[362] The government of Canada has recognized in a formal policy that the inherent right of Aboriginal peoples to self-government is an existing Aboriginal and treaty right under s. 35.[363] Since the right to self-government is a political aspect of the right of self-determination,[364] it would appear that these human rights are included in s. 35. The Declaration should be used to safeguard these principles and policies. Clearly, the incorporation of international principles of human rights into the rights of Aboriginal peoples would be appropriate if they serve to raise and reinforce existing standards in Canada.[365]

In Canada, as in other settler states of the Commonwealth, the Declaration on the Rights of Indigenous Peoples requires the Crown to develop, in consultation and collaboration with Indigenous peoples, a program of action for implementing the Declaration, consistent with Aboriginal peoples' constitutional rights, that deals with creating a just society. Justice Binnie of the Supreme Court has articulated this concept in Canadian law: "The fundamental objective of the modern law of aboriginal and treaty rights is the reconciliation of aboriginal peoples and non-aboriginal peoples and their respective claims, interests and ambitions."[366] This spirit of institutional reform is consistent with the alliance of our constitutional rights with our international human rights, using the word "spirit" in the Aboriginal legal tradition to mean the power to transcend any established human convention or order.

The design for an adequate national legal system on a rights-based approach has been described by the UN High Commissioner for Human Rights:

> An adequate national protection system is one in which international human rights norms are reflected in the national constitution and in national legislation; in which the courts can apply international human rights norms and jurisprudence; in which there is human rights education in the schools; in which there are specialized institutions such as human rights commissions or ombudspersons; and in which vulnerable parts of the population are watched over in order to detect and head off problems before they occur.[367]

This is a blueprint for our program of action, of what Canada's legal system must become to be a just postcolonial nation.

More than a decade ago, the Royal Commission on Aboriginal Peoples concluded that the right of self-determination gives Aboriginal peoples the right to initiate changes in their arrangements with Canada and to implement reforms by negotiation and agreement with other Canadian governments, which have the duty to negotiate in good faith and in light of fiduciary obligations owed by the Crown to Aboriginal peoples.[368] So far, Canada has avoided this process.[369]

11. Being a Self-Determining Human

TO LIVE UP TO THE CONCEPT OF SELF-DETERMINING human beings articulated in the Declaration is our responsibility as Indigenous peoples. The vision behind the Declaration was to create a means to reform and empower our traditions and humanities, to create a teaching that would make us greater, individually and collectively. The negotiations, endless and often humiliating, ultimately served our vision of lifting the burden of imposed poverty – the drudgery, infirmity, incapacity, weakness, and indignity that have resulted from the consistent denial of our human rights.[370] We must radiate these ideas and believe in human rights in our lives. We must learn to place our human rights and responsibilities ahead of our politics, morality, and economics. Our human rights are a guide for these behaviours, not a consequence of them. With the passage of the Declaration, we cannot continue to hide our distaste for political engagement under an alleged need for independence, sovereignty, self-determination. We must understand that the genuine core of empowerment is human responsibility and reconciliation. We must improve our people, our selves, and our consciences. We must re-imagine and remake our traditional institutions, and reconcile them with our vision of human rights.

Nothing will change for the better because of ink on paper – regardless of the authority of the paper, or of the ink. Nothing will change without a transformation in the sphere of human consciousness. Nothing will change unless Indigenous peoples become the spiritual crossroads of new, postcolonial sensibilities about the environment, false power, and humanity. This is our contribution to the international families of nations: to understand that the colonial ideologies are still destroying the planet that was entrusted to us, and are still destroying the mass of humanity for merely personal interests.

Indigenous peoples must create and sustain a political will in order for their program of action to counteract their lack of resources, the indifference of governments, and the vested interests of the rich and powerful. This is the art of transformative politics that we now have to teach and learn. This is not a new situation. We have used it in both national and international diplomacy, but, as self-determining peoples, we must create the commitment of nation-states to our human rights. This will require collective learning and institutional innovation. We should accept no proposals that fail to respect our self-determining personalities as distinct peoples. By making the Declaration a living document, a teaching, we can create a shared future with the nation-states, in dignity and respect.

More political inspiration and effort will have to be implemented if the Declaration is to end the effects of colonization, the human rights violations, and the deplorable conditions in which we live. It will require more than the familiar politics of short-term fixes and deals; it will require political mobilization and institutional reform.

Education about the rights of Indigenous peoples must be animated. Under the Declaration,[371] we need to push for education about Indigenous human rights, fundamental responsibilities, and state obligations.[372] The UN and NGOs have been silent on human rights education for Indigenous peoples in the past; we have not been consulted in creating curricula and pedagogy. The existing curricula used to teach human rights is not adequate for Indigenous peoples, as it is not directed to the specific concept of displacing colonial ideology or comprehending Indigenous peoples' rights and needs.[373] Teaching methods are not consistent with Indigenous learning. The existing pedagogy requires each people to respect the rights of others. This is directed at the dominant culture, rather than those whose rights have been ignored or violated. They focus on individual rather than collective rights. This pedagogy will not provide Indigenous peoples with the confidence and skills to assert, affirm, and live out their human rights.

The Aboriginal peoples of Canada, like Indigenous peoples across the world, have continually demonstrated that, through education and law, people can make a difference. We have developed the art of making visions come true, the art of the impossible. It has been difficult. We had to have many beliefs. We had to believe that the future remains open to global and national renewal and personal transformation. We had to believe that nothing in our heritage or culture could prevent us from lifting ourselves out of poverty. We had to believe that we could confront and transform the forces or interests that prevent us from living fully and freely. We had to comprehend that hope is more the consequence of action than observation.

We must now place action and hope above memory.

The art of achieving the impossible resides in a belief in the unlimited potential of problem solving through human effort, ingenuity, and dignity. The vast problems we confront – racial oppression, colonial prejudice, inequality, poverty – yield to the effect of many small solutions. You have to do what's necessary, then what's possible, and suddenly you are doing the impossible. That is the lesson of constitutional reform and the Declaration.

Aboriginal peoples have followed our ancient teachings and visions of a just society. We have embedded Aboriginal and treaty rights in the Constitution of Canada, established the Declaration in international law, and displaced the false assumptions of colonialism. These achievements had previously been considered impossible. They were made possible because visions of a just society touch the human spirit and animate intangible beliefs. Much work remains to be done, but it is no longer impossible. Rather, it is inevitable.

To unfold Canada's future – indeed, the global future – we have to care enough to reimagine and remake it into an extraordinary postcolonial nation. To create a just society, truth has to prevail over dogma, creativity over impossibility, constitutionalism over domination, hope over experience, prophecy over habit, kindness over the impersonal, place over time, solidarity over individualism, serenity over vulnerability, and caring and love over everything.

The enactment of the Declaration illustrates these processes. It witnesses that the old colonial ideology can be displaced by effort, but the same effort is needed to implement and actualize the new vision of human rights and a just society. This may leave many Indigenous peoples frustrated, but they have the spirit within them as self-determining people to make the transformation happen. Human consciousness and belief cannot be transformed overnight. It will take new forms of political mobilization and discussion based on the intellectual and spiritual dimension of politics to institute a new system of living based on constitutional and international human rights. This requires that we internalize our self-determination and human rights. We must comprehend our new responsibilities in new ways, and re-establish our relations with postcolonial politics in an age of international law and constitutionalism.

The effort of Indigenous diplomacy behind the Declaration is a model. At the end of the 20th century and the beginning of the 21st, it was the model developed by Indigenous people to create a new vision of a just global and national order. It prevailed over competing political ideology, and has created an innovative movement toward self-determination based on Indigenous traditions. It displays an Indigenous style of thinking and behaving, incorporating values of tenacity, patience, solidarity, creativity, co-operation, tolerance, courage, and deepening democracy. Our claims about human rights and our commitment to the indivisibility of freedom were viewed as impractical and idealistic by the nation-states, but we eventually succeeded in the real politics of the UN General Assembly. We will prevail also against the nation-states, regardless of power imbalances, political ideology, or economic dogma.

To awaken the inner spirit of decent politics, a need for an inclusive, vibrant democracy based on human rights is our responsibility. Everything now will depend on how we carry out our belief.

Notes

1 UN Declaration on the Rights of Indigenous Peoples, 2007, Doc. A/61/L.67. See Appendix I.

2 Russel Barsh, "The World's Indigenous Peoples." Paper submitted to Calvert Group by First Nations Development Institute/First Peoples Worldwide (1998) www.calvert.com/pdf/white_paper_barsh.pdf; José R. Martinez Cobo, *Study of the Problem of Discrimination against Indigenous Populations*, E/CN.4/Sub.2/1986/7/Add.4 (1987); Rodolfo Stavenhagen, "Indigenous Rights: Some Conceptual Problems," *Indigenous Peoples' Experience and Self-Government* (Copenhagen: IWGIA and the University of Amsterdam, 1994) 9-29 at 14-15; M. Battiste and J. Y. (Sa'ke'j) Henderson, *Protecting Indigenous Knowledge and Heritage: A Global Challenge* (Saskatoon: Purich Publishing, 2000) at 61-65; Maivan Clech Lam, *At the Edge of the State: Indigenous Peoples and Self-Determination* (Ardsley, NY: Transnational Publishers, 2000) at 2-10.

3 Robert A. Williams Jr., *The American Indian in Western Legal Thought: The Discourses of Conquest* (New York: Oxford University Press, 1990); James Anaya, *Indigenous Peoples in International Law* (New York: Oxford University Press, 1996) at 9-13; Antony Anghie, "Finding the Peripheries: Sovereignty and Colonialism in Nineteenth-Century International Law" (1999) 40 Harv. Int'l L. J. 1; N. Berman, "In the Wake of Empire" (1999) 14 Amer. U. Int'l L. Rev. 1515.

4 Michel de Montaigne (1533-1592), the great essayist of the French Renaissance, wrote that the indigenous Americans were the equals of Europeans and could be used to evaluate European society. He viewed indigenous Americans as representing the ideal of the child of nature, and was among the first to give expression to the notion of the noble savage, ruled by "the laws of nature" and "little corrupted by ours." D. M. Frame (Ed. and Trans.), *Montaigne's Essays and Selected Writing* (New York: St. Martin's Press, 1963) at 91-93; F. S. Cohen, "Americanizing the White Man" in L. K. Cohen (Ed.), *The Legal Conscience: Selected Papers of Felix S. Cohen* (New Haven: Yale University Press, 1960) at 319.

5 James (Sa'ke'j) Youngblood Henderson, *The Mi'kmaw Concordat* (Halifax: Fernwood, 1997) at ch. 4; *Indigenous Peoples in International Law*, *supra* note 3 at 9-13; Antony Anghie, "Francisco de Vitoria and the Colonial Origins of International Law" (1996) 5 Soc. and Legal Stud. 321.

6 "[D]iscovery applies to those things which belong to none." See *Indigenous Peoples in International Law*, *supra* note 3 at 12, n. 35, citing Hugo Grotius,

On the Law of War and Peace, Classics of International Law, edited and translated by Francis W. Kelsey (Washington, DC: Carnegie Endowment for International Peace, 1925) at 550. See, generally, Hersch Lauterpacht, "The Grotian Tradition in International Law" (1946) 23 Brit. Y. B. Int'l L. 1. The European doctrine of discovery was introduced in 1492 at the onset of colonialism; Keith D. Nunes, "We Can Do . . . Better: Rights of Singular Peoples and the United Nations Draft Declaration on the 'Rights of Indigenous Peoples'" (1995) 7, St. Thomas L. Rev. 521 at 534.

7 "According to the law of nature there is no degree a matter of doubt for the right to enter treaties is so common to all men that it does not admit of distinction arising from religion." See *Law of War and Peace*, *ibid.* at 38-39.

8 Thomas Hobbes, *Leviathan, or The Matter, Forme, and Power of a Common-wealth Ecclesiastical and Civill* (1651), C. B. Macpherson (Ed.) (Baltimore: Penguin Books, 1968) at 87-88; James (Sa'ke'j) Youngblood Henderson, "The Context of State of Nature," in Marie Battiste (Ed.), *Reclaiming Indigenous Voice and Vision* (Vancouver: University of British Columbia Press, 2000) at 11-38.

9 "Sovereignty and Colonialism," *supra* note 3; R. B. Porter, "The meaning of indigenous national sovereignty" (2002) 34(1) Arizona State L. J. 75; S. Russell, "The jurisprudence of colonialism" (2001) 25(3/4) Legal Studies Forum 605; J. T. Gathii, "Neoliberalism, colonialism and international governance: decentering the international law of governmental legitimacy" (2000) 98(6) Michigan L. Rev. 1996; A. Quentin-Baxter, "Human rights and decolonization" (1999) 30(2) Victoria University of Wellington L. Rev. 563-66; S. Wiessner, "Rights and status of indigenous peoples: a global comparative and international legal analysis (1999) 12 Harv. Hum. Rts. J. 57; Mark F. Lindley, *The Acquisition and Government of Backward Territory in International Law* (London: Longman, 1926).

10 E. Williams, *Capitalism and Slavery* (Chapel Hill: University of North Carolina Press, 1944); A. Césaire, *Discourse on Colonialism*, translated by J. Pinkham (New York: Modern Reader, 1972); Frantz Fanon, *The Wretched of the Earth*, translated by C. Farrington (New York: Grove Press, 1963), *A Dying Colonialism*, translated by H. Chevalier (New York: Grove Press, 1965), and *Black Skin, White Mask*, translated by C. L. Markman (London: MacGibbons and Kee, 1968); Max Horkheimer and Theodor Adorno, *Dialectic of Enlightenment*, translated by John Cumming (New York: Herder and Herder, 1972); Theodor Adorno, *Negative Dialectics*, translated by E. B. Ashton (New York: Seabury Press, 1973); and H. A. Bulhan, *Frantz Fanon and the Psychology of Oppression* (New York: Plenum Press, 1985) at 42–44.

11 A. Nandy, *The Intimate Enemy: Loss and Recovery of Self Under Colonization* (Delhi: Oxford University Press, 1983); R. M. Unger, *False Necessity: Anti-Necessitarian Social Theory in the Service of Radical Democracy.* Part I of *Politics, a Work in Constructive Social Theory* (Cambridge, UK: Cambridge University Press, 1987); Edward Said, *Orientalism: Western Concepts of the Orient* (Harmondsworth: Penguin, 1985) and *Culture and Imperialism* (Cambridge, Mass.: Harvard University Press, 1992); J. M. Blaut, *The Colonizer's Model of the World: Geographical Diffusionism and Eurocentric History* (New York: Guilford Press, 1993); L. Noël, *Intolerance: A General Survey*, translated by A. Bennet (Montreal and Kingston: McGill-Queen's University Press, 1994); James (Sa'ke'j) Youngblood Henderson, "Postcolonial Ghost Dancing: Diagnosing European Colonialism," in *Indigenous Voice and Vision*, *supra* note 8 at ch. 4.

12 Violence is difficult to define. *The Oxford English Dictionary* has a tame concept, which refers to the exercise of physical force so as to inflict injury on, or cause damage to, persons or property. In a different context, the exercise of physical force generates political order, terrorism, ethnic conflict, torture, oppression, war, and genocide. Definitions, however, are unimportant to the victims of these different forms of violence.

13 Norman Cohn argued in *Warrant for Genocide* (New York: Harper and Row, 1967) at 263-64: "However narrow, materialistic, or downright criminal their own motives may be, such men cannot operate without an ideology behind them. At least, when operating collectively, they need an ideology to legitimate their behaviour, for without it, they would have to see themselves and one another as what they really are – common thieves and murderers. And that apparently is something which even they cannot bear."

14 Neil MacCormick, *Questioning Sovereignty: Law, State, and Nation in the European Commonwealth* (Oxford: Oxford University Press, 1999) at 113; Michael Hardt and Antonio Negri, *Empire* (Cambridge, Mass.: Harvard University Press, 2000) at 132-34.

15 Ruth Gordon, "Saving Failed States: Sometimes a Neocolonialist Notion" (1997) 12 Am. U. J. Int'l L. & Pol'y 903; Nii Lante Wallace-Bruce, "Of Collapsed, Dysfunctional and Disoriented States: Challenges to International Law" (2000) 47 Nethl. Int'l L. Rev. 53.

16 E. Catellani, "Le droit international au commencement du XXE siècle" (1901) VIII Revue Générale de Droit International Public (RGDIP) at 585.

17 C. Solomon, *L'occupation des territoires sans maître: Etude de droit international* (Paris: Giard 1889) at 68.

18 Modernity involves essentialization of difference, but it is not a singular manifestation; it has many distinct local formations in the way that differences are constructed, manufactured, and viewed.

19 D. Maybury-Lewis, "Genocide Against Indigenous Peoples," in Alexander L. Hinton (Ed.), *Annihilating Difference: The Anthropology of Genocide* (Berkeley: University of California Press, 2002).

20 *Psychology of Oppression, supra* note 10 at 42–44; *Capitalism and Slavery, supra* note 10; J. Clay, "Genocide in the Age of Enlightenment" (1984) 12(3) Cultural Survival Quarterly 1; W. Churchill, *A Little Matter of Genocide: Holocaust and Denial in the Americas, 1492 to the Present* (San Francisco: City Lights Books, 1997).

21 J. Bodley, *Victims of Progress* (Mountain View, CA: Mayfield, 1999); D. Maybury-Lewis, *Indigenous People, Ethnic Groups, and the State* (Boston: Allyn and Bacon, 1997); Z. Bauman, *Modernity and the Holocaust* (NY: Cornell University Press, 1991).

22 Edward Shils, *Tradition* (Chicago: University of Chicago Press, 1981); H. Patrick Glenn, "Doin' the Transsystemic: Legal Systems and Legal Traditions" (2005) 50 McGill L. J. 863 at 871-72.

23 Albert Memmi, *The Colonizer and the Colonized*, translated by Howard Greenfield (New York: Orion Press, 1965), and "Attempt at a Definition," in A. Memmi, *Dominated Man: Notes Toward a Portrait* (Boston: Beacon Press, 1969) at 185; Emmanuel Levinas, "The Trace of the Other," in M. C. Taylor, (Ed.), *Deconstruction in Context* (Chicago: University of Chicago Press, 1986) at 346-47.

24 Samir Amin, *L'Eurocentrisme, critique d'une idéologie* (Paris: Anthropos, 1988); *The Colonizer's Model, supra* note 11; Vassilis Lambropoulos, *The Rise of Eurocentrism: Anatomy of Interpretation* (Princeton, NJ: Princeton University Press, 1993); Jose Rabasa, *Inventing America: Spanish Historiography and the Formation of Eurocentrism* (Oklahoma Project for Discourse and Theory, Vol. 2, University of Oklahoma Press, 1994); Ella Shohat and Robert Stam, *Unthinking Eurocentrism: Multiculturalism and the Media* (New York: Routledge, 1994); J. M. Blaut, *Eight Eurocentric Historians* (New York: Guilford Press, 2000); Dipesh Chakrabarty, *Provincializing Europe: Postcolonial Thought and Historical Difference* (Princeton: University of Princeton, 2000); Gerhard Hauck, *Die Gesellschaftstheorie und ihr Anderes : wider den Eurozentrismus der Sozialwissenschaften (The Social Theory and its Other: Opposition to the Eurocentrism of the Social Sciences)* (Münster: Westfälisches Dampfboot, 2003); Robert J. C. Young, *White Mythologies: Writing History and the West* (New York: Routledge, Chapman and Hall, 1990).

25 *The Colonizer's Model*, *supra* note 11 at 10.

26 Worldview refers to the collection of values, beliefs, and ideas held by a group, based on its ecological situation. Worldviews will differ based on gender, race, religion, nationality, political outlook, and place of residence. One would never desire, nor expect to find, consensus on worldviews, for they represent the core of who we are. Vamik Volkan in *Bloodlines: From Ethnic Pride to Ethnic Terrorism* (Boulder: Westview Press, 1998) argues the need to "preserve differences and delineate one group's members from another."

27 See R. Benedict, *Patterns of Culture* (Boston & New York: Houghton Mifflin, 1934). Cultural relativists sought to demonstrate that standards of morality and normalcy are culture-bound and called into question the ethnocentric assumption of European superiority. Alison Dundes Renteln, *International Human Rights: Universalism versus Relativism* (Newbury Park: Sage Publications, 1990) at 66; Shelley Wright, *International Human Rights, Decolonization and Globalisation: Becoming Human* (London, New York: Routledge, 2001).

28 Relativists claim that such universality is a cloak for the projection of culturally specific beliefs onto other cultures that possess different worldviews or "inner logic." *International Human Rights*, *ibid.* at 67-72.

29 *Intolerance*, *supra* note 11 at 147.

30 *Colonizer's Model*, *supra* note 11 at 10-11.

31 *Ibid.* at 12.

32 *Ibid.* at 14. There are a number of variants of this framework. The classical division was one between "civilization" and "savagery." Sometimes this dualism is treated as distinct, with a definite boundary between the two areas. (This familiar form of the model is sometimes called the Centre-Periphery Model of the World.) Alternatively, this dualism is expressed as a clear and definite centre, but outside it there is a gradual change in the degree of civilization, progressiveness, or innovativeness. Another variant depicts humanity as divided into zones, each representing a level of civilization or development. The classical division was "civilization," "barbarism," and "savagery." These views of cultural or social organization operating under relentless, irresistible forces has become less credible as the mass of historical knowledge and practical experience points to the conclusion that humanity does not have a ready-made script, a belief that structured Eurocentrism.

33 *Ibid.* at 15, chap. 2. See M. Weber, *The Protestant Ethic and the Spirit of Capitalism* (New York: Scribner's, 1958) at 30.

34 M. Foucault, *The Order of Things: An Archeology of the Human Sciences* (London: Tavistock, 1970) at 55.

35 J. R. Saul, *Voltaire's Bastards: The Dictatorship of Reason in the West* (Toronto: Penguin Books, 1993).

36 Roberto M. Unger, *Social Theory: Its Situation and Its Task. A Critical Introduction to Politics, a Work in Constructive Social Theory* (Cambridge: Cambridge University Press, 1987) at 5.

37 "Attempt at a Definition," *supra* note 23 at 185. See legal scholar Rob Williams's application of these principles to federal Indian law, "The Algebra of Federal Indian Law: The Hard Trail of Decolonizing and Americanizing the White Man's Indian Jurisprudence" (1986) Wis. L. Rev. 219.

38 "Everyone has felt the contempt implicit in the term 'native,' used to designate the inhabitants of a colonized country. The banker, the manufacturer, even the professor in the home country, are not natives of any country: they are not natives at all. The oppressed person, on the other hand, feels himself to be a native; each single event in his life repeats to him that he has not the right to exist." Jean-Paul Sartre, "Materialism and Revolution," in *Literary and Philosophical Essays*, translated by A. Michelson (London: Hutchinson, 1968) at 215.

39 *Psychology of Oppression*, *supra* note 10 at 42–44.

40 *Intimate Enemy*, *supra* note 11 at x; *False Necessity*, *supra* note 11; *Culture and Imperialism*, *supra* note 11.

41 *Colonizer's Model*, *supra* note 11 at 17.

42 *Ibid.* at ix, citing Albert Camus.

43 *Intolerance*, *supra* note 11 at 79.

44 UN Declaration on the Rights of Indigenous Peoples, *supra* note 1.

45 For the most accurate and insightful accounts, see the writings of Russel Lawrence Barsh, foreign affairs officer of the Mi'kmaw Nation and executive director of the Indigenous NGO, Four Directions Council: "Indigenous North America and Contemporary International Law" (1983) 62 Or. L. Rev. 73; "Evolving Conceptions of Group Rights in International Law" (1987) 13(1) Transnational Perspectives 6-10; "Indigenous Peoples: An Emerging Object of International Law" (1986) 80(2) Am. J. of Int'l Law 365; "United Nations Seminar on Indigenous Peoples and States" (1989) 83(3) Am. J. of Int'l Law 599; "United Nations and the Protection of Minorities" (1989) 58 Nordic J. Int'l L. 188; "Advocate's Guide to the Convention on Indigenous and Tribal Peoples" (1990) 15 Okla. City U. L. Rev. 209; "Right to Develop

as a Human Right: Results of the Global Consultation" (1991) 13 Hum. Rts. Q. 322; "Challenges of Indigenous Self-Determination" (1992-1993) 26 U. Mich. J. L. 277; "Democratization and Development" (1992) 14 Hum. Rts. Q. 120; "A 'New Partnership' for Indigenous Peoples: Can the United Nations Make a Difference?" (1993) 17(1) Am. Indian Culture and Research J. 197-227; "Indigenous People in the 1990s: From Object to Subject of International Law" (1994) 7 Harv. Hum. Rts. J. 33; "The Aboriginal Issue in Canadian Foreign Policy, 1984-94" (1995) 12 Int'l J. of Can. Studies 107; "Indigenous Peoples and the UN Commission on Human Rights: A Case of the Immovable Object and the Irresistible Force" (1996), 18 Hum. Rts. Q. 782; and "Indigenous Peoples and the Global Trade Regime: A Social Theory of Fair Trade, with Special Reference to Indigenous Peoples" (2002) 96 Am. Soc'y. Int'l L. Proc. 279.

46 *Covenant of the League of Nations* (1919) from Leland M. Goodrich, E. Hambro, and A. P. Simons, *Charter of the United Nations: Commentary and Documents*, 3rd rev. ed. (New York: Columbia University Press, 1969).

47 For the context of the Haudenosaunee claim, see Grace Li Xiu Woo, "Canada's Forgotten Founders: The Modern Significance of the Haudenosaunee (Iroquois) Application for Membership in the League of Nations" (2003), www2.warwick.ac.uk/fac/soc/law/elj/lgd/2003_1/woo. International courts at this time reached similar interpretations of Indigenous treaties; see *Island of Palmas Case, Netherlands* v. *United States* (1928), 2 R.I.A.A., 829 at 831 (Treaties between Native princes or chiefs and the Netherlands East India Company "are not, in the international law sense, treaties or conventions capable of creating rights and obligations such as may, in international law, arise out of treaties," because the Native princes or chiefs or people are not recognized as members of the community of nations [at 858]), reviewed in *Case Concerning Right of Passage over Indian Territory Portugal* v. *India*, [1960] I.C.J. Rep. 6 (the International Court of Justice held that Indigenous treaties were part of the law of nations and established the rule of construction for these treaties).

48 Charter of the United Nations, 26 June 1945, Can. T. S. (1945), No. 7.

49 *Ibid.*

50 UN General Assembly Res. 275 (III).

51 Convention Concerning the Protection and Integration of Indigenous and Other Tribal and Semi-Tribal Populations in Independent Countries, ILO Convention No. 107, 26 June 1957, reprinted in 328 UNT.S., 247.

52 UN Charter, *supra* note 48, Preamble, arts. 1, 2, and 55, and chapters XI, XII, and XIII.

53 *Declaration on the Granting of Independence to Colonial Countries and Peoples*, UN General Assembly Res. 1514 (XV) 1960.

54 *Ibid.*

55 *Indigenous Peoples in International Law*, *supra* note 3. Dr. Erica-Irene Daes, who chairs the Working Group on Indigenous Populations, in an explanatory note concerning the self-determination of Indigenous peoples, writes, "With few exceptions, indigenous peoples were never a part of State-building. They did not have an opportunity to participate in designing the modern constitutions of the States in which they live, or to share, in any meaningful way, in national decision-making. In some countries they have been excluded by law or by force, but in many countries . . . they have been separated by language, poverty, misery, and the prejudices of their non-indigenous neighbours. Whatever the reason, indigenous peoples in most countries have never been, and are not now, full partners in the political process and lack others' ability to use democratic means to defend their fundamental rights and freedoms."

56 At the end of colonialism, many Indigenous peoples were promised their own independent state, but this promise was never fulfilled. Examples include most of the treaty people of North America, the Naga of northeastern India and Burma, the Shan, the Karen, the Kachin, the Mon, the Karennie, the Arakanese, and others in Burma, and the Christianized peoples in southern Sudan in Africa.

57 Since the United Nations *Convention on the Prevention and Punishment of Crimes of Genocide* ([1948] 78 UNT.S., 277), five types of genocide against Indigenous peoples have been identified: cultural genocide, in which assimilation is the aim of the state; latent genocide, which is the result of activities that have unintended consequences, such as the spread of diseases; retributive genocide, in which states attempt to punish Indigenous or minority groups that challenge their legitimacy; utilitarian genocide, which involves the extermination of peoples to obtain control of economic resources; and optimal genocide, which is characterized by the slaughter of a people to achieve their obliteration. See, generally, F. Chalk and K. Jonassohn, *The History and Sociology of Genocide: Analyses and Case Studies* (New Haven: Yale University Press, 1990); Helen Fein, "Scenarios of Genocide: Models of Genocide and Critical Response," in I. W. Charney (Ed.), *Toward the Understanding and Prevention of Genocide: Proceedings of the International Conference on the Holocaust and Genocide* (Boulder, CO: Westview Press, 1984) at 3; and V. N. Dadrian, "A Topology of Genocide" (1975) 5 Int'l Rev. of Modern Sociology 201.

58 See, for example, J. Schirmer, *The Guatemalan Military Project: A Violence Called Democracy* (Philadelphia: University of Pennsylvania Press, 1998), on Guatemala's attempt to exterminate the Quiche Mayans from 1960-1996; S. H. Davis, *Victims of the Miracle: Development and the Indians of Brazil* (Cambridge: Cambridge University Press, 1977), and C. Levi-Strauss, *Saudades do Brasil* (Seattle: University of Washington Press, 1995), on Brazil's annihilation of more than 80 per cent of eighty Indigenous peoples within its borders between 1900-1957 for the purpose of control over natural resources; V. B. Saeedpour, "Establish State Motives for Genocide: Iraq and the Kurds" in H. Fein (Ed.), *Genocide Watch* (New Haven: Yale University Press, 1992), on Iraq's attempted extermination of the Kurds; R. Jahan, "Genocide in Bangladesh," in S. Totten, W. S. Parsons, and I. W. Charney (Eds.), *Century of Genocide: Eyewitness Accounts and Critical View* (New York: Garland Publishing, 1997), on Bangladesh's extermination of the Chittagong Hill Tribes; F. Helen (Ed.), *The Prevention of Genocide: Rwanda and Yugoslavia Reconsidered* (New York: Institute for the Study of Genocide, 1994), on the mutual genocide between Hutu and Tutsi peoples in Rwanda, and the ethnic cleansing of Serbs in Bosnia-Herzegovina, 1992-1995, with the collapse of the nation-state of Yugoslavia.

59 R. Stavenhagen, *The Return of the Natives: The Indigenous Challenge in Latin America* (London: Institute of Latin American Studies, 2002).

60 G. Psacharopoulos and H. A. Patrinos (Eds.), *Indigenous People and Poverty in Latin America: An Empirical Analysis* (Washington, DC: The World Bank, 1994) at 232. The Inter-American Development Bank (2002) concluded that poverty and underdevelopment had increased in Latin America over the past decade.

61 See George Manuel and Michael Posluns, *The Fourth World: An Indian Reality* (New York: The Free Press, 1974).

62 L. Henkin, *The Rights of Man Today* (Boulder, CO: Westview Press, 1978) at 96-97.

63 UN Charter, *supra* note 48, art. 1 paras. 1, 2, 3; and art. 55; *Indigenous Peoples in International Law*, *supra* note 3 at 41.

64 C. Lennox and I. Wildeboer, *Action Guide: A Human Rights Resource Manual for Secondary Schools* (Ottawa: United Nations Association in Canada, 1998) at 7.

65 Human Rights Committee, General Comment No. 12, art. 1, 21st session, A/39/40 (1984), para. 2: "Article 1 [of the International Covenant on Civil and Political Rights, *infra* note 79] enshrines an inalienable right of all peoples. . . ."

66 R. McCorquodale, "Human Rights and Self-Determination," in M. Sellers (Ed.), *The New World Order: Sovereignty, Human Rights, and the Self-Determination of Peoples* (Oxford/Washington, DC: Berg, 1996) at 11: ". . . it is certain that self-determination is now a human right in international law." See also I. Shearer, *Starke's International Law*, 11th Edition (London: Butterworths, 1994), at 338: ". . . a number of important human rights are not rights of individuals, but collective rights, i.e. the rights of groups or of peoples. This is clear so far as concerns the right of self-determination."

67 Vienna Declaration and Program of Action, adopted 25 June 1993 at the United Nations World Conference on Human Rights, UN Doc. A/CONF.157/24 (Part I) at 20 (1993), reprinted in (1993) 32 I.L.M. 1661, Part I, para. 5: "All human rights are universal, indivisible and interdependent and interrelated. The international community must treat human rights globally in a fair and equal manner, on the same footing, and with the same emphasis. While the significance of national and regional particularities and various historical, cultural and religious backgrounds must be borne in mind, it is the duty of States, regardless of their political, economic and cultural systems, to promote and protect all human rights and fundamental freedoms."

68 UN Sub-Commission on the Prevention of Discrimination and Protection of Minorities, *The Right to Self-Determination: Implementation of United Nations Resolutions*, UN Doc. E/CN.4/Sub.2/405/Rev.1 (1980) (H. Gros Espiell, Special Rapporteur) at 10, para. 59: ". . . human rights can only exist truly and fully when self-determination also exists. Such is the fundamental importance of self-determination as a human right and as a prerequisite for the enjoyment of all the other rights and freedoms." See also K. Mills, *Human Rights in the Emerging Global Order: A New Sovereignty?* (New York: St. Martin's Press, 1998) at 83: ". . . while self-determination is required for the development and enjoyment of human rights, human rights are also a precondition for communal self-determination. They cannot be divorced from each other. In this sense, self-determination is a human right along with civil, political, and economic rights which, taken as a whole, describe and guarantee the rights of human existence."

69 T. Franck, "The Emerging Right to Democratic Governance," (1992) 86 Am. J. Int'l L. 46 at 52.

70 R. Stavenhagen, "Self-Determination: Right or Demon?" in D. Clark and R. Williamson (Eds.), *Self-Determination: International Perspectives* (New York: St. Martin's Press, 1996) at 8.

71 20 Nov. 1963, UN General Assembly Res. 1904 (XVIII)

72 660 UN T.S. 195, entered into force 4 Jan. 1969.

73 *Ibid.*, art. 1

74 *Ibid.*, art. 1(4).

75 *Ibid.*

76 *Ibid.*

77 Canada, Department of Indian Affairs and Northern Development, Statement of the Government of Canada on Indian Policy, 1969 (Ottawa: Queen's Printer, 1969).

78 International Covenant on Economic, Social and Cultural Rights (1967), G.A. Res. 2200A (XXI), 21 UNGAOR, Supp. (No. 16) at 49, UN Doc. A/6316 (1966); Can. T. S. (1976, No. 46). Adopted by the UN General Assembly on 16 Dec. 1966 and entered into force on 3 Jan. 1976. Canada acceded to this covenant on 19 Aug. 1976. See Appendix IV.

79 International Covenant on Civil and Political Rights (1967) UN General Assembly Res. 2200A (XXI), 21 UN GAOR, Supp. (No. 16) at 52, UN Doc. A/6316, Can. T.S. 1976 No. 47 (1966). Adopted by the UN General Assembly on 16 Dec. 1966 and entered into force on 23 Mar. 1976. Canada acceded to this covenant on 19 Aug. 1976. See Appendix III.

80 Optional Protocol to the International Covenant on Civil and Political Rights. UN General Assembly Res. 2200A (XXI), 21 UN GAOR Supp. (No. 16) at 59, UN Doc. A/6316 (1966), 999 UNT.S. 302, entered into force 23 Mar. 1976. Canada acceded to this protocol on 19 Aug. 1976. See Appendix V.

81 "Human Rights and Self-Determination," *supra* note 66 at 9-10: The right to self-determination "now applies to all peoples in all territories, not just colonial territories, and to all peoples within a state"; Self-Determination, *supra* note 70.

82 *Discrimination Against Indigenous Populations*, *supra* note 2.

83 Raidza Torres, "The Rights of Indigenous Populations: The Emerging International Norm" (1991) 16 Yale J. Int'l L. 127 at 149, argues that the absence of international norms regarding Indigenous peoples made them seek recognition within the context of other legal rights under international and domestic law. Benedict Kingsbury, "Reconciling Five Competing Conceptual Structures of Indigenous Peoples' Claims in International and Comparative Law" (2001) 34 N.Y.U. J. Int'l L. & Pol. at 189-90, argued the claims were grounded in human rights, non-discrimination, self-determination, and historic sovereignty, and based on treaty and other agreements with the states.

84 *Sandra Lovelace* v. *Canada*, Communication No. R.6/24 (29 Dec. 1977), UN Doc. Supp. No. 40 (A/36/40) at 166 (1977-1981). See www.usask.ca/nativelaw/unhrfn/lovelace.php.

85 *The Mikmaq Tribal Society* v. *Canada*, Communication No. 78/1980. For the entire case and final decision (1991), see www.usask.ca/nativelaw/unhrfn/mikmaq.php. See also UN GAOR. Hum. Rts. Comm., 47th Session, Supp. No. 40, at 214, UN Doc. A/37/40 (1992).

86 *Chief Bernard Ominayak and the Lubicon Lake Band* v. *Canada*, Communication No. 167/1984, UN Doc. CCPR/C/38/D/167/1984 (1990). See also UN GAOR, Commission on Human Rights, 45th Session, No. 40, Vol. II, Annex 9, 27 UN Doc. A/45/40 (1990).

87 The procedure for sending communications to the UN Commission on Human Rights (CHR) is called the "1503 procedure." It is a paper communication, with no verbal hearing process. The CHR is now called the Human Rights Council (HRC), replacing the CHR in 2006 as part of the UN restructuring process. It retained its mandate to promote "universal respect for the protection of all human rights and fundamental freedoms for all," and "to address situations of violations of human rights, including gross and systematic violations, and make recommendations thereon. It should also promote the effective mainstreaming of human rights within the United Nations system." Under this procedure, the HRC may examine a consistent pattern of gross violations of human rights and fundamental freedoms occurring in any country. Any person or group claiming to be a victim of these violations, or any other person or group with direct knowledge of the violations, may file a communication. A communication cannot be anonymous. Each communication should describe the facts in detail, providing the names of alleged victims, dates, locations, and other evidence. It is desirable, if possible, for the victim to show that there has been a series or group of cases, because the procedure focuses primarily on patterns of violations of human rights. Victims should submit their communications within a reasonable period of time after the exhaustion of remedies available in their own country. Communications should not duplicate or overlap with other procedures in the UN system and they should not be politically motivated. The Secretariat, together with the Chair of the Working Group on Communications, performs an initial screening. If accepted, the communication will be forwarded to the Working Group on Communications and to the government concerned for comment (when forwarded, these communications are anonymous). After the Working Group on Communications has examined the communication and the government's response, and determined that it merits further attention, the communication is forwarded to the Working Group on Situations. This Working Group can forward the situation to the HRC, keep a situation pending, or close the file. The HRC, composed of representatives from state parties, considers the situations referred to it, and representatives of the gov-

ernment concerned are invited to address the HRC in writing and answer questions. The HRC can elect to keep a situation under review or appoint an independent expert. It may discontinue the matter under the 1503 procedure and take it up under a public procedure, or it may discontinue the matter. It may also make recommendations to the Economic and Social Council of the United Nations.

88 *Ominayak*, *supra* note 86. In regard to Aboriginal peoples, see Concluding Observations of the Human Rights Committee: Canada, UN Doc. CCPR/C/79/Add.105, 7 April 1999, para. 8: "... the Committee emphasizes that the right to self-determination requires, *inter alia*, that all peoples must be able to freely dispose of their natural wealth and resources and that they may not be deprived of their own means of subsistence," and para. 13.3: "... the Committee reaffirmed that the Covenant recognizes and protects in most resolute terms a people's right of self-determination and its right to dispose of its natural resources, as an essential condition for the effective guarantee and observance of individual human rights and for the promotion and strengthening of those rights."

89 *Indian Act*, s. 12(1)(b), R.S.C. 1970, C. I-6.

90 *Lovelace*, *supra* note 84. She claimed that Canada violated articles 23 (1) and (4), 26 and 27 of the International Covenant, entered into force in Canada on 19 Aug. 1976.

91 Civil and Political Rights, *supra* note 79.

92 *Ibid.* art. 27 provides that, "In those states in which ethnic, religious or linguistic minorities exist, persons belonging to such minorities shall not be denied the right, in community with the other members of their group, to enjoy their own culture, to profess and practice their own religion, or to use their own language."

93 *Mikmaq Society*, *supra* note 85. They submitted the communication on behalf of "the Mikmaq people," who claim as their territory the lands they possessed and governed at the time they entered into a protection treaty with Great Britain in 1752, and which are known today as Nova Scotia, Prince Edward Island, and parts of Newfoundland, New Brunswick, and the Gaspé Peninsula of Quebec. The communication further submitted that Canada has deprived the alleged victims of their means of subsistence and enacted and enforced laws and policies destructive of the family life of the Mi'kmaq and inimical to the proper education of their children. The communication rejected the applicability of article 27, concerning the rights of persons belonging to minorities. Like other Indigenous peoples, the Mi'kmaq have scrupulously maintained a legal and institutional distinction between them-

selves and minorities. There is a simple tactical reason for this: the "minority" category is larger, more complex, and far more controversial. See UN Declaration on the Rights of Persons Belonging to National or Ethnic, Religious, and Linguistic Minorities, UN General Assembly Res. 135, UN GAOR, 47th Session, at 3-6, UN Doc. A/Res.47/135 (1993).

94 *Mikmaq Society*, *ibid.* at 6.

95 *Ibid.* at 2-3.

96 *Ibid.* Beginning in 1985, the Supreme Court of Canada affirmed the protection of these treaty rights as constitutional rights under s. 35 of the *Canada Act, 1982* (UK), 1982, c. 11.

97 *Ibid.*

98 Admissibility decision, 21 Aug. 1990, *ibid.* doc. 29, para. 14.2 found this issue irrelevant.

99 *Ibid.*, doc. 29 at para. 14.2.

100 *Ibid.* at para. 14.4-15.

101 Final decision, 3 Dec. 1991, *ibid.* doc. 33 at paras. 5.3-6. The Committee stated at para. 5.5, "Invariably, the conduct of public affairs affects the interests of large segments of the population or even the population as a whole, while in other instances it affects more directly the interest of more specific groups of society. Although prior consultations, such as public hearings or consultations with the most interested groups may often be envisaged by law or have evolved as public policy . . . article 25(a) cannot be understood as meaning that any directly affected group, large or small, has the unconditional right to choose the modalities of [its] participation in the conduct of public affairs." Since the constitutional conferences had ended in 1987, the factual issue was moot by the time of the final decision. Also, as a matter of fact, in the communications, the Mi'kmaw did not demand an "unconditional" right to choose their means of participation in the constitutional conferences; they argued that Canadian officials could not discriminate against their constitutional rights, their Aboriginal and treaty rights affirmed and recognized by s. 35 of the new Constitution of Canada, by unilaterally recognizing only a select group of representatives of nationally funded organizations. The Supreme Court of Canada has affirmed the affirmative duty of the governments to consult with Aboriginal peoples on their constitutional rights, both actual and potential, under the constitutional doctrine of the honour of the Crown, *R.* v. *Sparrow*, [1990] 1 S.C.R. 1075; *Haida Nation* v. *British Columbia (Minister of Forests)*, [2004] 3 S.C.R. 511; *Mikisew Cree First Nation*, [2005] 3 S.C.R. 388.

102 *Ominayak*, *supra* note 86.

103 *Ibid.* Human Rights Committee, Concluding Observations of the Human Rights Committee, *supra* note 88, para. 8.

104 *Ibid.*

105 In 2005, the Committee found Canada still in violation of art. 27 of the Covenant, expanded its 1990 decision to include art. 1 of the Covenant, and urged Canada to "make every effort to resume negotiations with the Lubicon Lake Band with a view to finding a solution which respects the rights of the Band under the Covenant (on Civil and Political Rights), as already found by the Committee," and, in the meantime, to "consult with the Band before granting licences for economic exploitation of the disputed land and to ensure in no case such exploitation jeopardizes the rights recognized under the [International Covenant on Civil and Political Rights]" (CPR/C/CAN/CO/5). In 2006, the UN Committee on Economic, Social and Cultural Rights (UNCESCR) also dealt with the situation of the Lubicon Lake Indian Nation and "strongly recommend[ed] that the State party [Canada] resume negotiations with the Lubicon Lake Band with a view to finding a solution to the claims of the Band that ensures the enjoyment of their rights under the [International Covenant on Economic, Social and Cultural Rights]." The Committee also strongly recommended that Canada "conduct effective consultation with the Band prior to the grant of licences for economic purposes in the disputed land, and to ensure that such activities do not jeopardize the rights recognized under the International Covenant on Economic, Social and Cultural Rights" (UN document E/C.12/Q/CAN/CO/5).

106 *R. L. et. al.* v. *Canada*, Comm. No. 358/1989, UN GAOR, Hum Rts. Comm., 47th Session, Supp. No. 40, at 366, UN Doc. A/47/40 (1992).

107 *Ibid.* at para. 6.2: "the Committee has already decided that no claim for self-determination may be brought under the Optional Protocol. [Communication No. 167/1984 (*B. Ominayak* v. *Canada*), decision of 26 Mar. 1990, paragraph 32.1; communication No. 413/1990 (*A.B. et al.* v. *Italy*), inadmissibility decision of 2 Nov. 1990, paragraph 3.2.] Thus, this aspect of the communication is inadmissible under article 1 of the Optional Protocol."

108 *Ibid.* at paras. 6.2-7: "under article 5, paragraph 2(b), of the Optional Protocol" and "fears about the length of proceedings do not absolve authors from the requirement of at least making a reasonable effort to exhaust domestic remedies [*A. and S. N.* v. *Norway*, communication No. 224/1987, declared inadmissible on 11 July 1988, paragraph 6.2]."

109 See J. Y. Henderson, M. L. Benson, and I. M. Findlay, *Aboriginal Tenure in the Constitution of Canada* (Toronto: Carswell, 2000); James [Sa'ke'j] Youngblood Henderson, *First Nation Jurisprudences and Aboriginal Rights* (Saskatoon: Native Law Centre, 2006); James [Sa'ke'j] Youngblood Henderson, *Treaty Rights in the Constitution of Canada* (Toronto: Carswell, 2007).

110 The proposal for the creation of the Working Group on Indigenous Populations (WGIP) by the Sub-Commission on Prevention of Discrimination and Protection of Minorities was in its resolution 2 (XXXIV) of 8 Sept. 1981. The WGIP was established under Danish and Norwegian leadership, "Emerging Objects," *supra* note 45. The establishment of the WGIP was endorsed by the CHR in its resolution 1982/19 of 10 Mar. 1982 and authorized by the Economic and Social Council in its resolution 1982/34 of 7 May 1982. The existing Working Group on Indigenous Populations is a subsidiary body of the Commission's Sub-Commission on Prevention of Discrimination and Protection of Minorities. As such, it can only make recommendations, through the Sub-Commission, to the Commission, and it has no competence outside the field of human rights. Its reports are only distributed to UN human rights meetings, and it has no authority over other UN bodies.

111 In the recent reorganization of the UN, the Sub-Commission is now called the Expert Mechanism on the Rights of Indigenous Peoples of the HRC, see *infra* note 340.

112 See J. Crawford (Ed.), *The Rights of Peoples* (Oxford: Clarendon Press, 1988).

113 Francesco Capotorti, Special Rapporteur, *Study on the Rights of Persons Belonging to Ethnic, Religious and Linguistic Minorities* (New York: United Nations, 1991) at paras. 561–62.

114 *Discrimination Against Indigenous Populations*, *supra* note 2.

115 *On the Concept of "Indigenous People."* E/CN.4/Sub.2/AC.4/1996/2. Sub-Commission on Prevention of Discrimination and Protection of Minorities, Commission on Human Rights, United Nations Economic and Social Council.

116 "Conceptual Problems," *supra* note 2.

117 *Discrimination Against Indigenous Populations*, *supra* note 2 at para. 379.

118 *On the Concept of "Indigenous People," supra* note 115 at para. 10.

119 *Ibid.* at para. 11.

120 *Ibid.* at para. 73.

121 *Ibid.* at para. 69.

122 *Ibid.* at paras. 69-70.

123 "Conceptual Problems," *supra* note 2 at 17.

124 UNESCO Universal Declaration of Cultural Diversity (2001), and UNESCO Convention on the Protection and Promotion of the Diversity of Cultural Expressions (2005).

125 "Indigenous Peoples," *supra* note 2.

126 Russel Lawrence Barsh, "Political Diversification of the International Indigenous Movement" (1991) 5:1, Native Amer. Studies 7-10 and "Indigenous Peoples" *supra* note 2. The organizations included the Alaska Community Action on Toxics; the Aotearoa Indigenous Rights Trust (Aotearoa / New Zealand); the Arctic Indigenous Peoples and Nations Coalition (USA); the Asian Indigenous Peoples Pact (AIPP); Burkina Faso (West Africa); the Buffalo River Dene Nation (Canada); the *Comite Intertribal Memória e Ciêñcia Indígena*/ITC (Brazil); the *Centro de Asistencia Legal para los Pueblos Indígenas* (CEALP – Panama); the *Centro de Cooperación Indígena* (CECOIN – Colombia); the *Centro de Educación Ngobe-Bugle, Panamá*; the *Confederacion de las Nacionalidades Indigenas de Ecuador*/Confederation of Indigenous Nations of Ecuador (CONAIE); the Confederacy of Treaty 6 First Nations (Canada); the Cordillera Peoples Alliance (Philippines); the *Consejo de Pueblos Nahuas del Alto Balsas* (Mexico); the *Comisión de Juristas Indígenas* (Argentina); the *Centro para la autonomia y desarrollo de los pueblos indigenas* (CADPI – Nicaragua); the Dakota/Lakota/Nakota Human Rights Advocacy Coalition (USA); the *Dewanadat Apua Jayapura* (Papua); Earth Peoples; the *Fundacion para la Promocion del Conocimiento Indigena* (Panama); the Grand Council of the Crees (Canada); *Huicholes y Plaguicidas* (Mexico); Indigenous Environmental Network (USA); Indigenous Network on Economies and Trade (Canada); Indigenous Peoples from Africa Coordinating Committee (IPACC); the Indigenous World Association; the International Mohawk Nation of Kahnawake (North America); the International Indian Treaty Council (Americas); the *Inuit Tapirit Kanatami* (ITC – Canada); the Hmong Lao Human Rights Council (Southeast Asia); the *Organización Indígena Kus-Kurá Sociedad Civil* (Costa Rica); the Organization of Indigenous Resource Development (North America); the Nation of Hawaii; *Na Koa Ikaika Kalahui* (Hawaii); the Mainyoto Pastoralists Integrated Development Organization (MPIDO – Kenya); the *Movimiento de la Juventud Kuna* (Panama); the Pacific Concerns Resources Centre; the Russian Association of Indigenous Peoples of the North (RAIPON); the Saami Council (Norway, Sweden, Finland, and Russia); the *Servicios del Pueblo Mixe* (Mexico); the Society for Threatened

Peoples (Germany); the Sovereign Union of Aboriginal Nations and Peoples (Australia); the Tamaynut (Amazigh Peoples – Morroco); the Tebtebba Foundation (Philippines); the *Te Rau Aroha* (Aotearoa – New Zealand); the Tin Hinan/Indigenous Peoples of Africa Coordinating Committee (IPACC); the *Union de la Fuerza Indigena Campesina* (Mexico); and the *Yaquis Unidos por la Madre Tierra* (Sonora, Mexico).

The Grand Council of the Crees (Canada) was the first Indigenous nation to be accredited as an NGO with ECOSOC consultative status. Other Indigenous organizations that are accredited NGOs include the American Indian Law Alliance (USA); the *Asociacion Napguana* (Panama); the Asian Indigenous and Tribal Peoples Network (AITPN); the Assembly of First Nations (Canada); the Four Directions Council (North America); the Indigenous World Association (USA); the Indian Council of South America; the International Organization of Indigenous Resource Development (IOIRD); the Inuit Circumpolar Conference (North Arctic); the National Aboriginal and Islander Legal Services Secretariat (Australia); the National Indian Youth Council (Americas); the Native Women's Association of Canada; the Saami Council; the Union of British Columbia Indian Chiefs; the Western Shoshone Project (USA); the World Council of Indigenous Peoples (Canada); and the *Tupaj Amaru* (Indian Movement – Americas).

127 *Becoming Human*, *supra* note 27 at 36-50.

128 *Ibid.* at 47.

129 *Ibid.* at 44-45.

130 *Discrimination against Indigenous Populations*, *supra* note 2.

131 Many declarations of Indigenous peoples are related to Indigenous diplomacy. Also, Indigenous nations and institutes have ratified the declaration according to their legal traditions as part of their legal order and communicated that to the annual Working Group, since no repository exists for their ratifications. "We Can Do ... Better," *supra* note 6 at 554 argued that declarations by implementation can take the form of customary international law in the same way the UN Universal Declaration of Human Rights has now become part of customary international law).

132 Chidi Oguamanam, "Indigenous Peoples and International Law: The Making of a Regime" (2004) 30 Queen's L. J. 348-399; Siegfried Wiessner, "Joining Control to Authority: The Hardened 'Indigenous Norm'" (2000) 25 Yale J. Int'l L. 301; "Emerging Norm," *supra* note 83 at 149; "Emerging Object," *supra* note 45; "Indigenous North America," *supra* note 45 at 84-90.

133 "Aboriginal Issue," *supra* note 45.

134 See H. Patrick Glenn, *On Common Laws* (Oxford: Oxford University Press, 2005); M. Bellomo, *The Common Legal Past of Europe, 1000-1800*, translated by Lydia G. Cochrane (Washington, DC: The Catholic University of America Press, 1995). The different legal traditions of Europe have been know by many names, including *ius commune, le droit commun coutumier* of France, *el derecho cumún* of the *Siete Partiada, il diritto commune*, and *das gemeine Recht* of Germany.

135 These traditions were translated into arts. 34 and 46 of the UN Declaration on the Rights of Indigenous Peoples, *supra* note 1, as well as in the 1993 dialogue about art. 33 (now art. 34) in the final draft of the Indigenous declaration, *infra* note 160: the applicability of "universally recognized norms to Indigenous peoples' own autonomous institutions." Many Indigenous leaders argued that existing international standards were irrelevant or inappropriate; others took the position that all institutions and governments were capable of abusing power and must be subject to international scrutiny as the nation-states were. See R. Barsh, "Indigenous Peoples and the Idea of Individual Human Rights" (1995) 10(2) Native Studies Rev. 35-55.

136 "Indigenous Peoples," *supra* note 2.

137 The question of the "s" arose in the drafting of the Vienna Declaration on 25 June 1993, *supra* note 67. Perhaps the Austrian dialect intensified the battle, as it was difficult for Indigenous delegates to grasp the various "z" and "s" sounds of the discussion. Australia, supported by Colombia, Denmark, Mexico, New Zealand, Norway, and the Russian Federation, proposed that the declaration of the conference refer to indigenous "peoples" ("Object to Subject," *supra* note 45 at 49). When Canada opposed this position, taking the side of Indonesia and India, Aboriginal people at the conference expressed outrage (Rudy Platiel, UN Motions on Natives Stir Conflict, *Globe and Mail*, 24 Feb. 1988 at A3).

138 International Labour Organization, Convention Concerning Indigenous and Tribal Peoples No. 169, adopted by the General Conference of the International Labour Organization, Geneva, 27 June 1989, and entered into force 5 Sept. 1991, reprinted in 28 I.L.M. 1382 (1989), (1990) 15 Okla. City U.L. Rev., 127-53. See Appendix VI. Compare to Convention Concerning the Protection and Integration of Indigenous and Other Tribal and Semi-Tribal Populations in Independent Countries (1957), *supra* note 51. See "Advocate's Guide," *supra* note 45; compare with Sharon Venne, "The New Language of Assimilation: A Brief Analysis of ILO Convention 169" (1989) 3(2) *Without*

Prejudice 53-57. Canada is not yet a signatory to ILO Convention No. 169, though it is part of international law.

139 ILO Indigenous and Tribal Peoples Convention 169, *ibid.* at arts. 2(1), 4(2) and 6, and 33(2). During negotiations, some participants insisted on references to "self-determination," but the ILO committee ruled that the organization lacked competence to interpret article 1 of the UN Charter, *supra* note 48.

140 *Ibid.* at arts. 7(1), 5(b), 8(2), 6(1)(a), and 6(1)(c).

141 *Ibid.* at arts. 14(1), 13(2), 7(4), 16(1), and 18.

142 UN Conference on Environment and Development, Annex 1, Rio Declaration on the Environment, A/Conf/151/5/Rev.1 (1992), reprinted in 31 I.L.M. 874 (1992). See Appendix VII.

143 *Ibid.* at 7.

144 *Ibid.*

145 Agenda 21 of the UN Conference on Environment and Development is comprised of Annex 1, and is part of the Rio Declaration on the Environment, *supra* note 142. Also see Annex III, the Non-Legally Binding Authoritative Statement of Principles for Global Consensus on the Management, Conservation and Sustainable Development of All Types of Forests, a.k.a. the Forest Principles, 31 I.L.M. 881 (1992).

146 International Conference on Population and Development, Cairo (1994) at para. 26.1.

147 UN Convention on Biological Diversity, 1992 (CBD), 31 I.L.M. 818, and the Framework Convention on Climate Change, 31 I.L.M. 289 (1992). See Appendix VII.

148 UNESCO, The World Conference on Science for the Twenty-First Century: A New Commitment (1999). See Appendix VIII.

149 UN General Assembly Res. 45/164 (18 Dec. 1990); General Assembly Res. 46/128 (17 Dec. 1991). The official aim of the Year was "strengthening international co-operation for the solution of problems faced by Indigenous communities in such areas as human rights, the environment, development, education [and] health." In proclaiming the Year, the General Assembly called upon governments and UN agencies to "take fully into account the development needs of indigenous people," and to make "full use" of Indigenous peoples' expertise. The theme for the International Year was "A New Partnership," and in his remarks at the opening ceremony in Dec. 1992, UN Secretary-General Boutros-Ghali referred to the need for the UN to begin to listen to and work with Indigenous peoples at all levels of international

affairs. This spirit was reflected in the General Assembly's request that UN agencies consider giving Indigenous peoples an "important role in the planning, implementation and evaluation of projects which may affect them."

150 UN General Assembly Res. 48/163 (21 Dec. 1993), which also decided to celebrate an International Day of Indigenous People beginning in 1995. The Decade became part of Indigenous peoples' demands at the 1993 World Conference on Human Rights in the Vienna Declaration, *supra* note 67 at para. 32. The Decade had been the idea of Rigoberta Menchu, who served as Boutros-Ghali's Goodwill Ambassador for the Year. Menchu concluded that the process of building institutional support for Indigenous peoples within the UN would take not months, but years. In her view, a Decade was needed to continue the process of reform, and to encourage Indigenous peoples themselves to continue to increase their advocacy, visibility, and participation in UN meetings. A summit of Indigenous leaders held at Guatemala City in May 1993 supported her proposal in their Chimaltenango Declaration.

151 The Vienna Declaration, *supra* note 67, recommended the "permanent forum" to the General Assembly. The General Assembly requested the UN's CHR to give "priority consideration to the establishment of a permanent forum for indigenous peoples within the United Nations system," UN General Assembly Res. 48/163 (21 Dec. 1993) at para. 20. The term "permanent forum" was chosen to avoid any premature implications as to its institutional status, competence, or membership. Art. 41 of the Indigenous Declaration, *infra* note 160, authorized the establishment of "a body at the highest level with special competence in this field and with the direct participation of indigenous peoples."

152 Principles and Guidelines for the Protection of the Heritage of Indigenous Peoples, 1990-1995. E/CN.4/Sub.2/1995/26 and E/CN.4/Sub. 2/1995/31; UN Draft Principles and Guidelines for the Protection of the Heritage of Indigenous Peoples (2001) E/CN.4/Sub.2/1995/26 and E/CN.4/Sub. 2/1995/31, 2001 (see Appendix IX); *Protecting Indigenous Knowledge and Heritage: A Global Challenge, supra* note 2; S. Wiessner and Marie Battiste, "The 2000 Revision of the United Nations Draft Principles and Guidelines on the Protection of the Heritage of Indigenous People" (2000) 13 St. Thomas L. Rev. 383-90.

153 The Human Rights of Indigenous Peoples, Study on treaties, agreements and other constructive arrangements between States and indigenous populations; final report by Miguel Alfonso Martínez, Special Rapporteur, UN Doc. E/CN.4/Sub.2/1999/20 (1999).

154 Agenda item 9, adopted 8 Sept. 2001, Durban, South Africa; UN Doc. A/CONF.189/5 (2001). See Appendix X.

155 *Indigenous Peoples in International Law*, *supra* note 3; Object to Subject, *supra* note 45.

156 See www.un.org/esa/socdev/unpfii/; first approved by ECOSOC Res. 2000/22 of 28 July 2000, E/2000/INF/2/Add.2.

157 See J. Carey and S. Wiessner, "A New United Nations Subsidiary Organ: The Permanent Forum on Indigenous Issues," www.asil.org/insights/insigh67.htm. Other mandates of the Forum are to "(a) provide expert advice and recommendations on indigenous issues to the Council, as well as to programmes, funds and agencies of the United Nations, through the Council; (b) Raise awareness and promote the integration and coordination of activities relating to indigenous issues within the United Nations system; (c) Prepare and disseminate information on indigenous issues."

158 UN General Assembly Res. 59/174 of 20 Dec. 2004.

159 Erica-Irene A. Daes, "First International Day of the World's Indigenous People"; statement made to the Sub-Commission on Prevention of Discrimination and Protection of Minorities on the Occasion of the First International Day of the World's Indigenous People, Geneva, 9 Aug. 1995.

160 Discrimination Against Indigenous Peoples: Draft Declaration on the Rights of Indigenous Peoples, UN ESCOR, Commission on Hum. Rts., Sub-Commission on Prevention of Discrimination and Protection of Minorities, 45th Session, Agenda Item 14, UN Doc. E/CN.4/1995/2 E/CN.4/Sub.2/1994/56, 28 Oct. 1994, at art. 43. See Explanatory Note, *supra* note 55. See generally Erica-Irene A. Daes, "Some Considerations on the Rights of Indigenous Peoples to Self-Determination" (1993) 3 Transnational Law and Contemporary Problems 1; M. E. Turpel, "The Draft Declaration on the Rights of Indigenous Peoples – Commentaries" [1994] 1 C.N.L.R. 50; D. Sanders, "The Draft Declaration on the Rights of Indigenous Peoples – Commentaries" [1994] 1 C.N.L.R. 48.

161 B. Boutros-Ghali, Opening Statement by the United Nations Secretary-General, "Human Rights: The Common Language of Humanity," in World Conference on Human Rights, Vienna Declaration, *supra* note 67, UN DPI/1394-39399-August 1993-20 M.

162 Indigenous declaration, *supra* note 160 at arts. 3 and 31. Art. 3 is identical to art. 1 in the International Human Rights Covenants, *supra* notes 78-80, and art. 3 in the Decolonization Declaration, *supra* note 53.

163 Indigenous declaration, *Ibid.* at art. 2.

164 *Ibid.* at arts. 1, 37, and 40.

165 *Ibid.* at art. 45.

166 *Ibid.* at art. 43.

167 *Ibid.* at art. 42.

168 *Ibid.* at arts. 4, 8, and 34.

169 *Ibid.* at art. 31.

170 *Ibid.* at art. 21.

171 *Ibid.* at arts. 4, 26, 33, and 39.

172 *Ibid.* at art. 24.

173 *Ibid.* at arts. 4 and 36.

174 *Ibid.* at arts. 4, 9, and 32.

175 *Ibid.* at arts. 7 and 16.

176 *Ibid.* at art. 12.

177 *Ibid.* at art. 13.

178 *Ibid.* at art. 14.

179 *Ibid.* at art. 15.

180 *Ibid.* at art. 17.

181 *Ibid.* at art. 16.

182 *Ibid.* at arts. 10 and 25-30.

183 *Ibid.* at art. 28.

184 *Ibid.* at art. 11.

185 *Ibid.* at art. 6.

186 *Ibid.* at arts. 6 and 7.

187 *Ibid.* at arts. 4, 19, and 20.

188 *Ibid.* at art 38.

189 *Ibid.* at art. 39.

190 *Ibid.* at arts. 22 and 23.

191 *Ibid.* at art. 18.

192 *Ibid.* at arts. 23 and 24.

193 Sub-Commission Res. 46, UN EECOR, Commission on Hum. Rts., Sub-Commission on Prevention of Discrimination and Protection of Minorities (26 Aug. 1993). Three meetings of UN experts had previously reviewed and

supported the Indigenous declaration provisions; see "Object to Subject," *supra* note 45 at 56-58.

194 Sub-Commission, E/CN.4/1995/2.

195 Declaration on Principles of International Law Concerning Friendly Relations and Co-operation Among States in Accordance with the Charter of the United Nations (1970), UN General Assembly Res. 2625 (XXV), 24 Oct. 1970.

196 "First International Day," *supra* note 159.

197 *Ibid.*

198 *Ibid.*

199 *Ibid.*

200 *Ibid.*

201 *Ibid.*

202 *Ibid.*

203 "Immovable Object," *supra* note 45.

204 Annex 3, "Proposal by Norway: Amendment to Preambular Paragraph 15," draft WGDD consultations, Sept. 2002, p. 21. At the ninth session of the Working Group (2003), Australia, Canada, and New Zealand accepted the Norwegian proposal. For a summary of the debate, see *The Indigenous World*, 2001-2002, and 2002-2003, International Work Group for Indigenous Affairs (IWGIA).

205 "Always Indigenize! The Radical Humanities in the Postcolonial Canadian University," Ariel: A Review of International English Literature 31.1-2 (2000) 307-26 [Always Indigenize!]; Isobel Findlay, "Working for Postcolonial Legal Studies: Working with the Indigenous Humanities," Law, Social Justice & Global Development Journal (LGD) 2003 (1), www2.warwick.ac.uk/fac/soc/law/elj/lgd/2003_1/findlay/.

206 CHR resolution 2004/62 of 21 April 2004; see Official Records of the Economic and Social Council, 2004, Supplement No. 3 (E/2004/23), chap. II, s. A.

207 Decade, *supra* note 158; Supplement No. 3 and corrigenda (E/1995/23 and Corr.1 and 2), chap. II, s. A.

208 Second International Decade of the World's Indigenous Peoples (2005), UN A/Res/59/74 24 Feb. 2005.

209 *Ibid.*, art. 12.

210 Statement of Kofi Annan, UN Secretary General, at opening of the third session of the Permanent Forum on Indigenous Issues in New York on 10 May 2004.

211 Draft Declaration on the Rights of Indigenous Peoples (Revised Chairman's summary and proposal), in Luis-Enrique Chavez, Report of the Working Group established in accordance with CHR resolution 1995/32 of 3 Mar. 1995, UN Doc. E/CN.4/2006/79, Annex 1, at 10-55 (2006).

212 Human Rights Council Res. 2006/2, Working Group of the CHR to elaborate a draft declaration in accordance with para. 5 of the UN General Assembly Res. 49/214 of 23 Dec. 1994.

213 Azerbaijan, Bangladesh, Bhutan, Burundi, Colombia, Georgia, Kenya, Nigeria, Russian Federation, Samoa, and Ukraine.

214 Chad, Côte d'Ivoire, Equatorial Guinea, Eritrea, Ethiopia, Fiji, Gambia, Granada, Guinea-Bissau, Israel, Kiribati, Kyrgyzstan, Marshall Islands, Mauritania, Montenegro, Morocco, Nauru, Palau, Papua New Guinea, Romania, Rwanda, Saint Kitts and Nevis, Sao Tome and Principe, Seychelles, Solomon Islands, Somalia, Tajikistan, Togo, Tonga, Turkmenistan, Tuvalu, Uganda, Uzbekistan, and Vanuatu; UN Press Release GA 10612 and Resolution A/61/L.67.

215 UN Declaration on the Rights of Indigenous Peoples, *supra* note 1.

216 See "Aboriginal Issues" and "Object to Subject," *supra* note 45.

217 See *infra* note 330.

218 UN Declaration on the Rights of Indigenous Peoples, *supra* note 1 at art. 46(3).

219 *Ibid.* at art. 43.

220 *Ibid.* at art. 44. Compare with existing obligations in art. 3 in Civil and Political Rights, *supra* note 79, and art. 3 in Economic, Social and Cultural Rights, *supra* note 78.

221 *Ibid.* at arts. 21(2) and 22.

222 *Ibid.*

223 *Ibid.* at art. 46(3). Compare with existing obligations in art. 4 in Civil and Political Rights, *supra* note 78, and art. 4 in Economic, Social and Cultural Rights, *supra* note 79.

224 *Ibid.* at art. 1.

225 *Ibid.* at art. 2. Compare with existing obligations in art. 2, para. 2, and art. 26 in Civil and Political Rights, *supra* note 79, and art. 2, para. 2 in Economic, Social and Cultural Rights, *supra* note 78.

226 *Ibid.* at art. 6. Compare with existing obligations in art. 24(3) in Civil and Political Rights, *ibid.*

227 *Ibid.* at art. 9. Compare with existing obligations in arts. 22 and 27 in Civil and Political Rights, *ibid.* and art. 15(a), Economic, Social and Cultural Rights, *supra* note 78.

228 *Ibid.* at art. 9. Compare with existing obligations in art. 26 in Civil and Political Rights, *ibid.*

229 *Ibid.* at art. 5. Compare with existing obligations in arts. 25 and 27 in Civil and Political Rights, *ibid.* and art. 15(a) in Economic, Social and Cultural Rights, *supra* note 78.

230 *Ibid.* at art. 34. Compare with existing obligations in arts. 25 and 27 in Civil and Political Rights, *ibid.* and art. 15(a) in Economic, Social and Cultural Rights, *ibid.*

231 *Ibid.* at art. 20 (1). Compare with existing obligations in arts. 25 and 27 in Civil and Political Rights, *ibid.*, and art. 15(a) in Economic, Social and Cultural Rights, *ibid.*

232 *Ibid.* at art. 3. Identical with existing obligations in art. 1, para. 1 in Civil and Political Rights, *ibid.*, and art. 1, para. 1 in Economic, Social and Cultural Rights, *ibid.* This right is not afforded to persons belonging to minorities; see Minorities Declaration, *supra* note 93.

233 *Ibid.* at art. 4. The Minorities Declaration, *ibid.*, does not have this right.

234 *Ibid.* at art. 18. Compare with existing obligations in arts. 25 and 27 in Civil and Political Rights, *supra* note 79, and art. 15(a) in Economic, Social and Cultural Rights, *supra* note 78. The Minorities Declaration, *ibid.*, does not have this right to maintain and develop Indigenous institutions, but individuals have the right to participate in decision-making at regional levels where they live in a manner compatible with national legislation.

235 *Ibid.* at art. 33(1). Compare with existing obligations in arts. 25 and 27 in Civil and Political Rights, *ibid.*, and art. 15(a) in Economic, Social and Cultural Rights, *ibid.*

236 *Ibid.* at art. 33(2).

237 *Ibid.* at art. 35.

238 *Ibid.* at art. 36.

239 *Ibid.* at art. 37(2). This is consistent with both the sacred nature of the treaty in Indigenous legal traditions and the Vienna Convention on the Law of Treaties, 1155 UNT.S. 331, 8 I.L.M. 679, entered into force 27 Jan. 1980, arts. 26 ("Every treaty in force is binding upon the parties to it and must be performed by them in good faith") and 27 ("A party may not invoke the provisions of its internal law as justification for its failure to perform a treaty. This rule is without prejudice to article 46.") It is also consistent with the Supreme Court of Canada decisions on First Nation treaties with the Crown, *infra* note 358.

240 *Ibid.* at art. 37(2).

241 *Ibid.* at art. 45. Compare with existing obligations in arts. 4 and 5 in Civil and Political Rights, *supra* note 79, and art. 15(a) in Economic, Social and Cultural Rights, *supra* note 78.

242 *Ibid.* at art. 23. Compare with existing obligations in arts. 1 in Civil and Political Rights, *ibid.*, and arts 1, 6, 10, 11(a), and 15(1-2) in Economic, Social and Cultural Rights, *ibid.* The Minorities Declaration, *supra* note 93, does not recognize this right.

243 *Ibid.* at art. 23.

244 *Ibid.* at art. 17. Compare with existing obligations in arts. 8 and 22(3) in Civil and Political Rights, *supra* note 79, and art. 8 in Economic, Social and Cultural Rights, *supra* note 78.

245 *Ibid.* at art. 21(1). Compare with existing obligations in art. 1 in Civil and Political Rights, *ibid.*, and arts. 1, 10, 11, and 13 in Economic, Social and Cultural Rights, *ibid.*

246 *Ibid.* at art. 11. Compare with existing obligations in arts. 1 and 27 in Civil and Political Rights, *ibid.*, and art. 15(a) in Economic, Social and Cultural Rights, *ibid.*

247 *Ibid.* at art. 12.

248 *Ibid.* at art. 13.

249 *Ibid.* at art. 14. Compare with existing obligations in arts. 18(3) in Civil and Political Rights, *supra* note 79, and art. 10(1), 13, and 14 in Economic, Social and Cultural Rights, *supra* note 78. Further, government obligations to "adopt measures appropriate to the traditions and cultures of Indigenous peoples to make known to them their educational rights and duties" (ILO, 1969, *supra* note 138, art. 30) entail these commitments: education programs and services "shall incorporate their history, their knowledge and technologies, their value systems, and their further social, economic, and cultural as-

pirations" (ILO 169, *ibid.* art. 27(1)). Governments and competent authorities shall make efforts "to ensure that history textbooks and other educational material provide a fair, accurate, and informative portrayal of the societies and cultures of these peoples" (ILO 169, *ibid.* art. 31).

250 *Ibid.* at art. 15.

251 *Ibid.* at art. 16.

252 *Ibid.* at art. 11. See also UNESCO Universal Declaration of Cultural Diversity (2001), *supra* note 124, UNESCO Convention for the Safeguarding of the Intangible Cultural Heritage (2003), and UNESCO Convention on the Protection and Promotion of the Diversity of Cultural Expressions (2005), *supra* note 124, recognizing the importance of traditional knowledge as a source of intangible and material wealth, and in particular the knowledge systems of Indigenous peoples and their positive contribution to sustainable development, as well as the need for their adequate protection and promotion in the arts.

253 *Ibid.* at art. 31(1).

254 *Ibid.* at art. 7(2). Compare with existing obligations in arts. 2(a), 6, and 7 in Civil and Political Rights, *supra* note 79, and art. 5 in Economic, Social and Cultural Rights, *supra* note 78.

255 *Ibid.* at art. 8. Compare with existing obligations in art. 27 in Civil and Political Rights, *ibid.*, and art. 15(a) in Economic, Social and Cultural Rights, *ibid.*

256 *Ibid.* at art. 24(1).

257 *Ibid.* Compare with existing obligations in arts. 9 and 10(2) in Economic, Social and Cultural Rights, *supra* note 78.

258 *Ibid.* at art. 24(2). Compare with existing obligations in art. 6 in Economic, Social and Cultural Rights, *ibid.*

259 *Ibid.* at art. 7(1). Compare with existing obligations in arts. 6, 9, and 10 in Civil and Political Rights, *supra* note 79.

260 *Ibid.* at art. 25. Compare with existing obligations in arts. 1(2) and 47 in Civil and Political Rights, *ibid.*, and arts. 1(2), 2(1), 11(2)(a) and 25 in Economic, Social and Cultural Rights, *supra* note 78. The Minorities Declaration, *supra* note 93, does not ensure these rights.

261 *Ibid.* at art. 26(1).

262 *Ibid.* at art. 26(2).

263 *Ibid.* at art. 32.

264 *Ibid.* at art. 29.

265 *Ibid.* at art. 27. Compare with existing obligations in art. 2(3) in Civil and Political Rights, *supra* note 79.

266 *Ibid.* at art. 28(1).

267 *Ibid.* at art. 28(2).

268 *Ibid.* at art. 10.

269 *Ibid.* at art. 20(2). Compare with existing obligations in art 1(2) in Civil and Political Rights, *supra* note 79, and art. 10(3) in Economic, Social and Cultural Rights, *supra* note 78.

270 *Ibid.* at art. 46(1). This is balanced by art. 45 that provides that "Nothing in this Declaration may be construed as diminishing or extinguishing the rights indigenous people have now or may acquire in the future," which includes art. 3, the right to self-determination. Compare with existing obligations in arts. 46 and 47 in Civil and Political Rights, *ibid.* and arts. 24 and 25 in Economic, Social and Cultural Rights, *ibid.*

271 See art. 1(2) of the UN Charter, *supra* note 48: "To develop friendly relations among nations based on respect for the principle of equal rights and self-determination of peoples, and to take other appropriate measures to strengthen universal peace." Art. 55, *ibid.,* provides that the UN shall promote goals such as higher standards of living, full employment, and human rights "with a view to the creation of conditions of stability and well-being which are necessary for peaceful and friendly relations among nations based on respect for the principle of equal rights and self-determination of peoples." See also Friendly Relations Declaration, *supra* note 195: "By virtue of the principle of equal rights and self-determination of peoples enshrined in the Charter of the United Nations, all peoples have the right freely to determine, without external interference, their political status and to pursue their economic, social and cultural development, and every State has the duty to respect this right in accordance with the provisions of the Charter"; Final Act of the Conference on Security and Co-operation in Europe, 14 I.L.M. 1292 (1975) Part VIII: "The participating States will respect the equal rights of peoples and their right to self-determination, acting at all times in conformity with the purposes and principles of the Charter of the United Nations and with the relevant norms of international law, including those relating to territorial integrity of States. By virtue of the principle of equal rights and self-determination of peoples, all peoples always have the right, in full freedom, to determine, when and as they wish, their internal and external political status, without external interference, and to pursue as they wish their political, eco-

nomic, social and cultural development"; Vienna Meeting of the Conference on Security and Co-operation in Europe (1989) Principle 5: nation-states "confirm their commitment strictly and effectively to observe the principle of the territorial integrity of States. They will refrain from any violation of this principle and thus from any action aimed by direct or indirect means, in contravention of the purposes and principles of the Charter of the United Nations, other obligations under international law or the provisions of the [Helsinki] Final Act, at violating the territorial integrity, political independence or the unity of a State. No actions or situations in contravention of this principle will be recognized as legal by the participating States"; Vienna Declaration, *supra* note 67, art. 1: the right to self-determination is "not to be construed as authorizing or encouraging any action which would dismember or impair, totally or in part, the territorial integrity or political unity of sovereign and independent States conducting themselves in compliance with the principle of equal rights and self-determination of peoples as described above and thus possessed of a government representing the whole people belonging to the territory without distinction. . . ."

272 *Supra* note 79.

273 UN Declaration on the Rights of Indigenous Peoples, *supra* note 1 at art. 46(2). Compare with existing obligations in arts. 1(3) in Civil and Political Rights, *ibid.*, and art. 1(3) in Economic, Social and Cultural Rights, *supra* note 78.

274 *Ibid.* Compare with existing obligations in arts. 4(1) in Civil and Political Rights, *ibid.*

275 *Ibid.* at art. 46(3). Compare with existing obligations in arts. 13(3), 14(1), 18(3), 19(3)(a), 21, and 22(2) in Civil and Political Rights, *ibid.* and arts. 4, and 18(1)(a)(c) in Economic, Social and Cultural Rights, *supra* note 78.

276 *Ibid.* at art. 41. Compare with existing obligations in arts. 2(1), 6(2), 22, and 23 in Economic, Social and Cultural Rights, *ibid.*

277 *Ibid.*

278 *Ibid.* at art. 39. Compare to existing state obligations in art. 2(1) in Civil and Political Rights, *supra* note 79 and arts. 2(1), 6(2), 22, and 23 in Economic, Social and Cultural Rights, *supra* note 78.

279 UN Charter, *supra* note 48, art. 2, para. 2. The United Nations and member states also have a duty to promote universal respect for human rights. See L. B. Sohn, "The New International Law: Protection of the Rights of Individuals Rather than States" (1982) 32 Am. Univ. L. Rev. 1 at 13-14: "This constitution of the world [i.e. the peoples of the UN Charter], the highest

instrument in the intertwined hierarchy of international and domestic documents, prevails over all other treaties, and implicitly over all laws, anywhere in the world. . . . [H]uman rights are of international concern, and . . . the United Nations has the duty to promote 'universal respect for, and observance of, human rights and fundamental freedoms for all without distinction as to race, sex, language and religion.' [art. 55(c)] All members of the United Nations . . . have pledged to 'take joint and separate action,' [art. 56] in co-operation with the United Nations for the achievement of these great purposes."

280 *Ibid.*, art. 1, para. 3.

281 See identical arts. 1(3) and 2 in Civil and Political Rights, *supra* note 79; arts. 1(3) and 2 in Economic, Social and Cultural Rights, *supra* note 78; and the Optional Protocol, *supra* note 80.

282 See the Declaration on the Right and Responsibility of Individuals, Groups and Organs of Society to Promote and Protect Universally Recognized Human Rights and Fundamental Freedoms, UN General Assembly Res. 53/144, UN Doc. A/RES/53/144, 8 Mar. 1999, Annex, art. 2: "1. Each State has a prime responsibility and duty to protect, promote and implement all human rights and fundamental freedoms, *inter alia*, by adopting such steps as may be necessary to create all conditions necessary in the social, economic, political and other fields, as well as the legal guarantees required to ensure that all persons under its jurisdiction, individually and in association with others, are able to enjoy all those rights and freedoms in practice. 2. Each State shall adopt such legislative, administrative and other steps as may be necessary to ensure that the rights and freedoms referred to in the present Declaration are effectively guaranteed." Canada is committed to "seek to promote and give effect to" this Declaration; see Summit of the Americas, 2001, Plan of Action, adopted at the Third Summit of the Americas, Québec City, Canada, heading 2.

283 See the identical art. 2 in Civil and Political Rights, *supra* note 79, and art. 2 in Economic, Social and Cultural Rights, *supra* note 78.

284 This guarantee has also been described as a state obligation to guarantee the enjoyment of human rights; see Committee on the Elimination of Racial Discrimination, General Recommendation XX (48) concerning Non-discriminatory implementation of rights and freedoms (art. 5), 15 Mar. 1996 (contained in document A/51/18), para. 1: "Article 5 of the Convention contains the obligation of States Parties to guarantee the enjoyment of civil, political, economic, social and cultural rights and freedoms without racial discrimination. Note should be taken that the rights and freedoms mentioned in article 5 do not constitute an exhaustive list").

285 See *supra* notes 78 to 80. In 1998, the Human Rights Committee concluded: "17. The Committee is greatly concerned at the gross disparity between Aboriginal people and the majority of Canadians with respect to the enjoyment of Covenant rights. There has been little or no progress in the alleviation of social and economic deprivation among Aboriginal people. In particular, the Committee is deeply concerned at the shortage of adequate housing, the endemic mass unemployment and the high rate of suicide, especially among youth, in the Aboriginal communities. Another concern is the failure to provide safe and adequate drinking water to Aboriginal communities on reserves. The delegation of the State Party conceded that almost a quarter of Aboriginal household dwellings required major repairs and lacked basic amenities. . . . 18. The Committee views with concern the direct connection between Aboriginal economic marginalization and the ongoing dispossession of Aboriginal people from their lands, as recognized by RCAP, and endorses the recommendations of RCAP that policies which violate Aboriginal treaty obligations and the extinguishment, conversion or giving up of Aboriginal rights and title should on no account be pursued by the State Party. The Committee is greatly concerned that the recommendations of RCAP have not yet been implemented, in spite of the urgency of the situation" (Concluding observations of the UN Committee on Economic, Social and Cultural Rights: Canada. 10/12/98. E/C.12/1/Add.31, Dec. 1998.) In April 1999, the UN Human Rights Committee noted that, "as the State party acknowledged, the situation of the aboriginal peoples remains 'the most pressing human rights issue facing Canadians,'" *supra* note 88 at para. 8.

286 The idea of "binding" law is a recent judicial construct developed by imperial British courts. It is related to the emergence of the doctrine of *stare decisis* in the 19th century, the idea that first-instance judges are bound by decisions of the court of appeals. It is related to the positive concept of law as command rather than custom. H. Patrick Glenn, "Transsystemic," *supra* note 22 at 879-81, has noted that the idea of "binding" law on public servants is "incompatible with the idea of positive law and a legal system, as these concepts are explained by legal theory, and may now be reaching the end of its career"; . He notes that, on close "examination, we find that legal systems do not create any obligation [on public servants] to obey the law. They do not bind. This is because they exercise only persuasive authority," at 898.

287 UN Declaration on the Rights of Indigenous Peoples, *supra* note 1, Preamble at 5.

288 *Ibid.* at art. 13(2). Compare to arts. 2(3), 14, and 26 in Civil and Political Rights, *supra* note 79.

289 *Ibid.* at art. 42. Compare with art. 1(3) in Civil and Political Rights, *ibid.,* and art. 1(3) in Economic, Social and Cultural Rights, *supra* note 78.

290 *Ibid.* at art. 22 (1). Compare to Convention on the Rights of the Child, UN General Assembly Doc. A/RES/44/25 (12 Dec. 1989) at arts. 17(d), 29(d), and 30.

291 *Ibid.* at art. 39. Compare to existing state obligations in art. 2(1) in Civil and Political Rights, *supra* note 79, and arts. 2(1), 6(2), 22, and 23 in Economic, Social and Cultural Rights, *supra* note 78.

292 *Ibid.* at art. 32.

293 *Ibid.* at art. 38. Compare with art. 2(2) in Civil and Political Rights, *supra* note 79, and art. 2(1) in Economic, Social and Cultural Rights, *supra* note 78.

294 *Ibid.* at art. 19.

295 *Ibid.* at art. 15(1). See also ILO Indigenous and Tribal Peoples Convention 169, *supra* note 138 at arts. 26 (In the field of education, states and the teaching profession and unions have the obligation to ensure that Indigenous peoples "have the opportunity to acquire education at all levels on at least an equal footing with the rest of the national community"), 27(1) (States have the obligation to develop and implement "education programs and services in co-operation" with Indigenous peoples, and to foster "national and regional development"), and 31 ("These educational measures shall be taken among all sections of the national community, and particularly among those that are in most direct contact with the peoples concerned, with the object of eliminating prejudices that they may harbour in respect of Indigenous peoples").

296 *Ibid.* at art. 22(2). Compare with existing state obligations in art. 2(1) in Civil and Political Rights, *supra* note 79, and art. 2(2) in Economic, Social and Cultural Rights, *supra* note 78.

297 *Ibid.* at art. 14(2). Compare to existing state obligations in art. 2(1) in Civil and Political Rights, *ibid.*, and arts. 2(1), 13 in Economic, Social and Cultural Rights, *ibid.* See also ILO Indigenous and Tribal Peoples Convention 169, *supra* note 138 at arts. 26 and 27(1). It was not until the 1989 Convention on the Rights of the Child, *supra* note 290, 29(d) that "States Parties agree that the education of the child shall be directed to: [t]he preparation of the child for responsible life in a free society, in the spirit of understanding, peace, tolerance, equality of sexes, and friendship among all peoples, ethnic, national and religious groups and persons of indigenous origin").

298 *Ibid.* at art. 14(3). Compare to existing state obligations in arts. 2(1) and 27 in Civil and Political Rights, *ibid.*, and arts. 2(2), 13(3) and 15 in Economic, Social and Cultural Rights, *ibid.*; ILO Indigenous and Tribal Peoples

Convention 169, *ibid.*, at arts. 27(1) and 30(1); Convention on the Rights of the Child, *ibid.*, at arts. 17(d) and 30 (In those states in which ethnic, religious, or linguistic minorities or persons of indigenous origin exist, a child belonging to such a minority or who is indigenous shall not be denied the right, in community with other members of his or her group, to enjoy his or her own culture, to profess and practise his or her own religion, or to use his or her own language).

299 *Ibid.* at art. 17(2). Compare to existing state obligations in arts. 6 and 10(2-3) in Economic, Social and Cultural Rights, *ibid.*

300 *Ibid.* at art. 21.

301 *Ibid.* at art. 24(2). Compare to existing state obligations in art. 12 in Economic, Social and Cultural Rights, *supra* note 78.

302 *Ibid.* at art. 29(3). Compare to existing state obligations in art. 12 in Economic, Social and Cultural Rights, *ibid.*

303 *Ibid.* at art. 16(2). Compare to existing state obligations in art. 19 in Civil and Political Rights, *supra* note 79. See also UNESCO Universal Declaration of Cultural Diversity, (2001), *supra* note 124, arts. 2, 4, 5, and 6; Convention on the Rights of the Child, *supra* note 290 at art. 17(d) ("Encourage the mass media to have particular regard to the linguistic needs of the child who belongs to a minority group or who is Indigenous").

304 *Ibid.* at art. 40. Compare to existing state obligations in arts. 2 and 14 in Civil and Political Rights, *ibid.*

305 *Ibid.*

306 *Ibid.* at art. 8(2).

307 *Ibid.* at art. 26(3).

308 *Ibid.* at art. 29(1).

309 *Ibid.* at art. 27. Compare to existing state obligations in arts. 2, 14, and 47 in Civil and Political Rights, *supra* note 79.

310 *Ibid.* at art. 32(2). Compare to existing state obligations in art. 47 in Civil and Political Rights, *ibid.*, and art. 25 in Economic, Social and Cultural Rights, *supra* note 78.

311 *Ibid.* at art. 32(3).

312 *Ibid.* at art. 36(2).

313 *Ibid.* at art. 30.

314 *Ibid.* at art. 29.

315 *Ibid.* at art. 31. Compare to UNESCO Declaration on Race and Racial Prejudice (1978) at art. 5(2): states are required to ensure "that curricula and textbooks include scientific and ethical considerations concerning human unity and diversity and that no invidious distinctions are made with regard to any people" (UNESCO: The World Conference on Science for the Twenty First Century: A New Commitment, 1999), *supra* note 148.

316 *Ibid.* at art. 11(2).

317 *Ibid.* at art. 12(2).

318 First International Decade for the Eradication of Colonialism, 1990-2000, UN General Assembly Res. 43/47 (22 Nov. 1988); Second International Decade for the Eradication of Colonialism, 2001-2010, UN General Assembly Res. 55/146 (6 March 2001); Questions of American Samoa, Anguilla, Bermuda, the British Virgin Islands, the Cayman Islands, Guam, Montserrat, Pitcairn, Saint Helena, the Turks and Caicos Islands and the United States Virgin Islands, UN General Assembly Res. 59/134 A-B, 25 Jan. 2005. These documents reaffirm that, in the process of decolonization, there is no alternative to the principle of self-determination.

319 *Reference re Resolution to Amend the Constitution* [1981] 1 S.C.R., 753 at 874.

320 *Reference re Secession of Quebec* [1998] 2 S.C.R., 217 at para. 32.

321 *Ibid.* at para. 113.

322 *Ibid.* at para. 114.

323 *Ibid.* at para. 123.

324 *Ibid.* at para. 124.

325 See the identical art. 1(3) in Civil and Political Rights, *supra* note 79; art. 1(3) in Economic, Social and Cultural Rights, *supra* note 78; and art. 46, UN Declaration on the Rights of Indigenous People, *supra* note 1.

326 Optional Protocol, *supra* note 80.

327 *Lovelace*, *supra* note 84; *Mikmaq Society*, *supra* note 85; *Ominayak*, *supra* note 86.

328 Canada, *Final Report of the Royal Commission on Aboriginal Peoples* (Ottawa: Canada Communication Group, 1996); Governance: Restructuring the Relationship, vol. 2(1), ch. 3, 2.2 at 165-225; Recommendation 2.3.2. In April 1999, the UN Human Rights Committee, *supra* note 88, ruled on Canada as follows: "The Committee notes that, as the State party acknowledged, the situation of the aboriginal peoples remains 'the most pressing human rights issue facing Canadians.' In this connection, the Committee is particularly concerned that the State party has not yet implemented the recommenda-

tions of the Royal Commission on Aboriginal Peoples (RCAP). With reference to the conclusion by RCAP that without a greater share of lands and resources institutions of aboriginal self-government will fail, the Committee emphasizes that the right to self-determination requires, *inter alia*, that all peoples must be able to freely dispose of their natural wealth and resources and that they may not be deprived of their own means of subsistence (art. 1, para. 2). The Committee recommends that decisive and urgent action be taken towards the full implementation of the RCAP recommendations on land and resource allocation. The Committee also recommends that the practice of extinguishing inherent aboriginal rights be abandoned as incompatible with article 1 of the Covenant." See also Jennifer E. Dalton, "Aboriginal Self-Determination in Canada: Protections Afforded by the Judiciary and Government" (2006) 21:1 Can. J. of Law and Society 11-37.

329 Statements of the Canadian Delegation, CHR, 53rd Sess., Working Group established in accordance with CHR resolution 1995/32 of 3 Mar. 1995, 2nd Session, Geneva, 21 Oct.-1 Nov. 1996, cited in Consultations Between Canadian Aboriginal Organizations and DFAIT in Preparation for the 53rd Session of the UN CHR, 4 Feb. 1997 (statement on art. 3, right to self-determination, on 31 Oct. 1996). In 1994, the observer for Canada emphasized that Canada "supported the principle that indigenous people qualified for traditional rights of self-determination in international law on the same basis as non-indigenous people if they otherwise met the criteria of international law. The 'same basis' qualification was aimed at restricting the exercise of self-determination to classic colonial situations, preserving the territorial *status quo* of settled countries such as Canada. In all other cases 'self-determination' of indigenous people had to be granted within the framework of existing nation-states[.] The notion of self-determination as used in the draft declaration might imply the right of indigenous people to unilaterally determine their political, economic and social status within the existing State" (Explanatory note concerning the Draft Declaration on the Rights of Indigenous Peoples, UN Doc. E/CN.4/Sub.2/1993/26/ Add.1). In July 1992, Canadian diplomats stated, "Canada supports the principle of self-determination, within the framework of existing States, where there is an inter-relationship between indigenous and non-indigenous jurisdictions that gives indigenous people greater levels of autonomy over their own affairs but that also recognizes the jurisdiction of the state" (Denis Marantz, "Working Group on Indigenous Populations, Tenth Session; Statement of the Observer Delegation of Canada," Geneva, 21 July 1992).

330 First Nations/Federal Crown Political Accord on the Recognition and Implementation of First Nation Governments, 31 May 2005, www.afn.ca/cmslib/general/PolAcc.pdf.

331 *Ibid.* at art. 8.

332 Report of the Standing Senate Committee on Human Rights: Promises To Keep: Implementing Canada's Human Rights Obligations (2001) www.parl.gc.ca/37/1/parlbus/commbus/senate/Com-e/huma-e/rep-e/rep02dec01-e.htm: "These [Human Rights] Covenants exist as UN multi-party treaties that have turned the rights into customary international law. When rights are embedded in international law we speak of them as human rights; but when they are enacted in national law we more frequently describe them as civil or constitutional rights. As this illustrates, it is possible for a right to exist within more than one normative system at the same time. Enactment in national and international law is one of the ways in which human rights exist. But many have suggested that this is not the only way. One version of this idea is that people are born with rights, that human rights are somehow innate or inherent in human beings. One way that a normative status could be inherent in humans is by being God-given. Another view is that human rights exist independently of legal enactment by being part of actual human moralities, i.e., imperative norms of behaviour backed by reason and values. Another way of explaining the existence of human rights is to say that they exist in true or justified moralities, i.e., there are strong reasons for believing in them for moral and practical reasons, which exist independently of human construction."

333 *Suresh* v. *Canada (Minister of Citizenship and Immigration)*, [2002] 1 S.C.R. 3, at para. 60: "International treaty norms are not, strictly speaking, binding in Canada unless they have been incorporated into Canadian law by enactment. However, in seeking the meaning of the Canadian Constitution, the courts may be informed by international law. Our concern is not with Canada's international obligations *qua* obligations; rather, our concern is with the principles of fundamental justice. We look to international law as evidence of these principles and not as controlling in itself." See also Dickson, C. J. C. (dissenting) in *Re Public Service Employee Relations Act (Alta.)*, [1987] 1 S.C.R. 313 at 348-349: "Canada has thus obliged itself internationally to ensure within its borders the protection of certain fundamental rights and freedoms which are also contained in the Charter. The general principles of constitutional interpretation require that these international obligations be a relevant and persuasive factor in Charter interpretation."

334 S. J. Anaya, "Indigenous Rights Norms in Contemporary International Law" (1991) 8 Ariz. J. Int'l & Comp. Law 1 at 29-30: "self-determination is widely held to be a norm of general or customary international law, and arguably *jus cogens* (a peremptory norm)"; Human Rights and Self-Determination, *supra* note 66 at 858: "This right [of self-determination] has been declared in other international treaties and instruments, is generally accepted as customary international law and could even form part of *jus cogens*"; K. Doehring, "Self-Determination," in B. Simma (Ed.), *The Charter of the United Nations: A Commentary* (New York: Oxford University Press, 1994) 56 at 70: "The right of self-determination is overwhelmingly characterized as forming part of the peremptory norms of international law. However, this evaluation is also rejected by some. It can nevertheless be proved that such a qualification is correct"; A. Cassese, *Self-Determination of Peoples: A Legal Appraisal* (Cambridge: Cambridge University Press, 1995) at 140: "It is no coincidence that whenever States have referred to self-determination as belonging to *jus cogens*, they have not specified either the areas of application of self-determination, the means or the methods of its implementation, or the permissible outcome of self-determination. States have generically adverted to the 'principle'... or, more simply, to self-determination. It follows that the whole cluster of legal standards (the general principle and the customary rules) on self-determination should be regarded as belonging to the body of peremptory norms."

335 At the international level, a similar ruling is found in *Military and Paramilitary Activities in and against Nicaragua (Nicaragua* v. *United States)*, Merits, [1986] I.C.J. Rep. 14 (Merits), at 94-95, para. 177: "even if the customary norm and the treaty norm were to have exactly the same content, this would not be a reason for the Court to hold that the incorporation of the customary norm into treaty-law must deprive the customary norm of its applicability as distinct from that of the treaty norm.... More generally, there are no grounds for holding that when customary international law is comprised of rules identical to those of treaty law, the latter 'supervenes' the former, so that the customary international law has no further existence of its own."

336 Reply by the Attorney General of Canada to Questions Posed by the Supreme Court of Canada at para. 8, in *Quebec Secession Reference*, *supra* note 320. For a similar approach in the context of the Canadian Charter, *infra* note 354, see G. V. La Forest, "The Expanding Role of the Supreme Court of Canada in International Issues" (1996) 34 Can. Y. I.L. 89 at 97.

337 See, for example, the teachings of Graham Hingangaroa Smith, *Kaupapa Maori Theory and Praxis: A Critical theory approach to transformative praxis in intervening in Maori educational crises,* unpublished PhD diss., University of Auckland, 1997.

338 See J. Gledhill, *Power and Its Disguises: An Anthropological Perspective on Politics* (London: Pluto Press, 1994).

339 See John Rawls, *The Law of Peoples* (Cambridge: Harvard University Press, 1999); Martin van Crefeld, *The Rise and Decline of the State* (Cambridge: Cambridge University Press, 1999); Z. Skurbaty, *As if Peoples Mattered: A Critical Appraisal of "Peoples" and "Minorities" from the International Human Rights Perspective and Beyond* (The Hague: Martinus Nijhoff, 2000); "Transsystemic," *supra* note 22; L. M. Findlay, "Always Indigenize!" *supra* note 205.

340 HRC Resolution 6/36 (14 Dec. 2007) establishing a new Expert Mechanism on the Rights of Indigenous Peoples was adopted by consensus by the HRC. This was part of the reforming of the UN Human Rights machinery. The HRC adopted resolution 6/16 to request the Office of the High Commissioner for Human Rights to convene an informal meeting to discuss the most appropriate mechanisms to continue the work of the Working Group on Indigenous Populations. The informal meeting took place in Geneva on 6 Dec. and the morning of 7 Dec. 2007. The Consensus Recommendation was submitted by the Indigenous Peoples' Global Caucus addressing the work of the United Nations Human Rights Council and the establishment of an Expert Group on the Human Rights of Indigenous Peoples, IMWGIP/2007/CRP.3 and Draft Resolution submitted by the Indigenous Caucus, IMWGIP/2007/CRP.12.

341 H. L. A. Hart, *The Concept of Law*, 2nd Ed. (Oxford: Clarendon Press, 1994). This work, grounded in Eurocentrism, argues that the legal system eliminates "defects" of uncertainty, stasis, and inefficiency in "primitive communities" that did not have secondary rules on recognizing rules, *ibid.* at 91-95. This continues the "state of nature" presupposition, see *supra* note 8.

342 One of the defining features of the positivistic understanding of law is its insistence on the separation of law and morality. In other words, state or private action may be legal yet immoral, and vice versa, depending on the extent to which it is based on legal rules recognized as valid within the legal system in question. *The Concept of Law*, *ibid.* at 206-07; compare with Ronald Dworkin, *Taking Rights Seriously* (Cambridge, Mass: Harvard University Press, 1977) and *Law's Empire* (Cambridge, Mass: Harvard University Press, 1986).

343 *The Concept of Law*, *ibid.* at 60-66; Lon Fuller, *Morality of Law* (New Haven: Yale University Press, 1969) at 70-80; *Taking Rights Seriously*, *ibid.* at 247, 326; *Law's Empire, ibid.* at 101-8; Brian Z. Tamanaha, "Socio-legal Positivism and a General Jurisprudence" (2001) 20 Oxford J. Legal Stud. 1 at 12-13, and 19-20.

344 "Transsystemic," *supra* note 22 at 888-89.

345 *Ibid.* at 885. In the common law traditions, judicial review has traditionally been seen as the repository of all fundamental values; see David Dyzenhaus, Murray Hunt, and Michael Taggart, "The Principle of Legality in Administrative Law: Internationalisation as Constitutionalisation" [2001] Oxford University Commonwealth, L. J. 5. The discourses about common law reflect an awareness of plurality, an interdependence of many traditions, and the acceptance and accommodation of difference in a constant, dialogical tension.

346 See Paul Sieghart, *The Lawful Rights of Mankind: An Introduction to the International Legal Code of Human Rights* (Oxford: Oxford University Press, 1985).

347 On 7 April 2008 MP Irene Mathyssen (London-Fanshawe) introduced in the House of Commons a motion supported by MP Jean Crowder (Nanaimo-Cowichan) that the Third Report of the Standing Committee on the Status of Women, presented on 18 Feb., be concurred in. The motion was voted on the following day. See www.gcc.ca/newsarticle.php?id=133.

348 Supreme Court Justice Binnie's concurring opinion in *Mitchell* v. *Minister of National Revenue* [2001] 1 S.C.R., 911 at para. 164, spoke to the issue of territorial integrity and Canadian sovereignty in regard to Aboriginal rights to trade across the Canada-USA border: "Affirmation of the sovereign interest of Canadians as a whole, including aboriginal peoples, should not necessarily be seen as a loss of sufficient 'constitutional space for aboriginal peoples to be aboriginal'. . . . [T]he respondent's claim relates to national interests that all of us have in common rather than to distinctive interests that for some purposes differentiate an aboriginal community. In my view, reconciliation of these interests in this particular case favours an affirmation of our collective sovereignty."

349 *Ibid.* at paras. 126 and 130.

350 *Ibid.* at paras. 118-122. This provision is consistent with s. 46(1) in the UN Declaration on the Rights of Indigenous Peoples, *supra* note 1, and the legal tradition of many Indigenous peoples of living harmoniously with one another on the land.

351 *Ibid.*

352 *Ibid.*

353 Sections 35 and 52, *Constitution Act, 1982*, Schedule B to the *Canada Act 1982*, *supra* note 96, Part II. See also s. 25 of *Canadian Charter of Rights and Freedoms*, Part I of the *Constitution Act, 1982*, being Schedule B to the *Canada Act 1982*,

ibid. In 1983, a Mi'kmaq delegation asked for confirmation that Indigenous peoples enjoy the same right to self-determination as other "peoples" (United Nations 1983 Statement on Legal Standards by the Four Directions Council). In response, Canadian diplomats maintained that past injustices had been corrected and, in the fullness of time, Aboriginal peoples would be able to vindicate their rights under s. 35 of the *Constitution Act, 1982*.

354 *Aboriginal Tenure, supra* note 109 at 447: "Constitutional entrenchment of Aboriginal and treaty rights was intended to ensure that elected representatives, the administrative agencies, and the courts gave due regard and protection to the rights of Aboriginal peoples. It provided a safeguard for their distinct human rights and individual freedoms called 'Aboriginal rights'. . ." See also P. Joffe, "Assessing the *Delgamuukw* Principles: National Implications and Potential Effects in Québec" (2000) 45 McGill L. J. 155 at 182; C. P. Cohen (Ed.), *Human Rights of Indigenous Peoples* (Ardsley, NY: Transnational Publishers, 1998); M. E. Turpel, "Indigenous Peoples' Rights of Political Participation and Self-Determination: Recent International Legal Developments and the Continuing Struggle for Recognition," (1992) 25 Cornell Int'l L. J. 579; "Emerging Norm," *supra* note 83; D. Sanders, "Collective Rights" (1991) 13 Hum. Rts. Q. 368 at 379-80; and "Symposium, The Human Rights of Indigenous Peoples" (1982) 36 Colum. J. Int'l Aff. 1-161; B. Hocking (Ed.), *International Law and Aboriginal Human Rights* (Toronto: Carswell, 1988).

355 I. Cotler and F. P. Eliadis, (Eds.), *International Human Rights Law: Theory and Practice* (Montreal: Canadian Human Rights Foundation, 1992), 63 at 66.

356 In Canada, see also *Delgamuukw* v. *British Columbia* [1997] 3 S.C.R., 1010 at para. 115: "Aboriginal title cannot be held by individual aboriginal persons; it is a collective right to land held by all members of an aboriginal nation."

357 B. McLachlin, "Aboriginal Rights: International Perspectives," Order of Canada luncheon speech, Canadian Club of Vancouver, Vancouver, BC, 8 Feb. 2002.

358 *R.* v. *Sioui* [1990] 1 S.C.R., 1025 at 1063. *R.* v. *Badger* [1996] 1 S.C.R., 771 at para. 41 (per Cory J.); *R.* v. *Sundown* [1999] 1 S.C.R., 393. See also RCAP, *supra* note 328, vol. 2(1) at 53: "The consistent message emerging from the testimony of treaty nations is that the treaties are sacred and spiritual covenants that cannot be repudiated, any more than the cultures and identities of treaty nations can be repudiated."

359 *Treaty Rights, supra* note 109.

360 RCAP, *supra* note 328 at vol. 2(1) at 165-74; *Campbell* v. *British Columbia* [2000] B.C.J. No. 1524 (S.C.).

361 *Campbell*, *ibid.* at para. 52: "observance of and respect for these [underlying constitutional] principles is essential to the ongoing process of constitutional development and evolution of our Constitution as a 'living tree,' to invoke the famous description in *Edwards* v. *Attorney-General for Canada* [1930] A.C. 124 (P.C.), at 136"; *Reference re Provincial Electoral Boundaries (Sask.)* [1991] 2 S.C.R. 158 at 180: "The doctrine of the constitution as a living tree mandates that narrow technical approaches are to be eschewed. . . . The tree is rooted in past and present institutions, but must be capable of growth to meet the future." *Hunter* v. *Southam Inc.* [1984] 2 S.C.R. 145 at 155: "A constitution . . . is drafted with an eye to the future. . . . Once enacted, its provisions cannot easily be repealed or amended. It must, therefore, be capable of growth and development over time to meet new social, political and historical realities often unimagined by its framers. The judiciary is the guardian of the constitution and must, in interpreting its provisions, bear these considerations in mind."

362 *Charter*, *supra* note 353. Section 25 provides that "The guarantee in this Charter of certain rights and freedoms shall not be construed so as to abrogate or derogate from any aboriginal, treaty or other rights or freedoms that pertain to the aboriginal peoples of Canada including a) any rights or freedoms that have been recognized by the Royal Proclamation of October 7, 1763; and b) any rights or freedoms that now exist by way of land claims agreements or may be so acquired." Section 26 protects the human rights covenants: "The guarantee in this Charter of certain rights and freedoms shall not be construed as denying the existence of any other rights or freedoms that exist in Canada." Section 27 provides for interpretation of these human rights: "This Charter shall be interpreted in a manner consistent with the preservation and enhancement of the multicultural heritage of Canadians."

363 *The Government of Canada's Approach to Implementation of the Inherent Right and the Negotiation of Aboriginal Self-Government* (Ottawa: Minister of Public Works and Government Services Canada, 1995) at 3: "The Government of Canada recognizes the inherent right of self-government as an existing Aboriginal right under section 35 of the *Constitution Act, 1982*. It recognizes, as well, that the inherent right may find expression in treaties, and in the context of the Crown's relationship with treaty First Nations."

364 *Indigenous Peoples in International Law*, *supra* note 3 at 109: "Self-government is the overarching political dimension of ongoing self-determination." See also R. McCorquodale, "Self-Determination: A Human Rights Approach"

(1994) 43 Int'l & Comp. L.Q. 857 at 864; and the UN Declaration on the Rights of Indigenous Peoples, *supra* note 1, art. 4: "Indigenous peoples, as a specific form of exercising their right to self-determination, have the right to autonomy or self-government."

365 Art. 45 of the UN Declaration on the Rights of Indigenous Peoples, *ibid.* See also the revised set of basic principles and guidelines on the right to reparation for victims of gross violations of human rights and humanitarian law prepared by Theo van Boven, pursuant to Sub-Commission decision 1995/117, Annex, para. 3: "The human rights and humanitarian norms which every State has the duty to respect and to ensure respect for, are defined by international law and must be incorporated and in any event made effective in national law. In the event international and national norms differ, the State shall ensure that the norm providing the higher degree of protection shall be applicable."

366 *Mikisew Cree First Nation, supra* note 101 at para. 1.

367 UN CHR, Report of the United Nations High Commissioner for Human Rights and Follow-Up to the World, E/CN.4/2003/14, 26 Feb. 2003, at para. 11 and para. 53: "The rights-based approach must be the starting point for all our endeavours, whatever our spheres of operation: trade, finance, development, security, in both the public and private sectors. In a sense, this is an approach that involves human rights strategies of governance, namely, that we take the basic human rights as the starting point for governmental programs and the programs of national, regional and international institutions. What is at issue is a question of conscience: people matter, and the way we demonstrate this is by upholding the international minimum standards of protection of their human rights." See also B. McLachlin, "The Supreme Court and the Public Interest" (2001) 64 Sask. L. Rev. 309 at 313-314, in which the Chief Justice refers to the "rights-based nature of modern democracy" in Canada.

368 RCAP, *supra* note 328 at vol. 2(1) at 169-182.

369 For the government's position in voting against the UN Declaration on the Rights of Indigenous Peoples, see www.ainc-inac.gc.ca/nr/spch/unp/06/ddr_e.html. For a response to Canada's position, see Paul Joffe, "UN Declaration: Achieving Reconciliation and Effective Application in the Canadian Context" (2008), Aboriginal Law Conference, Paper 2.2, Continuing Legal Education Society of British Columbia (unpublished).

370 World Conference Against Racism, Racial Discrimination, Xenophobia and Related Intolerance Declaration. See Appendix X, para. 14: "We recognize that colonialism has led to racism, racial discrimination, xenophobia and related intolerance, and that ... indigenous peoples were victims of colonialism and continue to be victims of its consequences. We acknowledge the suffering caused by colonialism and affirm that, wherever and whenever it occurred, it must be condemned and its reoccurrence prevented"; Working Group on Indigenous Populations, "Principle Theme: Indigenous Peoples and Their Right to Development, Including Their Right to Participate in Development Affecting Them," note by the secretariat, E/CN.4/Sub.2/AC.4/2001/2, 20 June 2001, para. 11: "What are the causes of indigenous poverty? There are a number of explanations, which are often linked to each other. In some cases, it is the paucity of resources indigenous peoples have at their disposal for their own development processes, and the negative impacts of large-scale development projects on their lives and lands. In other cases, it is the marginal role they play in the national development process and the exclusion from the market, which prevents indigenous peoples from enjoying the same opportunities as others. In yet other situations, it is direct discrimination and exclusion from society that keeps indigenous peoples in poverty. Poverty is a denial of all human rights to an individual and group and erodes civil and political, as well as economic, social and cultural rights. As has been noted by the Working Group on numerous occasions, indigenous peoples form a disproportionately larger share among the poor"; UN CHR, Human rights and extreme poverty, Res. 2003/24, 22 April 2003, para. 1(c): "The existence of widespread absolute poverty inhibits the full and effective enjoyment of human rights and makes democracy and popular participation fragile. ..."; Vienna Declaration, *supra* note 67, Part I, para. 14: "the existence of widespread extreme poverty inhibits the full and effective enjoyment of human rights; its immediate alleviation and eventual elimination must remain a high priority for the international community"; "Statement of Reconciliation," in Indian Affairs and Northern Development, *Gathering Strength – Canada's Aboriginal Action Plan* (Ottawa: Minister of Public Works and Government Services, 1997) at 4: "Attitudes of racial and cultural superiority led to a suppression of Aboriginal culture and values. As a country, we are burdened by past actions that resulted in weakening the identity of Aboriginal peoples, suppressing their languages and cultures, and outlawing spiritual practices. . . . We must acknowledge that the result of these actions was the erosion of the political, economic and social systems of Aboriginal people and nations." James Tully, "The Struggles of Indigenous Peoples for and of Freedom," in D. Ivison, P. Patton, and W. Sanders (Eds.), *Political Theory and the Rights of Indigenous Peoples* (Cambridge/New York: Cambridge University Press,

2000) 36 at 39: "The long-term effects of [the processes of internal colonization] for the vast majority of native people in Canada has been to reduce formerly economically self-sufficient and interdependent native societies to tiny overcrowded reserves, inter-generational welfare dependency, sub-standard housing, diet, education and housing facilities, high levels of unemployment, low life expectancy, high rates of death at birth, and predictably, following these conditions on or off reserves that undermine their well-being and self-esteem, high levels of substance abuse, incarceration and suicide for native peoples"; R. Müllerson, "Reflections on the Future of Civil and Political Rights," in B. H. Weston and S. P. Marks (Eds.), *The Future of International Human Rights* (Ardsley, NY: Transnational Publishers, 1999), 225 at 235: "Existing poverty in some highly developed countries . . . [is] among the conditions that make the enjoyment of some civil and political rights for many people impossible, and thus, there still is some room for improvement in civil and political rights even in rich democratic countries in the sense of making the enjoyment of these rights real to everyone."

371 *Supra* note 1 at arts. 13, 14, 15, and 31; ILO Indigenous and Tribal Peoples Convention 169, *supra* note 138 at arts. 27(1) and 30(1).

372 Vienna Declaration, *supra* note 67 at paras. 78-82 (no mention of Indigenous peoples in human rights education). It was not until the Convention on the Rights of the Child, *supra* note 290, that express reference was made to Indigenous peoples, see art. 17(d), 29(d), and 30; First Decade, *supra* note 150 at paras. 3 and 22; Permanent Forum on Indigenous Issues, 2003 theme of Indigenous Children and Youth, Press Release HR/4676, 23 May 2003.

373 Paula Gerber, "Black Rights/White Curriculum: Human Rights Education for Indigenous Peoples" (2004) 9 Deakin L. Rev. 61; Lynda Frost, "Human Rights Education Programs for Indigenous People: Teaching Whose Human Rights?" (1995) 7 St. Thomas L. Rev. 699.

Appendices

Appendix I

United Nations Declaration on the Rights of Indigenous Peoples (2007)

United Nations A/61/L.67

The General Assembly,

Taking note of the recommendation of the Human Rights Council contained in its resolution 1/2 of 29 June 2006, by which the Council adopted the text of the United Nations Declaration on the Rights of Indigenous Peoples,

Recalling its resolution 61/178 of 20 December 2006, by which it decided to defer consideration of and action on the Declaration to allow time for further consultations thereon, and also decided to conclude its consideration before the end of the sixty-first session of the General Assembly,

Adopts the United Nations Declaration on the Rights of Indigenous Peoples as contained in the annex to the present resolution.

ANNEX

United Nations Declaration on the Rights of Indigenous Peoples

The General Assembly,

Guided by the purposes and principles of the Charter of the United Nations, and good faith in the fulfilment of the obligations assumed by States in accordance with the Charter,

Affirming that indigenous peoples are equal to all other peoples, while recognizing the right of all peoples to be different, to consider themselves different, and to be respected as such,

Affirming also that all peoples contribute to the diversity and richness of civilizations and cultures, which constitute the common heritage of humankind,

Affirming further that all doctrines, policies and practices based on or advocating superiority of peoples or individuals on the basis of national origin or racial, religious, ethnic or cultural differences are racist, scientifically false, legally invalid, morally condemnable and socially unjust,

Reaffirming that indigenous peoples, in the exercise of their rights, should be free from discrimination of any kind,

Concerned that indigenous peoples have suffered from historic injustices as a result of, *inter alia*, their colonization and dispossession of their lands, territories and resources, thus preventing them from exercising, in particular, their right to development in accordance with their own needs and interests,

Recognizing the urgent need to respect and promote the inherent rights of indigenous peoples which derive from their political, economic and social structures and from their cultures, spiritual traditions, histories and philosophies, especially their rights to their lands, territories and resources,

Recognizing also the urgent need to respect and promote the rights of indigenous peoples affirmed in treaties, agreements and other constructive arrangements with States,

Welcoming the fact that indigenous peoples are organizing themselves for political, economic, social and cultural enhancement and in order to bring to an end all forms of discrimination and oppression wherever they occur,

Convinced that control by indigenous peoples over developments affecting them and their lands, territories and resources will enable them to maintain and strengthen their institutions, cultures and traditions, and to promote their development in accordance with their aspirations and needs,

Recognizing that respect for indigenous knowledge, cultures and traditional practices contributes to sustainable and equitable development and proper management of the environment,

Emphasizing the contribution of the demilitarization of the lands and territories of indigenous peoples to peace, economic and social progress and development, understanding and friendly relations among nations and peoples of the world,

Recognizing in particular the right of indigenous families and communities to retain shared responsibility for the upbringing, training, education and well-being of their children, consistent with the rights of the child,

Considering that the rights affirmed in treaties, agreements and other constructive arrangements between States and indigenous peoples are, in some situations, matters of international concern, interest, responsibility and character,

Considering also that treaties, agreements and other constructive arrangements, and the relationship they represent, are the basis for a strengthened partnership between indigenous peoples and States,

Acknowledging that the Charter of the United Nations, the International Covenant on Economic, Social and Cultural Rights[1] and the International Covenant on Civil and Political Rights as well as the Vienna Declaration and Programme of Action,[2] affirm the fundamental importance of the right to self-determination of all peoples, by virtue of which they freely determine their political status and freely pursue their economic, social and cultural development,

Bearing in mind that nothing in this Declaration may be used to deny any peoples their right to self-determination, exercised in conformity with international law,

1. See resolution 2200 A (XXI), ANNEX.

2. Resolution 217 A (III).

Convinced that the recognition of the rights of indigenous peoples in this Declaration will enhance harmonious and co-operative relations between the State and indigenous peoples, based on principles of justice, democracy, respect for human rights, non-discrimination and good faith,

Encouraging States to comply with and effectively implement all their obligations as they apply to indigenous peoples under international instruments, in particular those related to human rights, in consultation and co-operation with the peoples concerned,

Emphasizing that the United Nations has an important and continuing role to play in promoting and protecting the rights of indigenous peoples,

Believing that this Declaration is a further important step forward for the recognition, promotion and protection of the rights and freedoms of indigenous peoples and in the development of relevant activities of the United Nations system in this field,

Recognizing and reaffirming that indigenous individuals are entitled without discrimination to all human rights recognized in international law, and that indigenous peoples possess collective rights which are indispensable for their existence, well-being and integral development as peoples,

Recognizing also that the situation of indigenous peoples varies from region to region and from country to country and that the significance of national and regional particularities and various historical and cultural backgrounds should be taken into consideration,

Solemnly proclaims the following United Nations Declaration on the Rights of Indigenous Peoples as a standard of achievement to be pursued in a spirit of partnership and mutual respect:

Article 1

Indigenous peoples have the right to the full enjoyment, as a collective or as individuals, of all human rights and fundamental freedoms as recognized in the Charter of the United Nations, the Universal Declaration of Human Rights[3] and international human rights law.

Article 2

Indigenous peoples and individuals are free and equal to all other peoples and individuals and have the right to be free from any kind of discrimination, in the exercise of their rights, in particular that based on their indigenous origin or identity.

Article 3

Indigenous peoples have the right to self-determination. By virtue of that right they freely determine their political status and freely pursue their economic, social and cultural development.

Article 4

Indigenous peoples, in exercising their right to self-determination, have the right to autonomy or self-government in matters relating to their internal and local affairs, as well as ways and means for financing their autonomous functions.

---

3. Resolution 217 A (III).

Article 5

Indigenous peoples have the right to maintain and strengthen their distinct political, legal, economic, social and cultural institutions, while retaining their right to participate fully, if they so choose, in the political, economic, social and cultural life of the State.

Article 6

Every indigenous individual has the right to a nationality.

Article 7

1. Indigenous individuals have the rights to life, physical and mental integrity, liberty and security of person.

2. Indigenous peoples have the collective right to live in freedom, peace and security as distinct peoples and shall not be subjected to any act of genocide or any other act of violence, including forcibly removing children of the group to another group.

Article 8

1. Indigenous peoples and individuals have the right not to be subjected to forced assimilation or destruction of their culture.

2. States shall provide effective mechanisms for prevention of, and redress for:

(a) Any action which has the aim or effect of depriving them of their integrity as distinct peoples, or of their cultural values or ethnic identities;

(b) Any action which has the aim or effect of dispossessing them of their lands, territories or resources;

(c) Any form of forced population transfer which has the aim or effect of violating or undermining any of their rights;

(d) Any form of forced assimilation or integration;

(e) Any form of propaganda designed to promote or incite racial or ethnic discrimination directed against them.

Article 9

Indigenous peoples and individuals have the right to belong to an indigenous community or nation, in accordance with the traditions and customs of the community or nation concerned. No discrimination of any kind may arise from the exercise of such a right.

Article 10

Indigenous peoples shall not be forcibly removed from their lands or territories. No relocation shall take place without the free, prior and informed consent of the indigenous peoples concerned and after agreement on just and fair compensation and, where possible, with the option of return.

Article 11

1. Indigenous peoples have the right to practise and revitalize their cultural traditions and customs. This includes the right to maintain, protect and develop the past, present and

future manifestations of their cultures, such as archaeological and historical sites, artefacts, designs, ceremonies, technologies and visual and performing arts and literature.

2. States shall provide redress through effective mechanisms, which may include restitution, developed in conjunction with indigenous peoples, with respect to their cultural, intellectual, religious and spiritual property taken without their free, prior and informed consent or in violation of their laws, traditions and customs.

Article 12

1. Indigenous peoples have the right to manifest, practice, develop and teach their spiritual and religious traditions, customs and ceremonies; the right to maintain, protect, and have access in privacy to their religious and cultural sites; the right to the use and control of their ceremonial objects; and the right to the repatriation of their human remains.

2. States shall seek to enable the access and/or repatriation of ceremonial objects and human remains in their possession through fair, transparent and effective mechanisms developed in conjunction with indigenous peoples concerned.

Article 13

1. Indigenous peoples have the right to revitalize, use, develop and transmit to future generations their histories, languages, oral traditions, philosophies, writing systems and literatures, and to designate and retain their own names for communities, places and persons.

2. States shall take effective measures to ensure that this right is protected and also to ensure that indigenous peoples can understand and be understood in political, legal and administrative proceedings, where necessary through the provision of interpretation or by other appropriate means.

Article 14

1. Indigenous peoples have the right to establish and control their educational systems and institutions providing education in their own languages, in a manner appropriate to their cultural methods of teaching and learning.

2. Indigenous individuals, particularly children, have the right to all levels and forms of education of the State without discrimination.

3. States shall, in conjunction with indigenous peoples, take effective measures, in order for indigenous individuals, particularly children, including those living outside their communities, to have access, when possible, to an education in their own culture and provided in their own language.

Article 15

1. Indigenous peoples have the right to the dignity and diversity of their cultures, traditions, histories and aspirations which shall be appropriately reflected in education and public information.

2. States shall take effective measures, in consultation and co-operation with the indigenous peoples concerned, to combat prejudice and eliminate discrimination and to promote tolerance, understanding and good relations among indigenous peoples and all other segments of society.

Article 16

1. Indigenous peoples have the right to establish their own media in their own languages and to have access to all forms of non-indigenous media without discrimination.

2. States shall take effective measures to ensure that State-owned media duly reflect indigenous cultural diversity. States, without prejudice to ensuring full freedom of expression, should encourage privately owned media to adequately reflect indigenous cultural diversity.

Article 17

1. Indigenous individuals and peoples have the right to enjoy fully all rights established under applicable international and domestic labour law.

2. States shall in consultation and co-operation with indigenous peoples take specific measures to protect indigenous children from economic exploitation and from performing any work that is likely to be hazardous or to interfere with the child's education, or to be harmful to the child's health or physical, mental, spiritual, moral or social development, taking into account their special vulnerability and the importance of education for their empowerment.

3. Indigenous individuals have the right not to be subjected to any discriminatory conditions of labour and, *inter alia*, employment or salary.

Article 18

Indigenous peoples have the right to participate in decision-making in matters which would affect their rights, through representatives chosen by themselves in accordance with their own procedures, as well as to maintain and develop their own indigenous decision-making institutions.

Article 19

States shall consult and co-operate in good faith with the indigenous peoples concerned through their own representative institutions in order to obtain their free, prior and informed consent before adopting and implementing legislative or administrative measures that may affect them.

Article 20

1. Indigenous peoples have the right to maintain and develop their political, economic and social systems or institutions, to be secure in the enjoyment of their own means of subsistence and development, and to engage freely in all their traditional and other economic activities.

2. Indigenous peoples deprived of their means of subsistence and development are entitled to just and fair redress.

Article 21

1. Indigenous peoples have the right, without discrimination, to the improvement of their economic and social conditions, including, *inter alia*, in the areas of education, employment, vocational training and retraining, housing, sanitation, health and social security.

2. States shall take effective measures and, where appropriate, special measures to ensure continuing improvement of their economic and social conditions. Particular attention shall be paid to the rights and special needs of indigenous elders, women, youth, children and persons with disabilities.

Article 22

1. Particular attention shall be paid to the rights and special needs of indigenous elders, women, youth, children and persons with disabilities in the implementation of this Declaration.

2. States shall take measures, in conjunction with indigenous peoples, to ensure that indigenous women and children enjoy the full protection and guarantees against all forms of violence and discrimination.

Article 23

Indigenous peoples have the right to determine and develop priorities and strategies for exercising their right to development. In particular, indigenous peoples have the right to be actively involved in developing and determining health, housing and other economic and social programmes affecting them and, as far as possible, to administer such programmes through their own institutions.

Article 24

1. Indigenous peoples have the right to their traditional medicines and to maintain their health practices, including the conservation of their vital medicinal plants, animals and minerals. Indigenous individuals also have the right to access, without any discrimination, to all social and health services.

2. Indigenous individuals have an equal right to the enjoyment of the highest attainable standard of physical and mental health. States shall take the necessary steps with a view to achieving progressively the full realization of this right.

Article 25

Indigenous peoples have the right to maintain and strengthen their distinctive spiritual relationship with their traditionally owned or otherwise occupied and used lands, territories, waters and coastal seas and other resources and to uphold their responsibilities to future generations in this regard.

Article 26

1. Indigenous peoples have the right to the lands, territories and resources which they have traditionally owned, occupied or otherwise used or acquired.

2. Indigenous peoples have the right to own, use, develop and control the lands, territories and resources that they possess by reason of traditional ownership or other traditional occupation or use, as well as those which they have otherwise acquired.

3. States shall give legal recognition and protection to these lands, territories and resources. Such recognition shall be conducted with due respect to the customs, traditions and land tenure systems of the indigenous peoples concerned.

Article 27

States shall establish and implement, in conjunction with indigenous peoples concerned, a fair, independent, impartial, open and transparent process, giving due recognition to indigenous peoples' laws, traditions, customs and land tenure systems, to recognize and adjudicate the rights of indigenous peoples pertaining to their lands, territories and resources, including those which were traditionally owned or otherwise occupied or used. Indigenous peoples shall have the right to participate in this process.

Article 28

1. Indigenous peoples have the right to redress, by means that can include restitution or, when this is not possible, just, fair and equitable compensation, for the lands, territories and resources which they have traditionally owned or otherwise occupied or used, and which have been confiscated, taken, occupied, used or damaged without their free, prior and informed consent.

2. Unless otherwise freely agreed upon by the peoples concerned, compensation shall take the form of lands, territories and resources equal in quality, size and legal status or of monetary compensation or other appropriate redress.

Article 29

1. Indigenous peoples have the right to the conservation and protection of the environment and the productive capacity of their lands or territories and resources. States shall establish and implement assistance programmes for indigenous peoples for such conservation and protection, without discrimination.

2. States shall take effective measures to ensure that no storage or disposal of hazardous materials shall take place in the lands or territories of indigenous peoples without their free, prior and informed consent.

3. States shall also take effective measures to ensure, as needed, that programmes for monitoring, maintaining and restoring the health of indigenous peoples, as developed and implemented by the peoples affected by such materials, are duly implemented.

Article 30

1. Military activities shall not take place in the lands or territories of indigenous peoples, unless justified by a relevant public interest or otherwise freely agreed with or requested by the indigenous peoples concerned.

2. States shall undertake effective consultations with the indigenous peoples concerned, through appropriate procedures and in particular through their representative institutions, prior to using their lands or territories for military activities.

Article 31

1. Indigenous peoples have the right to maintain, control, protect and develop their cultural heritage, traditional knowledge and traditional cultural expressions, as well as the manifestations of their sciences, technologies and cultures, including human and genetic resources, seeds, medicines, knowledge of the properties of fauna and flora, oral traditions, literatures, designs, sports and traditional games and visual and performing arts. They also

have the right to maintain, control, protect and develop their intellectual property over such cultural heritage, traditional knowledge, and traditional cultural expressions.

2. In conjunction with indigenous peoples, States shall take effective measures to recognize and protect the exercise of these rights.

Article 32

1. Indigenous peoples have the right to determine and develop priorities and strategies for the development or use of their lands or territories and other resources.

2. States shall consult and co-operate in good faith with the indigenous peoples concerned through their own representative institutions in order to obtain their free and informed consent prior to the approval of any project affecting their lands or territories and other resources, particularly in connection with the development, utilization or exploitation of mineral, water or other resources.

3. States shall provide effective mechanisms for just and fair redress for any such activities, and appropriate measures shall be taken to mitigate adverse environmental, economic, social, cultural or spiritual impact.

Article 33

1. Indigenous peoples have the right to determine their own identity or membership in accordance with their customs and traditions. This does not impair the right of indigenous individuals to obtain citizenship of the States in which they live.

2. Indigenous peoples have the right to determine the structures and to select the membership of their institutions in accordance with their own procedures.

Article 34

Indigenous peoples have the right to promote, develop and maintain their institutional structures and their distinctive customs, spirituality, traditions, procedures, practices and, in the cases where they exist, juridical systems or customs, in accordance with international human rights standards.

Article 35

Indigenous peoples have the right to determine the responsibilities of individuals to their communities.

Article 36

1. Indigenous peoples, in particular those divided by international borders, have the right to maintain and develop contacts, relations and co-operation, including activities for spiritual, cultural, political, economic and social purposes, with their own members as well as other peoples across borders.

2. States, in consultation and co-operation with indigenous peoples, shall take effective measures to facilitate the exercise and ensure the implementation of this right.

Article 37

1. Indigenous peoples have the right to the recognition, observance and enforcement of treaties, agreements and other constructive arrangements concluded with States or their successors and to have States honour and respect such treaties, agreements and other constructive arrangements.

2. Nothing in this Declaration may be interpreted as diminishing or eliminating the rights of indigenous peoples contained in treaties, agreements and other constructive arrangements.

Article 38

States in consultation and co-operation with indigenous peoples, shall take the appropriate measures, including legislative measures, to achieve the ends of this Declaration.

Article 39

Indigenous peoples have the right to have access to financial and technical assistance from States and through international co-operation, for the enjoyment of the rights contained in this Declaration.

Article 40

Indigenous peoples have the right to access to and prompt decision through just and fair procedures for the resolution of conflicts and disputes with States or other parties, as well as to effective remedies for all infringements of their individual and collective rights. Such a decision shall give due consideration to the customs, traditions, rules and legal systems of the indigenous peoples concerned and international human rights.

Article 41

The organs and specialized agencies of the United Nations system and other intergovernmental organizations shall contribute to the full realization of the provisions of this Declaration through the mobilization, *inter alia*, of financial co-operation and technical assistance. Ways and means of ensuring participation of indigenous peoples on issues affecting them shall be established.

Article 42

The United Nations, its bodies, including the Permanent Forum on Indigenous Issues, and specialized agencies, including at the country level, and States shall promote respect for and full application of the provisions of this Declaration and follow up the effectiveness of this Declaration.

Article 43

The rights recognized herein constitute the minimum standards for the survival, dignity and well-being of the indigenous peoples of the world.

Article 44

All the rights and freedoms recognized herein are equally guaranteed to male and female indigenous individuals.

Article 45

Nothing in this Declaration may be construed as diminishing or extinguishing the rights indigenous peoples have now or may acquire in the future.

Article 46

1. Nothing in this Declaration may be interpreted as implying for any State, people, group or person any right to engage in any activity or to perform any act contrary to the Charter of the United Nations or construed as authorizing or encouraging any action which would dismember or impair, totally or in part, the territorial integrity or political unity of sovereign and independent States.

2. In the exercise of the rights enunciated in the present Declaration, human rights and fundamental freedoms of all shall be respected. The exercise of the rights set forth in this Declaration shall be subject only to such limitations as are determined by law, and in accordance with international human rights obligations. Any such limitations shall be non-discriminatory and strictly necessary solely for the purpose of securing due recognition and respect for the rights and freedoms of others and for meeting the just and most compelling requirements of a democratic society.

3. The provisions set forth in this Declaration shall be interpreted in accordance with the principles of justice, democracy, respect for human rights, equality, non-discrimination, good governance and good faith.

Appendix II

Draft United Nations Declaration on the Rights of Indigenous Peoples

(1994/95)

The Sub-Commission on Prevention of Discrimination and Protection of Minorities,

Recalling its resolutions 1985/22 of 29 August 1985, 1991/30 of 29 August 1991, 1992/33 of 27 August 1992, 1993/46 of 26 August 1993,

Taking into account, in particular, paragraph 3 of its resolution 1993/46, in which it decided to postpone until its forty-sixth session consideration of the draft United Nations declaration on the rights of indigenous peoples agreed upon by the members of the Working Group on Indigenous Populations, to request the Secretary-General to submit the draft declaration to the appropriate services in the Centre for Human Rights for its technical revision, and to submit, if possible, the draft declaration to the Commission on Human Rights with the recommendation that the Commission adopt it at its fifty-first session,

Recalling Commission on Human Rights resolution 1994/29 of 4 March 1994, in which the Sub-Commission was urged to complete its consideration of the draft United Nations declaration at its forty-sixth session and to submit it to the Commission at its fifty-first session together with any recommendations thereon,

Bearing in mind General Assembly resolution 47/75 of 14 December 1992, paragraph 12 of Commission on Human Rights resolution 1993/30 of 5 March 1993, paragraph 6 (a) of Commission resolution 1993/31 of 5 March 1993 and paragraph II.28 of the Vienna Declaration and Programme of Action (A/Conf.157/23),

Having considered the report of the Working Group on Indigenous Populations on its twelfth session (E/CN.4/Sub.2/1994/30 and Corr.1), in particular the general comments on the draft declaration and the recommendations contained in chapters II and IX respectively of the report,

Taking into account the technical review of the draft declaration prepared by the Centre for Human Rights (E/CN.4/Sub.2/1994/2 and Add.1),

1. *Expresses its satisfaction* at the conclusion of the deliberations on the draft United Nations declaration on the rights of indigenous peoples by the Working Group on Indigenous Populations and the general views of the participants as reflected in the report of the Working Group on its twelfth session;

2. *Expresses its appreciation* to the Chairperson-Rapporteur of the Working Group, Ms. Erica-Irene Daes, and to the present and former members of the Working Group for their contributions to the process of elaboration of the draft declaration;

3. *Expresses its appreciation* to the Centre for Human Rights for its technical revision of the draft declaration;

4. *Decides*:

(a) To adopt the draft United Nations declaration on the rights of indigenous peoples agreed upon by members of the Working Group as contained in the annex to the present resolution;

(b) To submit the draft declaration to the Commission on Human Rights at its fifty-first session with the request that it consider the draft as expeditiously as possible;

(c) To request the Secretary-General to transmit the text of the draft declaration to indigenous peoples and organizations, Governments and intergovernmental organizations and to include in the note of transmittal the information that the draft declaration is to be submitted to the Commission on Human Rights at its fifty-first session;

5. *Recommends* that the Commission on Human Rights and the Economic and Social Council take effective measures to ensure that representatives of indigenous peoples are able to participate in the consideration of the draft declaration by these two bodies, regardless of their consultative status with the Economic and Social Council.

36th meeting
26 August 1994

[Adopted without a vote. See chap. XVI. E/CN.4/Sub.2/1994/56]

ANNEX

Draft United Nations Declaration on the Rights of Indigenous Peoples

Affirming that indigenous peoples are equal in dignity and rights to all other peoples, while recognizing the right of all peoples to be different, to consider themselves different, and to be respected as such,

Affirming also that all peoples contribute to the diversity and richness of civilizations and cultures, which constitute the common heritage of humankind,

Affirming further that all doctrines, policies and practices based on or advocating superiority of peoples or individuals on the basis of national origin, racial, religious, ethnic or cultural differences are racist, scientifically false, legally invalid, morally condemnable and socially unjust,

Reaffirming also that indigenous peoples, in the exercise of their rights, should be free from discrimination of any kind,

Concerned that indigenous peoples have been deprived of their human rights and fundamental freedoms, resulting, *inter alia*, in their colonization and dispossession of their lands, territories and resources, thus preventing them from exercising, in particular, their right to development in accordance with their own needs and interests,

Recognizing the urgent need to respect and promote the inherent rights and characteristics of indigenous peoples, especially their rights to their lands, territories and resources, which derive from their political, economic and social structures and from their cultures, spiritual traditions, histories and philosophies,

Welcoming the fact that indigenous peoples are organizing themselves for political, economic, social and cultural enhancement and in order to bring an end to all forms of discrimination and oppression wherever they occur,

Convinced that control by indigenous peoples over developments affecting them and their lands, territories and resources will enable them to maintain and strengthen their institutions, cultures and traditions, and to promote their development in accordance with their aspirations and needs,

Recognizing also that respect for indigenous knowledge, cultures and traditional practices contributes to sustainable and equitable development and proper management of the environment,

Emphasizing the need for demilitarization of the lands and territories of indigenous peoples, which will contribute to peace, economic and social progress and development, understanding and friendly relations among nations and peoples of the world,

Recognizing in particular the right of indigenous families and communities to retain shared responsibility for the upbringing, training, education and well-being of their children,

Recognizing also that indigenous peoples have the right freely to determine their relationships with States in a spirit of coexistence, mutual benefit and full respect,

Considering that treaties, agreements and other arrangements between States and indigenous peoples are properly matters of international concern and responsibility,

Acknowledging that the Charter of the United Nations, the International Covenant on Economic, Social and Cultural Rights and the International Covenant on Civil and Political Rights affirm the fundamental importance of the right of self-determination of all peoples, by virtue of which they freely determine their political status and freely pursue their economic, social and cultural development,

Bearing in mind that nothing in this Declaration may be used to deny any peoples their right of self-determination,

Encouraging States to comply with and effectively implement all international instruments, in particular those related to human rights, as they apply to indigenous peoples, in consultation and co-operation with the peoples concerned,

Emphasizing that the United Nations has an important and continuing role to play in promoting and protecting the rights of indigenous peoples,

Believing that this Declaration is a further important step forward for the recognition, promotion and protection of the rights and freedoms of indigenous peoples and in the development of relevant activities of the United Nations system in this field,

Solemnly proclaims the following United Nations Declaration on the Rights of Indigenous Peoples:

PART I

Article 1

Indigenous peoples have the right to the full and effective enjoyment of all human rights and fundamental freedoms recognized in the Charter of the United Nations, the Universal Declaration of Human Rights and international human rights law.

Article 2

Indigenous individuals and peoples are free and equal to all other individuals and peoples in dignity and rights, and have the right to be free from any kind of adverse discrimination, in particular that based on their indigenous origin or identity.

Article 3

Indigenous peoples have the right of self-determination. By virtue of that right they freely determine their political status and freely pursue their economic, social and cultural development.

Article 4

Indigenous peoples have the right to maintain and strengthen their distinct political, economic, social and cultural characteristics, as well as their legal systems, while retaining their rights to participate fully, if they so choose, in the political, economic, social and cultural life of the State.

Article 5

Every indigenous individual has the right to a nationality.

PART II

Article 6

Indigenous peoples have the collective right to live in freedom, peace and security as distinct peoples and to full guarantees against genocide or any other act of violence, including the removal of indigenous children from their families and communities under any pretext.

In addition, they have the individual rights to life, physical and mental integrity, liberty and security of person.

Article 7

Indigenous peoples have the collective and individual right not to be subjected to ethnocide and cultural genocide, including prevention of and redress for:

(a) Any action which has the aim or effect of depriving them of their integrity as distinct peoples, or of their cultural values or ethnic identities;

(b) Any action which has the aim or effect of dispossessing them of their lands, territories or resources;

(c) Any form of population transfer which has the aim or effect of violating or undermining any of their rights;

(d) Any form of assimilation or integration by other cultures or ways of life imposed on them by legislative, administrative or other measures;

(e) Any form of propaganda directed against them.

Article 8

Indigenous peoples have the collective and individual right to maintain and develop their distinct identities and characteristics, including the right to identify themselves as indigenous and to be recognized as such.

Article 9

Indigenous peoples and individuals have the right to belong to an indigenous community or nation, in accordance with the traditions and customs of the community or nation concerned. No disadvantage of any kind may arise from the exercise of such a right.

Article 10

Indigenous peoples shall not be forcibly removed from their lands or territories. No relocation shall take place without the free and informed consent of the indigenous peoples concerned and after agreement on just and fair compensation and, where possible, with the option of return.

Article 11

Indigenous peoples have the right to special protection and security in periods of armed conflict.

States shall observe international standards, in particular the Fourth Geneva Convention of 1949, for the protection of civilian populations in circumstances of emergency and armed conflict, and shall not:

(a) Recruit indigenous individuals against their will into the armed forces and, in particular, for use against other indigenous peoples;

(b) Recruit indigenous children into the armed forces under any circumstances;

(c) Force indigenous individuals to abandon their lands, territories or means of subsistence, or relocate them in special centres for military purposes;

(d) Force indigenous individuals to work for military purposes under any discriminatory conditions.

PART III

Article 12

Indigenous peoples have the right to practise and revitalize their cultural traditions and customs. This includes the right to maintain, protect and develop the past, present and future manifestations of their cultures, such as archaeological and historical sites, artifacts, designs, ceremonies, technologies and visual and performing arts and literature, as well as the right to the restitution of cultural, intellectual, religious and spiritual property taken without their free and informed consent or in violation of their laws, traditions and customs.

Article 13

Indigenous peoples have the right to manifest, practise, develop and teach their spiritual and religious traditions, customs and ceremonies; the right to maintain, protect, and have access in privacy to their religious and cultural sites; the right to the use and control of ceremonial objects; and the right to the repatriation of human remains.

States shall take effective measures, in conjunction with the indigenous peoples concerned, to ensure that indigenous sacred places, including burial sites, be preserved, respected and protected.

Article 14

Indigenous peoples have the right to revitalize, use, develop and transmit to future generations their histories, languages, oral traditions, philosophies, writing systems and literatures, and to designate and retain their own names for communities, places and persons.

States shall take effective measures, whenever any right of indigenous peoples may be threatened, to ensure this right is protected and also to ensure that they can understand and be understood in political, legal and administrative proceedings, where necessary through the provision of interpretation or by other appropriate means.

PART IV

Article 15

Indigenous children have the right to all levels and forms of education of the State. All indigenous peoples also have this right and the right to establish and control their educational systems and institutions providing education in their own languages, in a manner appropriate to their cultural methods of teaching and learning.

Indigenous children living outside their communities have the right to be provided access to education in their own culture and language.

States shall take effective measures to provide appropriate resources for these purposes.

Article 16

Indigenous peoples have the right to have the dignity and diversity of their cultures, traditions, histories and aspirations appropriately reflected in all forms of education and public information.

States shall take effective measures, in consultation with the indigenous peoples concerned, to eliminate prejudice and discrimination and to promote tolerance, understanding and good relations among indigenous peoples and all segments of society.

Article 17

Indigenous peoples have the right to establish their own media in their own languages. They also have the right to equal access to all forms of non-indigenous media.

States shall take effective measures to ensure that State-owned media duly reflect indigenous cultural diversity.

Article 18

Indigenous peoples have the right to enjoy fully all rights established under international labour law and national labour legislation.

Indigenous individuals have the right not to be subjected to any discriminatory conditions of labour, employment or salary.

PART V

Article 19

Indigenous peoples have the right to participate fully, if they so choose, at all levels of decision-making in matters which may affect their rights, lives and destinies through representatives chosen by themselves in accordance with their own procedures, as well as to maintain and develop their own indigenous decision-making institutions.

Article 20

Indigenous peoples have the right to participate fully, if they so choose, through procedures determined by them, in devising legislative or administrative measures that may affect them.

States shall obtain the free and informed consent of the peoples concerned before adopting and implementing such measures.

Article 21

Indigenous peoples have the right to maintain and develop their political, economic and social systems, to be secure in the enjoyment of their own means of subsistence and development, and to engage freely in all their traditional and other economic activities. Indigenous peoples who have been deprived of their means of subsistence and development are entitled to just and fair compensation.

Article 22

Indigenous peoples have the right to special measures for the immediate, effective and continuing improvement of their economic and social conditions, including in the areas of employment, vocational training and retraining, housing, sanitation, health and social security.

Particular attention shall be paid to the rights and special needs of indigenous elders, women, youth, children and disabled persons.

Article 23

Indigenous peoples have the right to determine and develop priorities and strategies for exercising their right to development. In particular, indigenous peoples have the right to determine and develop all health, housing and other economic and social programmes affecting them and, as far as possible, to administer such programmes through their own institutions.

Article 24

Indigenous peoples have the right to their traditional medicines and health practices, including the right to the protection of vital medicinal plants, animals and minerals.

They also have the right to access, without any discrimination, to all medical institutions, health services and medical care.

PART VI

Article 25

Indigenous peoples have the right to maintain and strengthen their distinctive spiritual and material relationship with the lands, territories, waters and coastal seas and other resources which they have traditionally owned or otherwise occupied or used, and to uphold their responsibilities to future generations in this regard.

Article 26

Indigenous peoples have the right to own, develop, control and use the lands and territories, including the total environment of the lands, air, waters, coastal seas, sea-ice, flora and fauna and other resources which they have traditionally owned or otherwise occupied or used. This includes the right to the full recognition of their laws, traditions and customs, land-tenure systems and institutions for the development and management of resources, and the right to effective measures by States to prevent any interference with, alienation of or encroachment upon these rights.

Article 27

Indigenous peoples have the right to the restitution of the lands, territories and resources which they have traditionally owned or otherwise occupied or used, and which have been confiscated, occupied, used or damaged without their free and informed consent. Where this is not possible, they have the right to just and fair compensation. Unless otherwise freely agreed upon by the peoples concerned, compensation shall take the form of lands, territories and resources equal in quality, size and legal status.

Article 28

Indigenous peoples have the right to the conservation, restoration and protection of the total environment and the productive capacity of their lands, territories and resources, as well as to assistance for this purpose from States and through international co-operation. Military activities shall not take place in the lands and territories of indigenous peoples, unless otherwise freely agreed upon by the peoples concerned.

States shall take effective measures to ensure that no storage or disposal of hazardous materials shall take place in the lands and territories of indigenous peoples.

States shall also take effective measures to ensure, as needed, that programmes for monitoring, maintaining and restoring the health of indigenous peoples, as developed and implemented by the peoples affected by such materials, are duly implemented.

Article 29

Indigenous peoples are entitled to the recognition of the full ownership, control and protection of their cultural and intellectual property.

They have the right to special measures to control, develop and protect their sciences, technologies and cultural manifestations, including human and other genetic resources, seeds, medicines, knowledge of the properties of fauna and flora, oral traditions, literatures, designs and visual and performing arts.

Article 30

Indigenous peoples have the right to determine and develop priorities and strategies for the development or use of their lands, territories and other resources, including the right to require that States obtain their free and informed consent prior to the approval of any project affecting their lands, territories and other resources, particularly in connection with the development, utilization or exploitation of mineral, water or other resources. Pursuant to agreement with the indigenous peoples concerned, just and fair compensation shall be provided for any such activities and measures taken to mitigate adverse environmental, economic, social, cultural or spiritual impact.

PART VII

Article 31

Indigenous peoples, as a specific form of exercising their right to self-determination, have the right to autonomy or self-government in matters relating to their internal and local affairs, including culture, religion, education, information, media, health, housing, employment, social welfare, economic activities, land and resources management, environment and entry by non-members, as well as ways and means for financing these autonomous functions.

Article 32

Indigenous peoples have the collective right to determine their own citizenship in accordance with their customs and traditions. Indigenous citizenship does not impair the right of indigenous individuals to obtain citizenship of the States in which they live.

Indigenous peoples have the right to determine the structures and to select the membership of their institutions in accordance with their own procedures.

Article 33

Indigenous peoples have the right to promote, develop and maintain their institutional structures and their distinctive juridical customs, traditions, procedures and practices, in accordance with internationally recognized human rights standards.

Article 34

Indigenous peoples have the collective right to determine the responsibilities of individuals to their communities.

Article 35

Indigenous peoples, in particular those divided by international borders, have the right to maintain and develop contacts, relations and co-operation, including activities for spiritual, cultural, political, economic and social purposes, with other peoples across borders.

States shall take effective measures to ensure the exercise and implementation of this right.

Article 36

Indigenous peoples have the right to the recognition, observance and enforcement of treaties, agreements and other constructive arrangements concluded with States or their successors, according to their original spirit and intent, and to have States honour and respect such treaties, agreements and other constructive arrangements. Conflicts and disputes which cannot otherwise be settled should be submitted to competent international bodies agreed to by all parties concerned.

PART VIII

Article 37

States shall take effective and appropriate measures, in consultation with the indigenous peoples concerned, to give full effect to the provisions of this Declaration. The rights recognized herein shall be adopted and included in national legislation in such a manner that indigenous peoples can avail themselves of such rights in practice.

Article 38

Indigenous peoples have the right to have access to adequate financial and technical assistance, from States and through international co-operation, to pursue freely their political, economic, social, cultural and spiritual development and for the enjoyment of the rights and freedoms recognized in this Declaration.

Article 39

Indigenous peoples have the right to have access to and prompt decision through mutually acceptable and fair procedures for the resolution of conflicts and disputes with States, as well as to effective remedies for all infringements of their individual and collective rights. Such a decision shall take into consideration the customs, traditions, rules and legal systems of the indigenous peoples concerned.

Article 40

The organs and specialized agencies of the United Nations system and other intergovernmental organizations shall contribute to the full realization of the provisions of this Declaration through the mobilization, *inter alia*, of financial co-operation and technical assistance. Ways and means of ensuring participation of indigenous peoples on issues affecting them shall be established.

Article 41

The United Nations shall take the necessary steps to ensure the implementation of this Declaration including the creation of a body at the highest level with special competence in this field and with the direct participation of indigenous peoples. All United Nations bodies shall promote respect for and full application of the provisions of this Declaration.

PART IX

Article 42

The rights recognized herein constitute the minimum standards for the survival, dignity and well-being of the indigenous peoples of the world.

Article 43

All the rights and freedoms recognized herein are equally guaranteed to male and female indigenous individuals.

Article 44

Nothing in this Declaration may be construed as diminishing or extinguishing existing or future rights indigenous peoples may have or acquire.

Article 45

Nothing in this Declaration may be interpreted as implying for any State, group or person any right to engage in any activity or to perform any act contrary to the Charter of the United Nations.

Appendix III

International Covenant on Civil and Political Rights

UNG.A. Res. 2200A (XXI), 21 UN GAOR Supp. (No. 16) at 52, UN Doc. A/6316 (1966), 999 UNT.S. 171, *entered into force* Mar. 23, 1976.

PREAMBLE

The States Parties to the present Covenant,

Considering that, in accordance with the principles proclaimed in the Charter of the United Nations, recognition of the inherent dignity and of the equal and inalienable rights of all members of the human family is the foundation of freedom, justice and peace in the world,

Recognizing that these rights derive from the inherent dignity of the human person,

Recognizing that, in accordance with the Universal Declaration of Human Rights, the ideal of free human beings enjoying civil and political freedom and freedom from fear and want can only be achieved if conditions are created whereby everyone may enjoy his civil and political rights, as well as his economic, social and cultural rights,

Considering the obligation of States under the Charter of the United Nations to promote universal respect for, and observance of, human rights and freedoms,

Realizing that the individual, having duties to other individuals and to the community to which he belongs, is under a responsibility to strive for the promotion and observance of the rights recognized in the present Covenant,

Agree upon the following articles:

PART I

Article 1

1. All peoples have the right of self-determination. By virtue of that right they freely determine their political status and freely pursue their economic, social and cultural development.

2. All peoples may, for their own ends, freely dispose of their natural wealth and resources without prejudice to any obligations arising out of international economic co-operation, based upon the principle of mutual benefit, and international law. In no case may a people be deprived of its own means of subsistence.

3. The States Parties to the present Covenant, including those having responsibility for the administration of Non-Self-Governing and Trust Territories, shall promote the realization of the right of self-determination, and shall respect that right, in conformity with the provisions of the Charter of the United Nations.

PART II

Article 2

1. Each State Party to the present Covenant undertakes to respect and to ensure to all individuals within its territory and subject to its jurisdiction the rights recognized in the present Covenant, without distinction of any kind, such as race, colour, sex, language, religion, political or other opinion, national or social origin, property, birth or other status.

2. Where not already provided for by existing legislative or other measures, each State Party to the present Covenant undertakes to take the necessary steps, in accordance with its constitutional processes and with the provisions of the present Covenant, to adopt such legislative or other measures as may be necessary to give effect to the rights recognized in the present Covenant.

3. Each State Party to the present Covenant undertakes:

(a) To ensure that any person whose rights or freedoms as herein recognized are violated shall have an effective remedy, notwithstanding that the violation has been committed by persons acting in an official capacity;

(b) To ensure that any person claiming such a remedy shall have his right thereto determined by competent judicial, administrative or legislative authorities, or by any other competent authority provided for by the legal system of the State, and to develop the possibilities of judicial remedy;

(c) To ensure that the competent authorities shall enforce such remedies when granted.

Article 3

The States Parties to the present Covenant undertake to ensure the equal right of men and women to the enjoyment of all civil and political rights set forth in the present Covenant.

Article 4

1. In time of public emergency which threatens the life of the nation and the existence of which is officially proclaimed, the States Parties to the present Covenant may take measures derogating from their obligations under the present Covenant to the extent strictly required by the exigencies of the situation, provided that such measures are not inconsistent with their other obligations under international law and do not involve discrimination solely on the ground of race, colour, sex, language, religion or social origin.

2. No derogation from articles 6, 7, 8 (paragraphs 1 and 2), 11, 15, 16 and 18 may be made under this provision.

3. Any State Party to the present Covenant availing itself of the right of derogation shall immediately inform the other States Parties to the present Covenant, through the intermediary of the Secretary-General of the United Nations, of the provisions from which it has derogated and of the reasons by which it was actuated. A further communication shall be made, through the same intermediary, on the date on which it terminates such derogation.

Article 5

1. Nothing in the present Covenant may be interpreted as implying for any State, group or person any right to engage in any activity or perform any act aimed at the destruction of any of the rights and freedoms recognized herein or at their limitation to a greater extent than is provided for in the present Covenant.

2. There shall be no restriction upon or derogation from any of the fundamental human rights recognized or existing in any State Party to the present Covenant pursuant to law, conventions, regulations or custom on the pretext that the present Covenant does not recognize such rights or that it recognizes them to a lesser extent.

PART III

Article 6

1. Every human being has the inherent right to life. This right shall be protected by law. No one shall be arbitrarily deprived of his life.

2. In countries which have not abolished the death penalty, sentence of death may be imposed only for the most serious crimes in accordance with the law in force at the time of the commission of the crime and not contrary to the provisions of the present Covenant and to the Convention on the Prevention and Punishment of the Crime of Genocide. This penalty can only be carried out pursuant to a final judgement rendered by a competent court.

3. When deprivation of life constitutes the crime of genocide, it is understood that nothing in this article shall authorize any State Party to the present Covenant to derogate in any way from any obligation assumed under the provisions of the Convention on the Prevention and Punishment of the Crime of Genocide.

4. Anyone sentenced to death shall have the right to seek pardon or commutation of the sentence. Amnesty, pardon or commutation of the sentence of death may be granted in all cases.

5. Sentence of death shall not be imposed for crimes committed by persons below eighteen years of age and shall not be carried out on pregnant women.

6. Nothing in this article shall be invoked to delay or to prevent the abolition of capital punishment by any State Party to the present Covenant.

Article 7

No one shall be subjected to torture or to cruel, inhuman or degrading treatment or punishment. In particular, no one shall be subjected without his free consent to medical or scientific experimentation.

Article 8

1. No one shall be held in slavery; slavery and the slave-trade in all their forms shall be prohibited.

2. No one shall be held in servitude.

3. (a) No one shall be required to perform forced or compulsory labour;

(b) Paragraph 3 (a) shall not be held to preclude, in countries where imprisonment with hard labour may be imposed as a punishment for a crime, the performance of hard labour in pursuance of a sentence to such punishment by a competent court;

(c) For the purpose of this paragraph the term "forced or compulsory labour" shall not include:

(i) Any work or service, not referred to in subparagraph (b), normally required of a person who is under detention in consequence of a lawful order of a court, or of a person during conditional release from such detention;

(ii) Any service of a military character and, in countries where conscientious objection is recognized, any national service required by law of conscientious objectors;

(iii) Any service exacted in cases of emergency or calamity threatening the life or well-being of the community;

(iv) Any work or service which forms part of normal civil obligations.

Article 9

1. Everyone has the right to liberty and security of person. No one shall be subjected to arbitrary arrest or detention. No one shall be deprived of his liberty except on such grounds and in accordance with such procedure as are established by law.

2. Anyone who is arrested shall be informed, at the time of arrest, of the reasons for his arrest and shall be promptly informed of any charges against him.

3. Anyone arrested or detained on a criminal charge shall be brought promptly before a judge or other officer authorized by law to exercise judicial power and shall be entitled to trial within a reasonable time or to release. It shall not be the general rule that persons awaiting trial shall be detained in custody, but release may be subject to guarantees to appear for trial, at any other stage of the judicial proceedings, and, should occasion arise, for execution of the judgement.

4. Anyone who is deprived of his liberty by arrest or detention shall be entitled to take proceedings before a court, in order that that court may decide without delay on the lawfulness of his detention and order his release if the detention is not lawful.

5. Anyone who has been the victim of unlawful arrest or detention shall have an enforceable right to compensation.

Article 10

1. All persons deprived of their liberty shall be treated with humanity and with respect for the inherent dignity of the human person.

2. (a) Accused persons shall, save in exceptional circumstances, be segregated from convicted persons and shall be subject to separate treatment appropriate to their status as unconvicted persons;

(b) Accused juvenile persons shall be separated from adults and brought as speedily as possible for adjudication.

3. The penitentiary system shall comprise treatment of prisoners the essential aim of which shall be their reformation and social rehabilitation. Juvenile offenders shall be segregated from adults and be accorded treatment appropriate to their age and legal status.

Article 11

No one shall be imprisoned merely on the ground of inability to fulfil a contractual obligation.

Article 12

1. Everyone lawfully within the territory of a State shall, within that territory, have the right to liberty of movement and freedom to choose his residence.

2. Everyone shall be free to leave any country, including his own.

3. The above-mentioned rights shall not be subject to any restrictions except those which are provided by law, are necessary to protect national security, public order (ordre public), public health or morals or the rights and freedoms of others, and are consistent with the other rights recognized in the present Covenant.

4. No one shall be arbitrarily deprived of the right to enter his own country.

Article 13

An alien lawfully in the territory of a State Party to the present Covenant may be expelled therefrom only in pursuance of a decision reached in accordance with law and shall, except where compelling reasons of national security otherwise require, be allowed to submit the reasons against his expulsion and to have his case reviewed by, and be represented for the purpose before, the competent authority or a person or persons especially designated by the competent authority.

Article 14

1. All persons shall be equal before the courts and tribunals. In the determination of any criminal charge against him, or of his rights and obligations in a suit at law, everyone shall be entitled to a fair and public hearing by a competent, independent and impartial tribunal established by law. The press and the public may be excluded from all or part of a trial for reasons of morals, public order (ordre public) or national security in a democratic society, or when the interest of the private lives of the parties so requires, or to the extent strictly necessary in the opinion of the court in special circumstances where publicity would prejudice the interests of justice; but any judgement rendered in a criminal case or in a suit at law shall be made public except where the interest of juvenile persons otherwise requires or the proceedings concern matrimonial disputes or the guardianship of children.

2. Everyone charged with a criminal offence shall have the right to be presumed innocent until proved guilty according to law.

3. In the determination of any criminal charge against him, everyone shall be entitled to the following minimum guarantees, in full equality:

(a) To be informed promptly and in detail in a language which he understands of the nature and cause of the charge against him;

(b) To have adequate time and facilities for the preparation of his defence and to communicate with counsel of his own choosing;

(c) To be tried without undue delay;

(d) To be tried in his presence, and to defend himself in person or through legal assistance of his own choosing; to be informed, if he does not have legal assistance, of this right; and to have legal assistance assigned to him, in any case where the interests of justice so require, and without payment by him in any such case if he does not have sufficient means to pay for it;

(e) To examine, or have examined, the witnesses against him and to obtain the attendance and examination of witnesses on his behalf under the same conditions as witnesses against him;

(f) To have the free assistance of an interpreter if he cannot understand or speak the language used in court;

(g) Not to be compelled to testify against himself or to confess guilt.

4. In the case of juvenile persons, the procedure shall be such as will take account of their age and the desirability of promoting their rehabilitation.

5. Everyone convicted of a crime shall have the right to his conviction and sentence being reviewed by a higher tribunal according to law.

6. When a person has by a final decision been convicted of a criminal offence and when subsequently his conviction has been reversed or he has been pardoned on the ground that a new or newly discovered fact shows conclusively that there has been a miscarriage of justice, the person who has suffered punishment as a result of such conviction shall be compensated according to law, unless it is proved that the non-disclosure of the unknown fact in time is wholly or partly attributable to him.

7. No one shall be liable to be tried or punished again for an offence for which he has already been finally convicted or acquitted in accordance with the law and penal procedure of each country.

Article 15

1. No one shall be held guilty of any criminal offence on account of any act or omission which did not constitute a criminal offence, under national or international law, at the time when it was committed. Nor shall a heavier penalty be imposed than the one that was applicable at the time when the criminal offence was committed. If, subsequent to the commission of the offence, provision is made by law for the imposition of the lighter penalty, the offender shall benefit thereby.

2. Nothing in this article shall prejudice the trial and punishment of any person for any act or omission which, at the time when it was committed, was criminal according to the general principles of law recognized by the community of nations.

Article 16

Everyone shall have the right to recognition everywhere as a person before the law.

Article 17

1. No one shall be subjected to arbitrary or unlawful interference with his privacy, family, home or correspondence, nor to unlawful attacks on his honour and reputation.

2. Everyone has the right to the protection of the law against such interference or attacks.

Article 18

1. Everyone shall have the right to freedom of thought, conscience and religion. This right shall include freedom to have or to adopt a religion or belief of his choice, and freedom, either individually or in community with others and in public or private, to manifest his religion or belief in worship, observance, practice and teaching.

2. No one shall be subject to coërcion which would impair his freedom to have or to adopt a religion or belief of his choice.

3. Freedom to manifest one's religion or beliefs may be subject only to such limitations as are prescribed by law and are necessary to protect public safety, order, health, or morals or the fundamental rights and freedoms of others.

4. The States Parties to the present Covenant undertake to have respect for the liberty of parents and, when applicable, legal guardians to ensure the religious and moral education of their children in conformity with their own convictions.

Article 19

1. Everyone shall have the right to hold opinions without interference.

2. Everyone shall have the right to freedom of expression; this right shall include freedom to seek, receive and impart information and ideas of all kinds, regardless of frontiers, either orally, in writing or in print, in the form of art, or through any other media of his choice.

3. The exercise of the rights provided for in paragraph 2 of this article carries with it special duties and responsibilities. It may therefore be subject to certain restrictions, but these shall only be such as are provided by law and are necessary:

(a) For respect of the rights or reputations of others;

(b) For the protection of national security or of public order (ordre public), or of public health or morals.

Article 20

1. Any propaganda for war shall be prohibited by law.

2. Any advocacy of national, racial or religious hatred that constitutes incitement to discrimination, hostility or violence shall be prohibited by law.

Article 21

The right of peaceful assembly shall be recognized. No restrictions may be placed on the exercise of this right other than those imposed in conformity with the law and which are necessary in a democratic society in the interests of national security or public safety, public order (ordre public), the protection of public health or morals or the protection of the rights and freedoms of others.

Article 22

1. Everyone shall have the right to freedom of association with others, including the right to form and join trade unions for the protection of his interests.

2. No restrictions may be placed on the exercise of this right other than those which are prescribed by law and which are necessary in a democratic society in the interests of national security or public safety, public order (ordre public), the protection of public health or morals or the protection of the rights and freedoms of others. This article shall not prevent the imposition of lawful restrictions on members of the armed forces and of the police in their exercise of this right.

3. Nothing in this article shall authorize States Parties to the International Labour Organization Convention of 1948 concerning Freedom of Association and Protection of the Right to Organize to take legislative measures which would prejudice, or to apply the law in such a manner as to prejudice, the guarantees provided for in that Convention.

Article 23

1. The family is the natural and fundamental group unit of society and is entitled to protection by society and the State.

2. The right of men and women of marriageable age to marry and to found a family shall be recognized.

3. No marriage shall be entered into without the free and full consent of the intending spouses.

4. States Parties to the present Covenant shall take appropriate steps to ensure equality of rights and responsibilities of spouses as to marriage, during marriage and at its dissolution. In the case of dissolution, provision shall be made for the necessary protection of any children.

Article 24

1. Every child shall have, without any discrimination as to race, colour, sex, language, religion, national or social origin, property or birth, the right to such measures of protection as are required by his status as a minor, on the part of his family, society and the State.

2. Every child shall be registered immediately after birth and shall have a name.

3. Every child has the right to acquire a nationality.

Article 25

Every citizen shall have the right and the opportunity, without any of the distinctions mentioned in article 2 and without unreasonable restrictions:

(a) To take part in the conduct of public affairs, directly or through freely chosen representatives;

(b) To vote and to be elected at genuine periodic elections which shall be by universal and equal suffrage and shall be held by secret ballot, guaranteeing the free expression of the will of the electors;

(c) To have access, on general terms of equality, to public service in his country.

Article 26

All persons are equal before the law and are entitled without any discrimination to the equal protection of the law. In this respect, the law shall prohibit any discrimination and guarantee to all persons equal and effective protection against discrimination on any ground such as race, colour, sex, language, religion, political or other opinion, national or social origin, property, birth or other status.

Article 27

In those States in which ethnic, religious or linguistic minorities exist, persons belonging to such minorities shall not be denied the right, in community with the other members of their group, to enjoy their own culture, to profess and practise their own religion, or to use their own language.

PART IV

Article 28

1. There shall be established a Human Rights Committee (hereafter referred to in the present Covenant as the Committee). It shall consist of eighteen members and shall carry out the functions hereinafter provided.

2. The Committee shall be composed of nationals of the States Parties to the present Covenant who shall be persons of high moral character and recognized competence in the field of human rights, consideration being given to the usefulness of the participation of some persons having legal experience.

3. The members of the Committee shall be elected and shall serve in their personal capacity.

Article 29

1 . The members of the Committee shall be elected by secret ballot from a list of persons possessing the qualifications prescribed in article 28 and nominated for the purpose by the States Parties to the present Covenant.

2. Each State Party to the present Covenant may nominate not more than two persons. These persons shall be nationals of the nominating State.

3. A person shall be eligible for renomination.

Article 30

1. The initial election shall be held no later than six months after the date of the entry into force of the present Covenant.

2. At least four months before the date of each election to the Committee, other than an election to fill a vacancy declared in accordance with article 34, the Secretary-General of the United Nations shall address a written invitation to the States Parties to the present Covenant to submit their nominations for membership of the Committee within three months.

3. The Secretary-General of the United Nations shall prepare a list in alphabetical order of all the persons thus nominated, with an indication of the States Parties which have nominated them, and shall submit it to the States Parties to the present Covenant no later than one month before the date of each election.

4. Elections of the members of the Committee shall be held at a meeting of the States Parties to the present Covenant convened by the Secretary General of the United Nations at the Headquarters of the United Nations. At that meeting, for which two thirds of the States Parties to the present Covenant shall constitute a quorum, the persons elected to the Committee shall be those nominees who obtain the largest number of votes and an absolute majority of the votes of the representatives of States Parties present and voting.

Article 31

1. The Committee may not include more than one national of the same State.

2. In the election of the Committee, consideration shall be given to equitable geographical distribution of membership and to the representation of the different forms of civilization and of the principal legal systems.

Article 32

1. The members of the Committee shall be elected for a term of four years. They shall be eligible for re-election if renominated. However, the terms of nine of the members elected at the first election shall expire at the end of two years; immediately after the first election, the names of these nine members shall be chosen by lot by the Chairman of the meeting referred to in article 30, paragraph 4.

2. Elections at the expiry of office shall be held in accordance with the preceding articles of this part of the present Covenant.

Article 33

1. If, in the unanimous opinion of the other members, a member of the Committee has ceased to carry out his functions for any cause other than absence of a temporary character, the Chairman of the Committee shall notify the Secretary-General of the United Nations, who shall then declare the seat of that member to be vacant.

2. In the event of the death or the resignation of a member of the Committee, the Chairman shall immediately notify the Secretary-General of the United Nations, who shall declare the seat vacant from the date of death or the date on which the resignation takes effect.

Article 34

1. When a vacancy is declared in accordance with article 33 and if the term of office of the member to be replaced does not expire within six months of the declaration of the vacancy, the Secretary-General of the United Nations shall notify each of the States Parties to the present Covenant, which may within two months submit nominations in accordance with article 29 for the purpose of filling the vacancy.

2. The Secretary-General of the United Nations shall prepare a list in alphabetical order of the persons thus nominated and shall submit it to the States Parties to the present

Covenant. The election to fill the vacancy shall then take place in accordance with the relevant provisions of this part of the present Covenant.

3. A member of the Committee elected to fill a vacancy declared in accordance with article 33 shall hold office for the remainder of the term of the member who vacated the seat on the Committee under the provisions of that article.

Article 35

The members of the Committee shall, with the approval of the General Assembly of the United Nations, receive emoluments from United Nations resources on such terms and conditions as the General Assembly may decide, having regard to the importance of the Committee's responsibilities.

Article 36

The Secretary-General of the United Nations shall provide the necessary staff and facilities for the effective performance of the functions of the Committee under the present Covenant.

Article 37

1. The Secretary-General of the United Nations shall convene the initial meeting of the Committee at the Headquarters of the United Nations.

2. After its initial meeting, the Committee shall meet at such times as shall be provided in its rules of procedure.

3. The Committee shall normally meet at the Headquarters of the United Nations or at the United Nations Office at Geneva.

Article 38

Every member of the Committee shall, before taking up his duties, make a solemn declaration in open committee that he will perform his functions impartially and conscientiously.

Article 39

1. The Committee shall elect its officers for a term of two years. They may be re-elected.

2. The Committee shall establish its own rules of procedure, but these rules shall provide, *inter alia*, that:

(a) Twelve members shall constitute a quorum;

(b) Decisions of the Committee shall be made by a majority vote of the members present.

Article 40

1. The States Parties to the present Covenant undertake to submit reports on the measures they have adopted which give effect to the rights recognized herein and on the progress made in the enjoyment of those rights:

(a) Within one year of the entry into force of the present Covenant for the States Parties concerned;

(b) Thereafter whenever the Committee so requests.

2. All reports shall be submitted to the Secretary-General of the United Nations, who shall transmit them to the Committee for consideration. Reports shall indicate the factors and difficulties, if any, affecting the implementation of the present Covenant.

3. The Secretary-General of the United Nations may, after consultation with the Committee, transmit to the specialized agencies concerned copies of such parts of the reports as may fall within their field of competence.

4. The Committee shall study the reports submitted by the States Parties to the present Covenant. It shall transmit its reports, and such general comments as it may consider appropriate, to the States Parties. The Committee may also transmit to the Economic and Social Council these comments along with the copies of the reports it has received from States Parties to the present Covenant.

5. The States Parties to the present Covenant may submit to the Committee observations on any comments that may be made in accordance with paragraph 4 of this article.

Article 41

1. A State Party to the present Covenant may at any time declare under this article that it recognizes the competence of the Committee to receive and consider communications to the effect that a State Party claims that another State Party is not fulfilling its obligations under the present Covenant. Communications under this article may be received and considered only if submitted by a State Party which has made a declaration recognizing in regard to itself the competence of the Committee. No communication shall be received by the Committee if it concerns a State Party which has not made such a declaration. Communications received under this article shall be dealt with in accordance with the following procedure:

(a) If a State Party to the present Covenant considers that another State Party is not giving effect to the provisions of the present Covenant, it may, by written communication, bring the matter to the attention of that State Party. Within three months after the receipt of the communication the receiving State shall afford the State which sent the communication an explanation, or any other statement in writing clarifying the matter which should include, to the extent possible and pertinent, reference to domestic procedures and remedies taken, pending, or available in the matter;

(b) If the matter is not adjusted to the satisfaction of both States Parties concerned within six months after the receipt by the receiving State of the initial communication, either State shall have the right to refer the matter to the Committee, by notice given to the Committee and to the other State;

(c) The Committee shall deal with a matter referred to it only after it has ascertained that all available domestic remedies have been invoked and exhausted in the matter, in conformity with the generally recognized principles of international law. This shall not be the rule where the application of the remedies is unreasonably prolonged;

(d) The Committee shall hold closed meetings when examining communications under this article;

(e) Subject to the provisions of subparagraph (c), the Committee shall make available its good offices to the States Parties concerned with a view to a friendly solution of the matter on the basis of respect for human rights and fundamental freedoms as recognized in the present Covenant;

(f) In any matter referred to it, the Committee may call upon the States Parties concerned, referred to in subparagraph (b), to supply any relevant information;

(g) The States Parties concerned, referred to in subparagraph (b), shall have the right to be represented when the matter is being considered in the Committee and to make submissions orally and/or in writing;

(h) The Committee shall, within twelve months after the date of receipt of notice under subparagraph (b), submit a report:

(i) If a solution within the terms of subparagraph (e) is reached, the Committee shall confine its report to a brief statement of the facts and of the solution reached;

(ii) If a solution within the terms of subparagraph (e) is not reached, the Committee shall confine its report to a brief statement of the facts; the written submissions and record of the oral submissions made by the States Parties concerned shall be attached to the report. In every matter, the report shall be communicated to the States Parties concerned.

2. The provisions of this article shall come into force when ten States Parties to the present Covenant have made declarations under paragraph 1 of this article. Such declarations shall be deposited by the States Parties with the Secretary-General of the United Nations, who shall transmit copies thereof to the other States Parties. A declaration may be withdrawn at any time by notification to the Secretary-General. Such a withdrawal shall not prejudice the consideration of any matter which is the subject of a communication already transmitted under this article; no further communication by any State Party shall be received after the notification of withdrawal of the declaration has been received by the Secretary-General, unless the State Party concerned has made a new declaration.

Article 42

1.

(a) If a matter referred to the Committee in accordance with article 41 is not resolved to the satisfaction of the States Parties concerned, the Committee may, with the prior consent of the States Parties concerned, appoint an ad hoc Conciliation Commission (hereinafter referred to as the Commission). The good offices of the Commission shall be made available to the States Parties concerned with a view to an amicable solution of the matter on the basis of respect for the present Covenant;

(b) The Commission shall consist of five persons acceptable to the States Parties concerned. If the States Parties concerned fail to reach agreement within three months on all or part of the composition of the Commission, the members of the Commission concerning whom no agreement has been reached shall be elected by secret ballot by a two-thirds majority vote of the Committee from among its members.

2. The members of the Commission shall serve in their personal capacity. They shall not be nationals of the States Parties concerned, or of a State not Party to the present Covenant, or of a State Party which has not made a declaration under article 41.

3. The Commission shall elect its own Chairman and adopt its own rules of procedure.

4. The meetings of the Commission shall normally be held at the Headquarters of the United Nations or at the United Nations Office at Geneva. However, they may be held at such other convenient places as the Commission may determine in consultation with the Secretary-General of the United Nations and the States Parties concerned.

5. The secretariat provided in accordance with article 36 shall also service the commissions appointed under this article.

6. The information received and collated by the Committee shall be made available to the Commission and the Commission may call upon the States Parties concerned to supply any other relevant information.

7. When the Commission has fully considered the matter, but in any event not later than twelve months after having been seized of the matter, it shall submit to the Chairman of the Committee a report for communication to the States Parties concerned:

(a) If the Commission is unable to complete its consideration of the matter within twelve months, it shall confine its report to a brief statement of the status of its consideration of the matter;

(b) If an amicable solution to the matter on the basis of respect for human rights as recognized in the present Covenant is reached, the Commission shall confine its report to a brief statement of the facts and of the solution reached;

(c) If a solution within the terms of subparagraph (b) is not reached, the Commission's report shall embody its findings on all questions of fact relevant to the issues between the States Parties concerned, and its views on the possibilities of an amicable solution of the matter. This report shall also contain the written submissions and a record of the oral submissions made by the States Parties concerned;

(d) If the Commission's report is submitted under subparagraph (c), the States Parties concerned shall, within three months of the receipt of the report, notify the Chairman of the Committee whether or not they accept the contents of the report of the Commission.

8. The provisions of this article are without prejudice to the responsibilities of the Committee under article 41.

9. The States Parties concerned shall share equally all the expenses of the members of the Commission in accordance with estimates to be provided by the Secretary-General of the United Nations.

10. The Secretary-General of the United Nations shall be empowered to pay the expenses of the members of the Commission, if necessary, before reimbursement by the States Parties concerned, in accordance with paragraph 9 of this article.

Article 43

The members of the Committee, and of the ad hoc conciliation commissions which may be appointed under article 42, shall be entitled to the facilities, privileges and immunities of experts on mission for the United Nations as laid down in the relevant sections of the Convention on the Privileges and Immunities of the United Nations.

Article 44

The provisions for the implementation of the present Covenant shall apply without prejudice to the procedures prescribed in the field of human rights by or under the constituent instruments and the conventions of the United Nations and of the specialized agencies and shall not prevent the States Parties to the present Covenant from having recourse to other procedures for settling a dispute in accordance with general or special international agreements in force between them.

Article 45

The Committee shall submit to the General Assembly of the United Nations, through the Economic and Social Council, an annual report on its activities.

PART V

Article 46

Nothing in the present Covenant shall be interpreted as impairing the provisions of the Charter of the United Nations and of the constitutions of the specialized agencies which define the respective responsibilities of the various organs of the United Nations and of the specialized agencies in regard to the matters dealt with in the present Covenant.

Article 47

Nothing in the present Covenant shall be interpreted as impairing the inherent right of all peoples to enjoy and utilize fully and freely their natural wealth and resources.

PART VI

Article 48

1. The present Covenant is open for signature by any State Member of the United Nations or member of any of its specialized agencies, by any State Party to the Statute of the International Court of Justice, and by any other State which has been invited by the General Assembly of the United Nations to become a Party to the present Covenant.

2. The present Covenant is subject to ratification. Instruments of ratification shall be deposited with the Secretary-General of the United Nations.

3. The present Covenant shall be open to accession by any State referred to in paragraph 1 of this article.

4. Accession shall be effected by the deposit of an instrument of accession with the Secretary-General of the United Nations.

5. The Secretary-General of the United Nations shall inform all States which have signed this Covenant or acceded to it of the deposit of each instrument of ratification or accession.

Article 49

1. The present Covenant shall enter into force three months after the date of the deposit with the Secretary-General of the United Nations of the thirty-fifth instrument of ratification or instrument of accession.

2. For each State ratifying the present Covenant or acceding to it after the deposit of the thirty-fifth instrument of ratification or instrument of accession, the present Covenant shall enter into force three months after the date of the deposit of its own instrument of ratification or instrument of accession.

Article 50

The provisions of the present Covenant shall extend to all parts of federal States without any limitations or exceptions.

Article 51

1. Any State Party to the present Covenant may propose an amendment and file it with the Secretary-General of the United Nations. The Secretary-General of the United Nations shall thereupon communicate any proposed amendments to the States Parties to the present Covenant with a request that they notify him whether they favour a conference of States Parties for the purpose of considering and voting upon the proposals. In the event that at least one third of the States Parties favours such a conference, the Secretary-General shall convene the conference under the auspices of the United Nations. Any amendment adopted by a majority of the States Parties present and voting at the conference shall be submitted to the General Assembly of the United Nations for approval.

2. Amendments shall come into force when they have been approved by the General Assembly of the United Nations and accepted by a two-thirds majority of the States Parties to the present Covenant in accordance with their respective constitutional processes.

3. When amendments come into force, they shall be binding on those States Parties which have accepted them, other States Parties still being bound by the provisions of the present Covenant and any earlier amendment which they have accepted.

Article 52

Irrespective of the notifications made under article 48, paragraph 5, the Secretary-General of the United Nations shall inform all States referred to in paragraph I of the same article of the following particulars:

(a) Signatures, ratifications and accessions under article 48;

(b) The date of the entry into force of the present Covenant under article 49 and the date of the entry into force of any amendments under article 51.

Article 53

1. The present Covenant, of which the Chinese, English, French, Russian and Spanish texts are equally authentic, shall be deposited in the archives of the United Nations.

2. The Secretary-General of the United Nations shall transmit certified copies of the present Covenant to all States referred to in article 48.

Appendix IV

International Covenant on Economic, Social and Cultural Rights

UN G.A. Res. 2200A (XXI), 21 UNGAOR Supp. (No. 16) at 49, UN Doc. A/6316 (1966), 993 UNT.S. 3, *entered into force* 3 Jan. 1976.

Preamble

The States Parties to the present Covenant,

Considering that, in accordance with the principles proclaimed in the Charter of the United Nations, recognition of the inherent dignity and of the equal and inalienable rights of all members of the human family is the foundation of freedom, justice and peace in the world,

Recognizing that these rights derive from the inherent dignity of the human person,

Recognizing that, in accordance with the Universal Declaration of Human Rights, the ideal of free human beings enjoying freedom from fear and want can only be achieved if conditions are created whereby everyone may enjoy his economic, social and cultural rights, as well as his civil and political rights,

Considering the obligation of States under the Charter of the United Nations to promote universal respect for, and observance of, human rights and freedoms,

Realizing that the individual, having duties to other individuals and to the community to which he belongs, is under a responsibility to strive for the promotion and observance of the rights recognized in the present Covenant,

Agree upon the following articles:

PART I

Article 1

1. All peoples have the right of self-determination. By virtue of that right they freely determine their political status and freely pursue their economic, social and cultural development.

2. All peoples may, for their own ends, freely dispose of their natural wealth and resources without prejudice to any obligations arising out of international economic co-operation, based upon the principle of mutual benefit, and international law. In no case may a people be deprived of its own means of subsistence.

3. The States Parties to the present Covenant, including those having responsibility for the administration of Non-Self-Governing and Trust Territories, shall promote the realization of the right of self-determination, and shall respect that right, in conformity with the provisions of the Charter of the United Nations.

PART II

Article 2

1. Each State Party to the present Covenant undertakes to take steps, individually and through international assistance and co-operation, especially economic and technical, to

the maximum of its available resources, with a view to achieving progressively the full realization of the rights recognized in the present Covenant by all appropriate means, including particularly the adoption of legislative measures.

2. The States Parties to the present Covenant undertake to guarantee that the rights enunciated in the present Covenant will be exercised without discrimination of any kind as to race, colour, sex, language, religion, political or other opinion, national or social origin, property, birth or other status.

3. Developing countries, with due regard to human rights and their national economy, may determine to what extent they would guarantee the economic rights recognized in the present Covenant to non-nationals.

Article 3

The States Parties to the present Covenant undertake to ensure the equal right of men and women to the enjoyment of all economic, social and cultural rights set forth in the present Covenant.

Article 4

The States Parties to the present Covenant recognize that, in the enjoyment of those rights provided by the State in conformity with the present Covenant, the State may subject such rights only to such limitations as are determined by law only in so far as this may be compatible with the nature of these rights and solely for the purpose of promoting the general welfare in a democratic society.

Article 5

1. Nothing in the present Covenant may be interpreted as implying for any State, group or person any right to engage in any activity or to perform any act aimed at the destruction of any of the rights or freedoms recognized herein, or at their limitation to a greater extent than is provided for in the present Covenant.

2. No restriction upon or derogation from any of the fundamental human rights recognized or existing in any country in virtue of law, conventions, regulations or custom shall be admitted on the pretext that the present Covenant does not recognize such rights or that it recognizes them to a lesser extent.

PART III

Article 6

1. The States Parties to the present Covenant recognize the right to work, which includes the right of everyone to the opportunity to gain his living by work which he freely chooses or accepts, and will take appropriate steps to safeguard this right.

2. The steps to be taken by a State Party to the present Covenant to achieve the full realization of this right shall include technical and vocational guidance and training programmes, policies and techniques to achieve steady economic, social and cultural development and full and productive employment under conditions safeguarding fundamental political and economic freedoms to the individual.

Article 7

The States Parties to the present Covenant recognize the right of everyone to the enjoyment of just and favourable conditions of work which ensure, in particular:

(a) Remuneration which provides all workers, as a minimum, with:

(i) Fair wages and equal remuneration for work of equal value without distinction of any kind, in particular women being guaranteed conditions of work not inferior to those enjoyed by men, with equal pay for equal work;

(ii) A decent living for themselves and their families in accordance with the provisions of the present Covenant;

(b) Safe and healthy working conditions;

(c) Equal opportunity for everyone to be promoted in his employment to an appropriate higher level, subject to no considerations other than those of seniority and competence;

(d) Rest, leisure and reasonable limitation of working hours and periodic holidays with pay, as well as remuneration for public holidays.

Article 8

1. The States Parties to the present Covenant undertake to ensure:

(a) The right of everyone to form trade unions and join the trade union of his choice, subject only to the rules of the organization concerned, for the promotion and protection of his economic and social interests. No restrictions may be placed on the exercise of this right other than those prescribed by law and which are necessary in a democratic society in the interests of national security or public order or for the protection of the rights and freedoms of others;

(b) The right of trade unions to establish national federations or confederations and the right of the latter to form or join international trade-union organizations;

(c) The right of trade unions to function freely subject to no limitations other than those prescribed by law and which are necessary in a democratic society in the interests of national security or public order or for the protection of the rights and freedoms of others;

(d) The right to strike, provided that it is exercised in conformity with the laws of the particular country.

2. This article shall not prevent the imposition of lawful restrictions on the exercise of these rights by members of the armed forces or of the police or of the administration of the State.

3. Nothing in this article shall authorize States Parties to the International Labour Organization Convention of 1948 concerning Freedom of Association and Protection of the Right to Organize to take legislative measures which would prejudice, or apply the law in such a manner as would prejudice, the guarantees provided for in that Convention.

Article 9

The States Parties to the present Covenant recognize the right of everyone to social security, including social insurance.

Article 10

The States Parties to the present Covenant recognize that:

1. The widest possible protection and assistance should be accorded to the family, which is the natural and fundamental group unit of society, particularly for its establishment and while it is responsible for the care and education of dependent children. Marriage must be entered into with the free consent of the intending spouses.

2. Special protection should be accorded to mothers during a reasonable period before and after childbirth. During such period working mothers should be accorded paid leave or leave with adequate social security benefits.

3. Special measures of protection and assistance should be taken on behalf of all children and young persons without any discrimination for reasons of parentage or other conditions. Children and young persons should be protected from economic and social exploitation. Their employment in work harmful to their morals or health or dangerous to life or likely to hamper their normal development should be punishable by law. States should also set age limits below which the paid employment of child labour should be prohibited and punishable by law.

Article 11

1. The States Parties to the present Covenant recognize the right of everyone to an adequate standard of living for himself and his family, including adequate food, clothing and housing, and to the continuous improvement of living conditions. The States Parties will take appropriate steps to ensure the realization of this right, recognizing to this effect the essential importance of international co-operation based on free consent.

2. The States Parties to the present Covenant, recognizing the fundamental right of everyone to be free from hunger, shall take, individually and through international co-operation, the measures, including specific programmes, which are needed:

(a) To improve methods of production, conservation and distribution of food by making full use of technical and scientific knowledge, by disseminating knowledge of the principles of nutrition and by developing or reforming agrarian systems in such a way as to achieve the most efficient development and utilization of natural resources;

(b) Taking into account the problems of both food-importing and food-exporting countries, to ensure an equitable distribution of world food supplies in relation to need.

Article 12

1. The States Parties to the present Covenant recognize the right of everyone to the enjoyment of the highest attainable standard of physical and mental health.

2. The steps to be taken by the States Parties to the present Covenant to achieve the full realization of this right shall include those necessary for:

(a) The provision for the reduction of the stillbirth-rate and of infant mortality and for the healthy development of the child;

(b) The improvement of all aspects of environmental and industrial hygiene;

(c) The prevention, treatment and control of epidemic, endemic, occupational and other diseases;

(d) The creation of conditions which would assure to all medical service and medical attention in the event of sickness.

Article 13

1. The States Parties to the present Covenant recognize the right of everyone to education. They agree that education shall be directed to the full development of the human personality and the sense of its dignity, and shall strengthen the respect for human rights and fundamental freedoms. They further agree that education shall enable all persons to participate effectively in a free society, promote understanding, tolerance and friendship among all nations and all racial, ethnic or religious groups, and further the activities of the United Nations for the maintenance of peace.

2. The States Parties to the present Covenant recognize that, with a view to achieving the full realization of this right:

(a) Primary education shall be compulsory and available free to all;

(b) Secondary education in its different forms, including technical and vocational secondary education, shall be made generally available and accessible to all by every appropriate means, and in particular by the progressive introduction of free education;

(c) Higher education shall be made equally accessible to all, on the basis of capacity, by every appropriate means, and in particular by the progressive introduction of free education;

(d) Fundamental education shall be encouraged or intensified as far as possible for those persons who have not received or completed the whole period of their primary education;

(e) The development of a system of schools at all levels shall be actively pursued, an adequate fellowship system shall be established, and the material conditions of teaching staff shall be continuously improved.

3. The States Parties to the present Covenant undertake to have respect for the liberty of parents and, when applicable, legal guardians to choose for their children schools, other than those established by the public authorities, which conform to such minimum educational standards as may be laid down or approved by the State and to ensure the religious and moral education of their children in conformity with their own convictions.

4. No part of this article shall be construed so as to interfere with the liberty of individuals and bodies to establish and direct educational institutions, subject always to the observance of the principles set forth in paragraph 1 of this article and to the requirement that the education given in such institutions shall conform to such minimum standards as may be laid down by the State.

Article 14

Each State Party to the present Covenant which, at the time of becoming a Party, has not been able to secure in its metropolitan territory or other territories under its jurisdiction compulsory primary education, free of charge, undertakes, within two years, to work out and adopt a detailed plan of action for the progressive implementation, within a reasonable number of years, to be fixed in the plan, of the principle of compulsory education free of charge for all.

Article 15

1. The States Parties to the present Covenant recognize the right of everyone:

(a) To take part in cultural life;

(b) To enjoy the benefits of scientific progress and its applications;

(c) To benefit from the protection of the moral and material interests resulting from any scientific, literary or artistic production of which he is the author.

2. The steps to be taken by the States Parties to the present Covenant to achieve the full realization of this right shall include those necessary for the conservation, the development and the diffusion of science and culture.

3. The States Parties to the present Covenant undertake to respect the freedom indispensable for scientific research and creative activity.

4. The States Parties to the present Covenant recognize the benefits to be derived from the encouragement and development of international contacts and co-operation in the scientific and cultural fields.

PART IV

Article 16

1. The States Parties to the present Covenant undertake to submit in conformity with this part of the Covenant reports on the measures which they have adopted and the progress made in achieving the observance of the rights recognized herein.

2. (a) All reports shall be submitted to the Secretary-General of the United Nations, who shall transmit copies to the Economic and Social Council for consideration in accordance with the provisions of the present Covenant;

(b) The Secretary-General of the United Nations shall also transmit to the specialized agencies copies of the reports, or any relevant parts therefrom, from States Parties to the present Covenant which are also members of these specialized agencies in so far as these reports, or parts therefrom, relate to any matters which fall within the responsibilities of the said agencies in accordance with their constitutional instruments.

Article 17

1. The States Parties to the present Covenant shall furnish their reports in stages, in accordance with a programme to be established by the Economic and Social Council within one year of the entry into force of the present Covenant after consultation with the States Parties and the specialized agencies concerned.

2. Reports may indicate factors and difficulties affecting the degree of fulfilment of obligations under the present Covenant.

3. Where relevant information has previously been furnished to the United Nations or to any specialized agency by any State Party to the present Covenant, it will not be necessary to reproduce that information, but a precise reference to the information so furnished will suffice.

Article 18

Pursuant to its responsibilities under the Charter of the United Nations in the field of human rights and fundamental freedoms, the Economic and Social Council may make arrangements with the specialized agencies in respect of their reporting to it on the progress made in achieving the observance of the provisions of the present Covenant falling within the scope of their activities. These reports may include particulars of decisions and recommendations on such implementation adopted by their competent organs.

Article 19

The Economic and Social Council may transmit to the Commission on Human Rights for study and general recommendation or, as appropriate, for information the reports concerning human rights submitted by States in accordance with articles 16 and 17, and those concerning human rights submitted by the specialized agencies in accordance with article 18.

Article 20

The States Parties to the present Covenant and the specialized agencies concerned may submit comments to the Economic and Social Council on any general recommendation under article 19 or reference to such general recommendation in any report of the Commission on Human Rights or any documentation referred to therein.

Article 21

The Economic and Social Council may submit from time to time to the General Assembly reports with recommendations of a general nature and a summary of the information received from the States Parties to the present Covenant and the specialized agencies on the measures taken and the progress made in achieving general observance of the rights recognized in the present Covenant.

Article 22

The Economic and Social Council may bring to the attention of other organs of the United Nations, their subsidiary organs and specialized agencies concerned with furnishing technical assistance any matters arising out of the reports referred to in this part of the present Covenant which may assist such bodies in deciding, each within its field of competence, on the advisability of international measures likely to contribute to the effective progressive implementation of the present Covenant.

Article 23

The States Parties to the present Covenant agree that international action for the achievement of the rights recognized in the present Covenant includes such methods as the conclusion of conventions, the adoption of recommendations, the furnishing of technical assistance and the holding of regional meetings and technical meetings for the purpose of consultation and study organized in conjunction with the Governments concerned.

Article 24

Nothing in the present Covenant shall be interpreted as impairing the provisions of the Charter of the United Nations and of the constitutions of the specialized agencies which define the respective responsibilities of the various organs of the United Nations and of the specialized agencies in regard to the matters dealt with in the present Covenant.

Article 25

Nothing in the present Covenant shall be interpreted as impairing the inherent right of all peoples to enjoy and utilize fully and freely their natural wealth and resources.

PART V

Article 26

1. The present Covenant is open for signature by any State Member of the United Nations or member of any of its specialized agencies, by any State Party to the Statute of the International Court of Justice, and by any other State which has been invited by the General Assembly of the United Nations to become a party to the present Covenant.

2. The present Covenant is subject to ratification. Instruments of ratification shall be deposited with the Secretary-General of the United Nations.

3. The present Covenant shall be open to accession by any State referred to in paragraph 1 of this article.

4. Accession shall be effected by the deposit of an instrument of accession with the Secretary-General of the United Nations.

5. The Secretary-General of the United Nations shall inform all States which have signed the present Covenant or acceded to it of the deposit of each instrument of ratification or accession.

Article 27

1. The present Covenant shall enter into force three months after the date of the deposit with the Secretary-General of the United Nations of the thirty-fifth instrument of ratification or instrument of accession.

2. For each State ratifying the present Covenant or acceding to it after the deposit of the thirty-fifth instrument of ratification or instrument of accession, the present Covenant shall enter into force three months after the date of the deposit of its own instrument of ratification or instrument of accession.

Article 28

The provisions of the present Covenant shall extend to all parts of federal States without any limitations or exceptions.

Article 29

1. Any State Party to the present Covenant may propose an amendment and file it with the Secretary-General of the United Nations. The Secretary-General shall thereupon communicate any proposed amendments to the States Parties to the present Covenant with a request that they notify him whether they favour a conference of States Parties for the purpose of considering and voting upon the proposals. In the event that at least one third of the States Parties favours such a conference, the Secretary-General shall convene the conference under the auspices of the United Nations. Any amendment adopted by a majority of the States Parties present and voting at the conference shall be submitted to the General Assembly of the United Nations for approval.

2. Amendments shall come into force when they have been approved by the General Assembly of the United Nations and accepted by a two-thirds majority of the States Parties to the present Covenant in accordance with their respective constitutional processes.

3. When amendments come into force they shall be binding on those States Parties which have accepted them, other States Parties still being bound by the provisions of the present Covenant and any earlier amendment which they have accepted.

Article 30

Irrespective of the notifications made under article 26, paragraph 5, the Secretary-General of the United Nations shall inform all States referred to in paragraph 1 of the same article of the following particulars:

(a) Signatures, ratifications and accessions under article 26;

(b) The date of the entry into force of the present Covenant under article 27 and the date of the entry into force of any amendments under article 29.

Article 31

1. The present Covenant, of which the Chinese, English, French, Russian and Spanish texts are equally authentic, shall be deposited in the archives of the United Nations.

2. The Secretary-General of the United Nations shall transmit certified copies of the present Covenant to all States referred to in article 26.

Appendix V

Optional Protocol to the International Covenant on Civil and Political Rights

UNG.A. Res. 2200A (XXI), 21 UN GAOR Supp. (No. 16) at 59, UN Doc. A/6316 (1966), 999 UNT.S. 302, *entered into force* March 23, 1976.

The States Parties to the present Protocol,

Considering that in order further to achieve the purposes of the International Covenant on Civil and Political Rights (hereinafter referred to as the Covenant) and the implementation of its provisions it would be appropriate to enable the Human Rights Committee set up in part IV of the Covenant (hereinafter referred to as the Committee) to receive and consider, as provided in the present Protocol, communications from individuals claiming to be victims of violations of any of the rights set forth in the Covenant.

Have agreed as follows:

Article 1

A State Party to the Covenant that becomes a Party to the present Protocol recognizes the competence of the Committee to receive and consider communications from individuals subject to its jurisdiction who claim to be victims of a violation by that State Party of any of the rights set forth in the Covenant. No communication shall be received by the Committee if it concerns a State Party to the Covenant which is not a Party to the present Protocol.

Article 2

Subject to the provisions of article 1, individuals who claim that any of their rights enumerated in the Covenant have been violated and who have exhausted all available domestic remedies may submit a written communication to the Committee for consideration.

Article 3

The Committee shall consider inadmissible any communication under the present Protocol which is anonymous, or which it considers to be an abuse of the right of submission of such communications or to be incompatible with the provisions of the Covenant.

Article 4

1. Subject to the provisions of article 3, the Committee shall bring any communications submitted to it under the present Protocol to the attention of the State Party to the present Protocol alleged to be violating any provision of the Covenant.

2. Within six months, the receiving State shall submit to the Committee written explanations or statements clarifying the matter and the remedy, if any, that may have been taken by that State.

Article 5

1. The Committee shall consider communications received under the present Protocol in the light of all written information made available to it by the individual and by the State Party concerned.

2. The Committee shall not consider any communication from an individual unless it has ascertained that:

(a) The same matter is not being examined under another procedure of international investigation or settlement;

(b) The individual has exhausted all available domestic remedies. This shall not be the rule where the application of the remedies is unreasonably prolonged.

3. The Committee shall hold closed meetings when examining communications under the present Protocol.

4. The Committee shall forward its views to the State Party concerned and to the individual.

Article 6

The Committee shall include in its annual report under article 45 of the Covenant a summary of its activities under the present Protocol.

Article 7

Pending the achievement of the objectives of resolution 1514(XV) adopted by the General Assembly of the United Nations on 14 December 1960 concerning the Declaration on the Granting of Independence to Colonial Countries and Peoples, the provisions of the present Protocol shall in no way limit the right of petition granted to these peoples by the Charter of the United Nations and other international conventions and instruments under the United Nations and its specialized agencies.

Article 8

1. The present Protocol is open for signature by any State which has signed the Covenant.

2. The present Protocol is subject to ratification by any State which has ratified or acceded to the Covenant. Instruments of ratification shall be deposited with the Secretary-General of the United Nations.

3. The present Protocol shall be open to accession by any State which has ratified or acceded to the Covenant.

4. Accession shall be effected by the deposit of an instrument of accession with the Secretary-General of the United Nations.

5. The Secretary-General of the United Nations shall inform all States which have signed the present Protocol or acceded to it of the deposit of each instrument of ratification or accession.

Article 9

1. Subject to the entry into force of the Covenant, the present Protocol shall enter into force three months after the date of the deposit with the Secretary-General of the United Nations of the tenth instrument of ratification or instrument of accession.

2. For each State ratifying the present Protocol or acceding to it after the deposit of the tenth instrument of ratification or instrument of accession, the present Protocol shall enter into force three months after the date of the deposit of its own instrument of ratification or instrument of accession.

Article 10

The provisions of the present Protocol shall extend to all parts of federal States without any limitations or exceptions.

Article 11

1. Any State Party to the present Protocol may propose an amendment and file it with the Secretary-General of the United Nations. The Secretary-General shall thereupon communicate any proposed amendments to the States Parties to the present Protocol with a request that they notify him whether they favour a conference of States Parties for the purpose of considering and voting upon the proposal. In the event that at least one third of the States Parties favours such a conference, the Secretary-General shall convene the conference under the auspices of the United Nations. Any amendment adopted by a majority of the States Parties present and voting at the conference shall be submitted to the General Assembly of the United Nations for approval.

2. Amendments shall come into force when they have been approved by the General Assembly of the United Nations and accepted by a two-thirds majority of the States Parties to the present Protocol in accordance with their respective constitutional processes.

3. When amendments come into force, they shall be binding on those States Parties which have accepted them, other States Parties still being bound by the provisions of the present Protocol and any earlier amendment which they have accepted.

Article 12

1. Any State Party may denounce the present Protocol at any time by written notification addressed to the Secretary-General of the United Nations. Denunciation shall take effect three months after the date of receipt of the notification by the Secretary-General.

2. Denunciation shall be without prejudice to the continued application of the provisions of the present Protocol to any communication submitted under article 2 before the effective date of denunciation.

Article 13

Irrespective of the notifications made under article 8, paragraph 5, of the present Protocol, the Secretary-General of the United Nations shall inform all States referred to in article 48, paragraph 1, of the Covenant of the following particulars:

(a) Signatures, ratifications and accessions under article 8;

(b) The date of the entry into force of the present Protocol under article 9 and the date of the entry into force of any amendments under article 11;

(c) Denunciations under article 12.

Article 14

1. The present Protocol, of which the Chinese, English, French, Russian and Spanish texts are equally authentic, shall be deposited in the archives of the United Nations.

2. The Secretary-General of the United Nations shall transmit certified copies of the present Protocol to all States referred to in article 48 of the Covenant.

Appendix VI

International Labour Organization Convention Concerning Indigenous and Tribal Peoples in Independent Countries (ILO no. 169)

72 ILO Official Bull. 59, *entered into force* Sept. 5, 1991.

The General Conference of the International Labour Organization,

Having been convened at Geneva by the Governing Body of the International Labour Office, and having met in its seventy-sixth session on 7 June 1989, and

Noting the international standards contained in the Indigenous and Tribal Populations Convention and Recommendation, 1957, and

Recalling the terms of the Universal Declaration of Human Rights, the International Covenant on Economic, Social and Cultural Rights, the International Covenant on Civil and Political Rights, and the many international instruments on the prevention of discrimination, and

Considering that the developments which have taken place in international law since 1957, as well as developments in the situation of indigenous and tribal peoples in all regions of the world, have made it appropriate to adopt new international standards on the subject with a view to removing the assimilationist orientation of the earlier standards, and

Recognizing the aspirations of these peoples to exercise control over their own institutions, ways of life and economic development and to maintain and develop their identities, languages and religions, within the framework of the States in which they live, and

Noting that in many parts of the world these peoples are unable to enjoy their fundamental human rights to the same degree as the rest of the population of the States within which they live, and that their laws, values, customs and perspectives have often been eroded, and

Calling attention to the distinctive contributions of indigenous and tribal peoples to the cultural diversity and social and ecological harmony of humankind and to international co-operation and understanding, and

Noting that the following provisions have been framed with the co-operation of the United Nations, the Food and Agriculture Organization of the United Nations, the United Nations Educational, Scientific and Cultural Organization and the World Health Organization, as well as of the Inter-American Indian Institute, at appropriate levels and in their respective fields and that it is proposed to continue this co-operation in promoting and securing the application of these provisions, and

Having decided upon the adoption of certain proposals with regard to the partial revision of the Indigenous and Tribal Populations Convention, 1957 (No. 107), which is the fourth item on the agenda of the session, and

Having determined that these proposals shall take the form of an international Convention revising the Indigenous and Tribal Populations Convention, 1957,

Adopts this twenty-seventh day of June of the year one thousand nine hundred and eighty-nine the following Convention, which may be cited as the Indigenous and Tribal Peoples Convention, 1989:

PART I. GENERAL POLICY

Article 1

1. This Convention applies to:

(a) Tribal peoples in independent countries whose social, cultural and economic conditions distinguish them from other sections of the national community, and whose status is regulated wholly or partially by their own customs or traditions or by special laws or regulations;

(b) Peoples in independent countries who are regarded as indigenous on account of their descent from the populations which inhabited the country, or a geographical region to which the country belongs, at the time of conquest or colonization or the establishment of present State boundaries and who, irrespective of their legal status, retain some or all of their own social, economic, cultural and political institutions.

2. Self-identification as indigenous or tribal shall be regarded as a fundamental criterion for determining the groups to which the provisions of this Convention apply.

3. The use of the term "peoples" in this Convention shall not be construed as having any implications as regards the rights which may attach to the term under international law.

Article 2

1. Governments shall have the responsibility for developing, with the participation of the peoples concerned, coordinated and systematic action to protect the rights of these peoples and to guarantee respect for their integrity.

2. Such action shall include measures for:

(a) Ensuring that members of these peoples benefit on an equal footing from the rights and opportunities which national laws and regulations grant to other members of the population;

(b) Promoting the full realization of the social, economic and cultural rights of these peoples with respect for their social and cultural identity, their customs and traditions and their institutions;

(c) Assisting the members of the peoples concerned to eliminate socio-economic gaps that may exist between indigenous and other members of the national community, in a manner compatible with their aspirations and ways of life.

Article 3

1. Indigenous and tribal peoples shall enjoy the full measure of human rights and fundamental freedoms without hindrance or discrimination. The provisions of the Convention shall be applied without discrimination to male and female members of these peoples.

2. No form of force or coërcion shall be used in violation of the human rights and fundamental freedoms of the peoples concerned, including the rights contained in this Convention.

Article 4

1. Special measures shall be adopted as appropriate for safeguarding the persons, institutions, property, labour, cultures and environment of the peoples concerned.

2. Such special measures shall not be contrary to the freely-expressed wishes of the peoples concerned.

3. Enjoyment of the general rights of citizenship, without discrimination, shall not be prejudiced in any way by such special measures.

Article 5

In applying the provisions of this Convention:

(a) The social, cultural, religious and spiritual values and practices of these peoples shall be recognized and protected, and due account shall be taken of the nature of the problems which face them both as groups and as individuals;

(b) The integrity of the values, practices and institutions of these peoples shall be respected;

(c) Policies aimed at mitigating the difficulties experienced by these peoples in facing new conditions of life and work shall be adopted, with the participation and co-operation of the peoples affected.

Article 6

1. In applying the provisions of this Convention, Governments shall:

(a) Consult the peoples concerned, through appropriate procedures and in particular through their representative institutions, whenever consideration is being given to legislative or administrative measures which may affect them directly;

(b) Establish means by which these peoples can freely participate, to at least the same extent as other sectors of the population, at all levels of decision-making in elective institutions and administrative and other bodies responsible for policies and programmes which concern them;

(c) Establish means for the full development of these peoples' own institutions and initiatives, and in appropriate cases provide the resources necessary for this purpose.

2. The consultations carried out in application of this Convention shall be undertaken, in good faith and in a form appropriate to the circumstances, with the objective of achieving agreement or consent to the proposed measures.

Article 7

1. The peoples concerned shall have the right to decide their own priorities for the process of development as it affects their lives, beliefs, institutions and spiritual well-being and the lands they occupy or otherwise use, and to exercise control, to the extent possible, over

their own economic, social and cultural development. In addition, they shall participate in the formulation, implementation and evaluation of plans and programmes for national and regional development which may affect them directly.

2. The improvement of the conditions of life and work and levels of health and education of the peoples concerned, with their participation and co-operation, shall be a matter of priority in plans for the overall economic development of areas they inhabit. Special projects for development of the areas in question shall also be so designed as to promote such improvement.

3. Governments shall ensure that, whenever appropriate, studies are carried out, in co-operation with the peoples concerned, to assess the social, spiritual, cultural and environmental impact on them of planned development activities. The results of these studies shall be considered as fundamental criteria for the implementation of these activities.

4. Governments shall take measures, in co-operation with the peoples concerned, to protect and preserve the environment of the territories they inhabit.

Article 8

1. In applying national laws and regulations to the peoples concerned, due regard shall be had to their customs or customary laws.

2. These peoples shall have the right to retain their own customs and institutions, where these are not incompatible with fundamental rights defined by the national legal system and with internationally recognized human rights. Procedures shall be established, whenever necessary, to resolve conflicts which may arise in the application of this principle.

3. The application of paragraphs 1 and 2 of this Article shall not prevent members of these peoples from exercising the rights granted to all citizens and from assuming the corresponding duties.

Article 9

1. To the extent compatible with the national legal system and internationally recognised human rights. the methods customarily practised by the peoples concerned for dealing with offences committed by their members shall be respected.

2. The customs of these peoples in regard to penal matters shall be taken into consideration by the authorities and courts dealing with such cases.

Article 10

1. In imposing penalties laid down by general law on members of these peoples account shall be taken of their economic, social and cultural characteristics.

2. Preference shall be given to methods of punishment other than confinement in prison.

Article 11

The exaction from members of the peoples concerned of compulsory personal services in any form, whether paid or unpaid, shall be prohibited and punishable by law, except in cases prescribed by law for all citizens.

Article 12

The peoples concerned shall be safeguarded against the abuse of their rights and shall be able to take legal proceedings, either individually or through their representative bodies, for the effective protection of these rights. Measures shall be taken to ensure that members of these peoples can understand and be understood in legal proceedings, where necessary through the provision of interpretation or by other effective means.

PART II. LAND

Article 13

1. In applying the provisions of this Part of the Convention governments shall respect the special importance for the cultures and spiritual values of the peoples concerned of their relationship with the lands or territories, or both as applicable, which they occupy or otherwise use, and in particular the collective aspects of this relationship.

2. The use of the term "lands" in Articles 15 and 16 shall include the concept of territories, which covers the total environment of the areas which the peoples concerned occupy or otherwise use.

Article 14

1. The rights of ownership and possession of the peoples concerned over the lands which they traditionally occupy shall be recognized. In addition, measures shall be taken in appropriate cases to safeguard the right of the peoples concerned to use lands not exclusively occupied by them, but to which they have traditionally had access for their subsistence and traditional activities. Particular attention shall be paid to the situation of nomadic peoples and shifting cultivators in this respect.

2. Governments shall take steps as necessary to identify the lands which the peoples concerned traditionally occupy, and to guarantee effective protection of their rights of ownership and possession.

3. Adequate procedures shall be established within the national legal system to resolve land claims by the peoples concerned.

Article 15

1. The rights of the peoples concerned to the natural resources pertaining to their lands shall be specially safeguarded. These rights include the right of these peoples to participate in the use, management and conservation of these resources.

2. In cases in which the State retains the ownership of mineral or sub-surface resources or rights to other resources pertaining to lands, governments shall establish or maintain procedures through which they shall consult these peoples, with a view to ascertaining whether and to what degree their interests would be prejudiced, before undertaking or permitting any programmes for the exploration or exploitation of such resources pertaining to their lands. The peoples concerned shall wherever possible participate in the benefits of such activities, and shall receive fair compensation for any damages which they may sustain as a result of such activities.

Article 16

1. Subject to the following paragraphs of this Article, the peoples concerned shall not be removed from the lands which they occupy.

2. Where the relocation of these peoples is considered necessary as an exceptional measure, such relocation shall take place only with their free and informed consent. Where their consent cannot be obtained, such relocation shall take place only following appropriate procedures established by national laws and regulations, including public inquiries where appropriate, which provide the opportunity for effective representation of the peoples concerned.

3. Whenever possible, these peoples shall have the right to return to their traditional lands, as soon as the grounds for relocation cease to exist.

4. When such return is not possible, as determined by agreement or, in the absence of such agreement, through appropriate procedures, these peoples shall be provided in all possible cases with lands of quality and legal status at least equal to that of the lands previously occupied by them, suitable to provide for their present needs and future development. Where the peoples concerned express a preference for compensation in money or in kind, they shall be so compensated under appropriate guarantees.

5. Persons thus relocated shall be fully compensated for any resulting loss or injury.

Article 17

1. Procedures established by the peoples concerned for the transmission of land rights among members of these peoples shall be respected.

2. The peoples concerned shall be consulted whenever consideration is being given to their capacity to alienate their lands or otherwise transmit their rights outside their own community.

3. Persons not belonging to these peoples shall be prevented from taking advantage of their customs or of lack of understanding of the laws on the part of their members to secure the ownership, possession or use of land belonging to them.

Article 18

Adequate penalties shall be established by law for unauthorized intrusion upon, or use of, the lands of the peoples concerned, and governments shall take measures to prevent such offences.

Article 19

National agrarian programmes shall secure to the peoples concerned treatment equivalent to that accorded to other sectors of the population with regard to:

(a) The provision of more land for these peoples when they have not the area necessary for providing the essentials of a normal existence, or for any possible increase in their numbers;

(b) The provision of the means required to promote the development of the lands which these peoples already possess.

PART III. RECRUITMENT AND CONDITIONS OF EMPLOYMENT

Article 20

1. Governments shall, within the framework of national laws and regulations, and in cooperation with the peoples concerned, adopt special measures to ensure the effective protection with regard to recruitment and conditions of employment of workers belonging to these peoples, to the extent that they are not effectively protected by laws applicable to workers in general.

2. Governments shall do everything possible to prevent any discrimination between workers belonging to the peoples concerned and other workers, in particular as regards:

(a) Admission to employment, including skilled employment, as well as measures for promotion and advancement;

(b) Equal remuneration for work of equal value;

(c) Medical and social assistance, occupational safety and health, all social security benefits and any other occupationally related benefits, and housing;

(d) The right of association and freedom for all lawful trade union activities, and the right to conclude collective agreements with employers or employers' organizations.

3. The measures taken shall include measures to ensure:

(a) That workers belonging to the peoples concerned, including seasonal, casual and migrant workers in agricultural and other employment, as well as those employed by labour contractors, enjoy the protection afforded by national law and practice to other such workers in the same sectors, and that they are fully informed of their rights under labour legislation and of the means of redress available to them;

(b) That workers belonging to these peoples are not subjected to working conditions hazardous to their health, in particular through exposure to pesticides or other toxic substances;

(c) That workers belonging to these peoples are not subjected to coërcive recruitment systems, including bonded labour and other forms of debt servitude;

(d) That workers belonging to these peoples enjoy equal opportunities and equal treatment in employment for men and women, and protection from sexual harassment.

4. Particular attention shall be paid to the establishment of adequate labour inspection services in areas where workers belonging to the peoples concerned undertake wage employment, in order to ensure compliance with the provisions of this Part of this Convention.

PART IV. VOCATIONAL TRAINING, HANDICRAFTS, AND RURAL INDUSTRIES

Article 21

Members of the peoples concerned shall enjoy opportunities at least equal to those of other citizens in respect of vocational training measures.

Article 22

1. Measures shall be taken to promote the voluntary participation of members of the peoples concerned in vocational training programmes of general application.

2. Whenever existing programmes of vocational training of general application do not meet the special needs of the peoples concerned, governments shall, with the participation of these peoples, ensure the provision of special training programmes and facilities.

3. Any special training programmes shall be based on the economic environment, social and cultural conditions and practical needs of the peoples concerned. Any studies made in this connection shall be carried out in co-operation with these peoples, who shall be consulted on the organization and operation of such programmes. Where feasible, these peoples shall progressively assume responsibility for the organization and operation of such special training programmes, if they so decide.

Article 23

1. Handicrafts, rural and community-based industries, and subsistence economy and traditional activities of the peoples concerned, such as hunting, fishing, trapping and gathering, shall be recognized as important factors in the maintenance of their cultures and in their economic self-reliance and development. Governments shall, with the participation of these peoples and whenever appropriate, ensure that these activities are strengthened and promoted.

2. Upon the request of the peoples concerned, appropriate technical and financial assistance shall be provided wherever possible, taking into account the traditional technologies and cultural characteristics of these peoples, as well as the importance of sustainable and equitable development.

PART V. SOCIAL SECURITY AND HEALTH

Article 24

Social security schemes shall be extended progressively to cover the peoples concerned, and applied without discrimination against them.

Article 25

1. Governments shall ensure that adequate health services are made available to the peoples concerned, or shall provide them with resources to allow them to design and deliver such services under their own responsibility and control, so that they may enjoy the highest attainable standard of physical and mental health.

2. Health services shall, to the extent possible, be community-based. These services shall be planned and administered in co-operation with the peoples concerned and take into account their economic, geographic, social and cultural conditions as well as their traditional preventive care, healing practices and medicines.

3. The health care system shall give preference to the training and employment of local community health workers, and focus on primary health care while maintaining strong links with other levels of health care services.

4. The provision of such health services shall be coordinated with other social, economic and cultural measures in the country.

PART VI. EDUCATION AND MEANS OF COMMUNICATION

Article 26

Measures shall be taken to ensure that members of the peoples concerned have the opportunity to acquire education at all levels on at least an equal footing with the rest of the national community.

Article 27

1. Education programmes and services for the peoples concerned shall be developed and implemented in co-operation with them to address their special needs, and shall incorporate their histories, their knowledge and technologies, their value systems and their further social, economic and cultural aspirations.

2. The competent authority shall ensure the training of members of these peoples and their involvement in the formulation and implementation of education programmes, with a view to the progressive transfer of responsibility for the conduct of these programmes to these peoples as appropriate.

3. In addition, governments shall recognize the right of these peoples to establish their own educational institutions and facilities, provided that such institutions meet minimum standards established by the competent authority in consultation with these peoples. Appropriate resources shall be provided for this purpose.

Article 28

1. Children belonging to the peoples concerned shall, wherever practicable, be taught to read and write in their own indigenous language or in the language most commonly used by the group to which they belong. When this is not practicable, the competent authorities shall undertake consultations with these peoples with a view to the adoption of measures to achieve this objective.

2. Adequate measures shall be taken to ensure that these peoples have the opportunity to attain fluency in the national language or in one of the official languages of the country.

3. Measures shall be taken to preserve and promote the development and practice of the indigenous languages of the peoples concerned.

Article 29

The imparting of general knowledge and skills that will help children belonging to the peoples concerned to participate fully and on an equal footing in their own community and in the national community shall be an aim of education for these peoples.

Article 30

1. Governments shall adopt measures appropriate to the traditions and cultures of the peoples concerned, to make known to them their rights and duties, especially in regard

to labour, economic opportunities, education and health matters, social welfare and their rights deriving from this Convention.

2. If necessary, this shall be done by means of written translations and through the use of mass communications in the languages of these peoples.

Article 31

Educational measures shall be taken among all sections of the national community, and particularly among those that are in most direct contact with the peoples concerned, with the object of eliminating prejudices that they may harbour in respect of these peoples. To this end, efforts shall be made to ensure that history textbooks and other educational materials provide a fair, accurate and informative portrayal of the societies and cultures of these peoples.

PART VII. CONTACTS AND CO-OPERATION ACROSS BORDERS

Article 32

Governments shall take appropriate measures, including by means of international agreements, to facilitate contacts and co-operation between indigenous and tribal peoples across borders, including activities in the economic, social, cultural, spiritual and environmental fields.

PART VIII. ADMINISTRATION

Article 33

1. The governmental authority responsible for the matters covered in this Convention shall ensure that agencies or other appropriate mechanisms exist to administer the programmes affecting the peoples concerned, and shall ensure that they have the means necessary for the proper fulfilment of the functions assigned to them.

2. These programmes shall include:

(a) The planning, coordination, execution and evaluation, in co-operation with the peoples concerned, of the measures provided for in this Convention;

(b) The proposing of legislative and other measures to the competent authorities and supervision of the application of the measures taken, in co-operation with the peoples concerned.

PART IX. GENERAL PROVISIONS

Article 34

The nature and scope of the measures to be taken to give effect to this Convention shall be determined in a flexible manner, having regard to the conditions characteristic of each country.

Article 35

The application of the provisions of this Convention shall not adversely affect rights and benefits of the peoples concerned pursuant to other Conventions and Recommendations, international instruments, treaties, or national laws, awards, custom or agreements.

PART X. FINAL PROVISIONS

Article 36

This Convention revises the Indigenous and Tribal Populations Convention, 1957.

Article 37

The formal ratifications of this Convention shall be communicated to the Director-General of the International Labour Office for registration.

Article 38

1. This Convention shall be binding only upon those Members of the International Labour Organization whose ratifications have been registered with the Director-General.

2. It shall come into force twelve months after the date on which the ratifications of two Members have been registered with the Director General.

3. Thereafter, this Convention shall come into force for any Member twelve months after the date on which its ratification has been registered.

Article 39

1. A Member which has ratified this Convention may denounce it after the expiration of ten years from the date on which the Convention first comes into force, by an act communicated to the Director-General of the International Labour Office for registration. Such denunciation shall not take effect until one year after the date on which it is registered.

2. Each Member which has ratified this Convention and which does not, within the year following the expiration of the period of ten years mentioned in the preceding paragraph, exercise the right of denunciation provided for in this Article, will be bound for another period of ten years and, thereafter, may denounce this Convention at the expiration of each period of ten years under the terms provided for in this Article.

Article 40

1. The Director-General of the International Labour Office shall notify all Members of the International Labour Organization of the registration of all ratifications and denunciations communicated to him by the Members of the Organization.

2. When notifying the Members of the Organization of the registration of the second ratification communicated to him, the Director-General shall draw the attention of the Members of the Organization to the date upon which the Convention will come into force.

Article 41

The Director-General of the International Labour Office shall communicate to the Secretary-General of the United Nations for registration in accordance with Article 102 of the Charter of the United Nations full particulars of all ratifications and acts of denunciation registered by him in accordance with the provisions of the preceding Articles.

Article 42

At such times as it may consider necessary the Governing Body of the International Labour Office shall present to the General Conference a report on the working of this Convention and shall examine the desirability of placing on the agenda of the Conference the question of its revision in whole or in part.

Article 43

1. Should the Conference adopt a new Convention revising this Convention in whole or in part, then, unless the new Convention otherwise provides:

(a) The ratification by a Member of the new revising Convention shall *ipso jure* involve the immediate denunciation of this Convention, notwithstanding the provisions of Article 39 above, if and when the new revising Convention shall have come into force:

(b) As from the date when the new revising Convention comes into force this Convention shall cease to be open to ratification by the Members.

2. This Convention shall in any case remain in force in its actual form and content for those Members which have ratified it but have not ratified the revising Convention.

Article 44

The English and French versions of the text of this Convention are equally authoritative.

Appendix VII

UN Convention on Biological Diversity, 1992

31 I.L.M 818

Preamble

The Contracting Parties,

Conscious of the intrinsic value of biological diversity and of the ecological, genetic, social, economic, scientific, educational, cultural, recreational and aesthetic values of biological diversity and its components,

Conscious also of the importance of biological diversity for evolution and for maintaining life sustaining systems of the biosphere,

Affirming that the conservation of biological diversity is a common concern of humankind,

Reaffirming that States have sovereign rights over their own biological resources,

Reaffirming also that States are responsible for conserving their biological diversity and for using their biological resources in a sustainable manner,

Concerned that biological diversity is being significantly reduced by certain human activities,

Aware of the general lack of information and knowledge regarding biological diversity and of the urgent need to develop scientific, technical and institutional capacities to provide the basic understanding upon which to plan and implement appropriate measures,

Noting that it is vital to anticipate, prevent and attack the causes of significant reduction or loss of biological diversity at source,

Noting also that where there is a threat of significant reduction or loss of biological diversity, lack of full scientific certainty should not be used as a reason for postponing measures to avoid or minimize such a threat,

Noting further that the fundamental requirement for the conservation of biological diversity is the *in-situ* conservation of ecosystems and natural habitats and the maintenance and recovery of viable populations of species in their natural surroundings,

Noting further that *ex-situ* measures, preferably in the country of origin, also have an important role to play,

Recognizing the close and traditional dependence of many indigenous and local communities embodying traditional lifestyles on biological resources, and the desirability of sharing equitably benefits arising from the use of traditional knowledge, innovations and practices relevant to the conservation of biological diversity and the sustainable use of its components,

Recognizing also the vital role that women play in the conservation and sustainable use of biological diversity and affirming the need for the full participation of women at all levels of policy-making and implementation for biological diversity conservation,

Stressing the importance of, and the need to promote, international, regional and global co-operation among States and intergovernmental organizations and the non-governmental sector for the conservation of biological diversity and the sustainable use of its components,

Acknowledging that the provision of new and additional financial resources and appropriate access to relevant technologies can be expected to make a substantial difference in the world's ability to address the loss of biological diversity,

Acknowledging further that special provision is required to meet the needs of developing countries, including the provision of new and additional financial resources and appropriate access to relevant technologies,

Noting in this regard the special conditions of the least developed countries and small island States,

Acknowledging that substantial investments are required to conserve biological diversity and that there is the expectation of a broad range of environmental, economic and social benefits from those investments,

Recognizing that economic and social development and poverty eradication are the first and overriding priorities of developing countries,

Aware that conservation and sustainable use of biological diversity is of critical importance for meeting the food, health and other needs of the growing world population, for which purpose access to and sharing of both genetic resources and technologies are essential,

Noting that, ultimately, the conservation and sustainable use of biological diversity will strengthen friendly relations among States and contribute to peace for humankind,

Desiring to enhance and complement existing international arrangements for the conservation of biological diversity and sustainable use of its components, and

Determined to conserve and sustainably use biological diversity for the benefit of present and future generations,

Have agreed as follows:

Article 1. Objectives

The objectives of this Convention, to be pursued in accordance with its relevant provisions, are the conservation of biological diversity, the sustainable use of its components and the fair and equitable sharing of the benefits arising out of the utilization of genetic resources, including by appropriate access to genetic resources and by appropriate transfer of relevant technologies, taking into account all rights over those resources and to technologies, and by appropriate funding.

[...]

Article 8. In-situ Conservation

Each Contracting Party shall, as far as possible and as appropriate:

(a) Establish a system of protected areas or areas where special measures need to be taken to conserve biological diversity;

(b) Develop, where necessary, guidelines for the selection, establishment and management of protected areas or areas where special measures need to be taken to conserve biological diversity;

[...]

(j) Subject to its national legislation, respect, preserve and maintain knowledge, innovations and practices of indigenous and local communities embodying traditional lifestyles relevant for the conservation and sustainable use of biological diversity and promote their wider application with the approval and involvement of the holders of such knowledge, innovations and practices and encourage the equitable sharing of the benefits arising from the utilization of such knowledge, innovations and practices;

[...]

(m) Co-operate in providing financial and other support for *in-situ* conservation outlined in subparagraphs (a) to (l) above, particularly to developing countries.

[...]

Article 10. Sustainable Use of Components of Biological Diversity

Each Contracting Party shall, as far as possible and as appropriate:

(a) Integrate consideration of the conservation and sustainable use of biological resources into national decision-making;

(b) Adopt measures relating to the use of biological resources to avoid or minimize adverse impacts on biological diversity;

(c) Protect and encourage customary use of biological resources in accordance with traditional cultural practices that are compatible with conservation or sustainable use requirements;

(d) Support local populations to develop and implement remedial action in degraded areas where biological diversity has been reduced; and

(e) Encourage co-operation between its governmental authorities and its private sector in developing methods for sustainable use of biological resources.

[...]

Article 16. Access to and Transfer of Technology

1. Each Contracting Party, recognizing that technology includes biotechnology, and that both access to and transfer of technology among Contracting Parties are essential elements for the attainment of the objectives of this Convention, undertakes subject to the provisions of this Article to provide and/or facilitate access for and transfer to other Contracting Parties of technologies that are relevant to the conservation and sustainable use of biological diversity or make use of genetic resources and do not cause significant damage to the environment.

[...]

Article 17. Exchange of Information

1. The Contracting Parties shall facilitate the exchange of information, from all publicly

available sources, relevant to the conservation and sustainable use of biological diversity, taking into account the special needs of developing countries.

2. Such exchange of information shall include exchange of results of technical, scientific and socio-economic research, as well as information on training and surveying programmes, specialized knowledge, indigenous and traditional knowledge as such and in combination with the technologies referred to in Article 16, paragraph 1. It shall also, where feasible, include repatriation of information.

Article 18. Technical and Scientific Co-operation

1. The Contracting Parties shall promote international technical and scientific co-operation in the field of conservation and sustainable use of biological diversity, where necessary, through the appropriate international and national institutions.

2. Each Contracting Party shall promote technical and scientific co-operation with other Contracting Parties, in particular developing countries, in implementing this Convention, *inter alia*, through the development and implementation of national policies. In promoting such co-operation, special attention should be given to the development and strengthening of national capabilities, by means of human resources development and institution building.

3. The Conference of the Parties, at its first meeting, shall determine how to establish a clearing-house mechanism to promote and facilitate technical and scientific co-operation.

4. The Contracting Parties shall, in accordance with national legislation and policies, encourage and develop methods of co-operation for the development and use of technologies, including indigenous and traditional technologies, in pursuance of the objectives of this Convention. For this purpose, the Contracting Parties shall also promote co-operation in the training of personnel and exchange of experts.

5. The Contracting Parties shall, subject to mutual agreement, promote the establishment of joint research programmes and joint ventures for the development of technologies relevant to the objectives of this Convention.

[...]

Agenda 21. UN Conference on Environment and Development

A/Conf/151/5/Rev.1 (1992), reprinted in 31 I.L.M 874 (1992)

ANNEX I: RIO DECLARATION ON THE ENVIRONMENT

Having met at Rio de Janeiro from 3 to 14 June 1992,

Reaffirming the Declaration of the United Nations Conference on the Human Environment, adopted at Stockholm on 16 June 1972, a/ and seeking to build upon it,

With the goal of establishing a new and equitable global partnership through the creation of new levels of co-operation among States, key sectors of societies and people,

Working towards international agreements which respect the interests of all and protect the integrity of the global environmental and developmental system,

Recognizing the integral and interdependent nature of the Earth, our home,

Proclaims that:

Principle 1

Human beings are at the centre of concerns for sustainable development. They are entitled to a healthy and productive life in harmony with nature.

Principle 2

States have, in accordance with the Charter of the United Nations and the principles of international law, the sovereign right to exploit their own resources pursuant to their own environmental and developmental policies, and the responsibility to ensure that activities within their jurisdiction or control do not cause damage to the environment of other States or of areas beyond the limits of national jurisdiction.

Principle 3

The right to development must be fulfilled so as to equitably meet developmental and environmental needs of present and future generations.

Principle 4

In order to achieve sustainable development, environmental protection shall constitute an integral part of the development process and cannot be considered in isolation from it.

Principle 5

All States and all people shall co-operate in the essential task of eradicating poverty as an indispensable requirement for sustainable development, in order to decrease the disparities in standards of living and better meet the needs of the majority of the people of the world.

Principle 6

The special situation and needs of developing countries, particularly the least developed and those most environmentally vulnerable, shall be given special priority. International actions in the field of environment and development should also address the interests and needs of all countries.

Principle 7

States shall co-operate in a spirit of global partnership to conserve, protect and restore the health and integrity of the Earth's ecosystem. In view of the different contributions to global environmental degradation, States have common but differentiated responsibilities. The developed countries acknowledge the responsibility that they bear in the international pursuit of sustainable development in view of the pressures their societies place on the global environment and of the technologies and financial resources they command.

Principle 8

To achieve sustainable development and a higher quality of life for all people, States should reduce and eliminate unsustainable patterns of production and consumption and promote appropriate demographic policies.

[...]

Principle 22

Indigenous people and their communities and other local communities have a vital role in environmental management and development because of their knowledge and traditional practices. States should recognize and duly support their identity, culture and interests and enable their effective participation in the achievement of sustainable development.

Principle 23

The environment and natural resources of people under oppression, domination and occupation shall be protected.

Principle 24

Warfare is inherently destructive of sustainable development. States shall therefore respect international law providing protection for the environment in times of armed conflict and co-operate in its further development, as necessary.

Principle 25

Peace, development and environmental protection are interdependent and indivisible.

Principle 26

States shall resolve all their environmental disputes peacefully and by appropriate means in accordance with the Charter of the United Nations.

Principle 27

States and people shall co-operate in good faith and in a spirit of partnership in the fulfilment of the principles embodied in this Declaration and in the further development of international law in the field of sustainable development.

ANNEX III: NON-LEGALLY BINDING AUTHORITATIVE STATEMENT OF PRINCIPLES FOR A GLOBAL CONSENSUS ON THE MANAGEMENT, CONSERVATION AND SUSTAINABLE DEVELOPMENT OF ALL TYPES OF FORESTS

Preamble

(a) The subject of forests is related to the entire range of environmental and development issues and opportunities, including the right to socio-economic development on a sustainable basis.

(b) The guiding objective of these principles is to contribute to the management, conservation and sustainable development of forests and to provide for their multiple and complementary functions and uses.

(c) Forestry issues and opportunities should be examined in a holistic and balanced manner within the overall context of environment and development, taking into consideration the multiple functions and uses of forests, including traditional uses, and the likely economic and social stress when these uses are constrained or restricted, as well as the potential for development that sustainable forest management can offer.

(d) These principles reflect a first global consensus on forests. In committing themselves to the prompt implementation of these principles, countries also decide to keep them under assessment for their adequacy with regard to further international co-operation on forest issues.

(e) These principles should apply to all types of forests, both natural and planted, in all geographical regions and climatic zones, including austral, boreal, subtemperate, temperate, subtropical and tropical.

(f) All types of forests embody complex and unique ecological processes which are the basis for their present and potential capacity to provide resources to satisfy human needs as well as environmental values, and as such their sound management and conservation is of concern to the Governments of the countries to which they belong and are of value to local communities and to the environment as a whole.

(g) Forests are essential to economic development and the maintenance of all forms of life.

(h) Recognizing that the responsibility for forest management, conservation and sustainable development is in many States allocated among federal/national, state/provincial and local levels of government, each State, in accordance with its constitution and/or national legislation, should pursue these principles at the appropriate level of government.

Principles/Elements

1. (a) States have, in accordance with the Charter of the United Nations and the principles of international law, the sovereign right to exploit their own resources pursuant to their own environmental policies and have the responsibility to ensure that activities within their jurisdiction or control do not cause damage to the environment of other States or of areas beyond the limits of national jurisdiction.

(b) The agreed full incremental cost of achieving benefits associated with forest conservation and sustainable development requires increased international co-operation and should be equitably shared by the international community.

2. (a) States have the sovereign and inalienable right to utilize, manage and develop their forests in accordance with their development needs and level of socio-economic development and on the basis of national policies consistent with sustainable development and legislation, including the conversion of such areas for other uses within the overall socio-economic development plan and based on rational land-use policies.

(b) Forest resources and forest lands should be sustainably managed to meet the social, economic, ecological, cultural and spiritual needs of present and future generations. These needs are for forest products and services, such as wood and wood products, water, food, fodder, medicine, fuel, shelter, employment, recreation, habitats for wildlife, landscape diversity, carbon sinks and reservoirs, and for other forest products. Appropriate measures should be taken to protect forests against harmful effects of pollution, including air-borne pollution, fires, pests and diseases, in order to maintain their full multiple value.

(c) The provision of timely, reliable and accurate information on forests and forest ecosystems is essential for public understanding and informed decision-making and should be ensured.

(d) Governments should promote and provide opportunities for the participation of interested parties, including local communities and indigenous people, industries, labour, non-governmental organizations and individuals, forest dwellers and women, in the development, implementation and planning of national forest policies.

[...]

4. The vital role of all types of forests in maintaining the ecological processes and balance at the local, national, regional and global levels through, *inter alia*, their role in protecting fragile ecosystems, watersheds and freshwater resources and as rich storehouses of biodiversity and biological resources and sources of genetic material for biotechnology products, as well as photosynthesis, should be recognized.

5. (a) National forest policies should recognize and duly support the identity, culture and the rights of indigenous people, their communities and other communities and forest dwellers. Appropriate conditions should be promoted for these groups to enable them to have an economic stake in forest use, perform economic activities, and achieve and maintain cultural identity and social organization, as well as adequate levels of livelihood and well-being, through, *inter alia*, those land tenure arrangements which serve as incentives for the sustainable management of forests.

(b) The full participation of women in all aspects of the management, conservation and sustainable development of forests should be actively promoted.

[...]

12. (a) Scientific research, forest inventories and assessments carried out by national institutions which take into account, where relevant, biological, physical, social and economic variables, as well as technological development and its application in the field of sustainable forest management, conservation and development, should be strengthened through effective modalities, including international co-operation. In this context, attention should also be given to research and development of sustainably harvested non-wood products.

(b) National and, where appropriate, regional and international institutional capabilities in education, training, science, technology, economics, anthropology and social aspects of forests and forest management are essential to the conservation and sustainable development of forests and should be strengthened.

(c) International exchange of information on the results of forest and forest management research and development should be enhanced and broadened, as appropriate, making full use of education and training institutions, including those in the private sector.

(d) Appropriate indigenous capacity and local knowledge regarding the conservation and sustainable development of forests should, through institutional and financial support and in collaboration with the people in the local communities concerned, be recognized, respected, recorded, developed and, as appropriate, introduced in the implementation of programmes. Benefits arising from the utilization of indigenous knowledge should therefore be equitably shared with such people.

Appendix VIII

UNESCO Declaration on Science and the Use of Scientific Knowledge

Text adopted by the World Conference on Science
1 July 1999. Definitive version (edited)

Preamble

1. We all live on the same planet and are part of the biosphere. We have come to recognize that we are in a situation of increasing interdependence, and that our future is intrinsically linked to the preservation of the global life-support systems and to the survival of all forms of life. The nations and the scientists of the world are called upon to acknowledge the urgency of using knowledge from all fields of science in a responsible manner to address human needs and aspirations without misusing this knowledge. We seek active collaboration across all the fields of scientific endeavour, that is the natural sciences such as the physical, earth and biological sciences, the biomedical and engineering sciences, and the social and human sciences. While the *Framework for Action* emphasizes the promise and the dynamism of the natural sciences but also their potential adverse effects, and the need to understand their impact on and relations with society, the commitment to science, as well as the challenges and the responsibilities set out in this Declaration, pertain to all fields of the sciences. All cultures can contribute scientific knowledge of universal value. The sciences should be at the service of humanity as a whole, and should contribute to providing everyone with a deeper understanding of nature and society, a better quality of life and a sustainable and healthy environment for present and future generations.

[...]

Considering:

[...]

8. that in the twenty-first century science must become a shared asset benefiting all peoples on a basis of solidarity, that science is a powerful resource for understanding natural and social phenomena, and that its role promises to be even greater in the future as the growing complexity of the relationship between society and the environment is better understood,

[...]

23. that the pursuit of science and the use of scientific knowledge should respect and maintain life in all its diversity, as well as the life-support systems of our planet,

24. that there is a historical imbalance in the participation of men and women in all science-related activities,

25. that there are barriers which have precluded the full participation of other groups, of both sexes, including disabled people, indigenous peoples and ethnic minorities, hereafter referred to as disadvantaged groups,

26. that traditional and local knowledge systems, as dynamic expressions of perceiving and understanding the world, can make, and historically have made, a valuable contribu-

tion to science and technology, and that there is a need to preserve, protect, research and promote this cultural heritage and empirical knowledge,

27. that a new relationship between science and society is necessary to cope with such pressing global problems as poverty, environmental degradation, inadequate public health, and food and water security, in particular those associated with population growth,

Proclaim the following:

[. . .]

31. The essence of scientific thinking is the ability to examine problems from different perspectives and seek explanations of natural and social phenomena, constantly submitted to critical analysis. Science thus relies on critical and free thinking, which is essential in a democratic world. The scientific community, sharing a long-standing tradition that transcends nations, religions and ethnicity, should promote, as stated in the Constitution of UNESCO, the "intellectual and moral solidarity of mankind," which is the basis of a culture of peace.

[. . .]

33. [. . .] Investment in science and technology aimed both at these objectives and at a better understanding and safeguarding of the planet's natural resource base, biodiversity and life-support systems must be increased. The objective should be a move towards sustainable development strategies through the integration of economic, social, cultural and environmental dimensions.

34. Science education, in the broad sense, without discrimination and encompassing all levels and modalities, is a fundamental prerequisite for democracy and for ensuring sustainable development. In recent years, worldwide measures have been undertaken to promote basic education for all. It is essential that the fundamental role played by women in the application of scientific development to food production and health care be fully recognized, and efforts made to strengthen their understanding of scientific advances in these areas. It is on this platform that science education, communication and popularization need to be built. Special attention still needs to be given to marginalized groups.

35. The building of scientific capacity should be supported by regional and international co-operation, to ensure both equitable development and the spread and utilization of human creativity without discrimination of any kind against countries, groups or individuals. Co-operation between developed and developing countries should be carried out in conformity with the principles of full and open access to information, equity and mutual benefit. In all efforts of co-operation, diversity of traditions and cultures should be given due consideration.

[. . .]

38. [. . .] There is also a need to further develop appropriate national legal frameworks to accommodate the specific requirements of developing countries and traditional knowledge and its sources and products, to ensure their recognition and adequate protection on the basis of the informed consent of the customary or traditional owners of this knowledge.

42. [. . .] The difficulties encountered by women, constituting over half of the world's population, in entering, pursuing and advancing in a career in the sciences and in partici-

pating in decision-making in science and technology should be addressed urgently. There is an equally urgent need to address the difficulties faced by disadvantaged groups which preclude their full and effective participation.

[. . .]

We, participants in the *World Conference on Science for the Twenty-first Century: A New Commitment*, commit ourselves to making every effort to promote dialogue between the scientific community and society, to remove all discrimination with respect to education for and the benefits of science, to act ethically and co-operatively within our own spheres of responsibility, to strengthen scientific culture and its peaceful application throughout the world, and to promote the use of scientific knowledge for the well-being of populations and for sustainable peace and development, taking into account the social and ethical principles illustrated above.

We consider that the Conference document *Science Agenda - Framework for Action* gives practical expression to a new commitment to science, and can serve as a strategic guide for partnership within the United Nations system and between all stakeholders in the scientific endeavour in the years to come.

We therefore adopt this *Declaration on Science and the Use of Scientific Knowledge* and agree upon the *Science Agenda - Framework for Action* as a means of achieving the goals set forth in the Declaration, and call upon UNESCO and ICSU to submit both documents to the General Conference of UNESCO and to the General Assembly of ICSU. The United Nations General Assembly will also be seized of these documents. The purpose is to enable both UNESCO and ICSU to identify and implement follow-up action in their respective programmes, and to mobilize the support of all partners, particularly those in the United Nations system, in order to reinforce international coordination and co-operation in science.

Appendix IX

Draft Principles and Guidelines for the Protection of the Heritage of Indigenous People

Commission on Human Rights, Economic and Social Council,
e/cn.4/sub.2/2000/26 19 June 2000

Principles

1. The effective protection of the heritage of the indigenous peoples of the world benefits all humanity. Its diversity is essential to the adaptability, sustainability and creativity of the human species as a whole.

2. To be effective, the protection of indigenous peoples' heritage should be based broadly on the principle of self-determination, which includes the right of indigenous peoples to maintain and develop their own cultures and knowledge systems, and forms of social organization.

3. Indigenous peoples should be the source, the guardians and the interpreters of their heritage, whether created in the past, or developed by them in the future.

4. Recognizing, respecting and valuing their customs, rules and practices for the transmission of their heritage to future generations is essential to indigenous peoples, their identity and dignity.

5. Indigenous peoples' ownership and custody of their heritage should be collective, permanent and inalienable, or as prescribed by the customs, rules and practices of each people.

6. The discovery, use and teaching of indigenous peoples' heritage is inextricably connected with the traditional lands and territories of each people. Control over traditional territories and resources is essential to the continued transmission of indigenous peoples' heritage to future generations, and its full protection.

7. To protect and preserve their heritage, indigenous peoples must control their own forms of cultural transmission and education. This includes their right to the continued use and, wherever applicable, the restoration of their own languages and orthographies.

8. To protect and preserve their heritage, indigenous peoples must also exercise control over all research conducted on their people and any aspect of their heritage within their territories.

9. The prior, free and informed consent of the owners should be an essential precondition of any agreements which may be made for the recording, study, display, access, and use, in any form whatsoever, of indigenous peoples' heritage.

10. Any agreements which may be made for the recording, study, use or display of indigenous peoples' heritage must ensure that the peoples concerned continue to be the principal beneficiaries of any use or application.

11. Nothing in this declaration may be construed as diminishing or extinguishing existing or future rights indigenous peoples may have or acquire under national or international law; neither may it be construed as violating universal standards of human rights.

Guidelines

Definitions

12. The heritage of indigenous peoples has a collective character and is comprised of all objects, sites and knowledge including languages, the nature or use of which has been transmitted from generation to generation, and which is regarded as pertaining to a particular people or its territory of traditional natural use. The heritage of indigenous peoples also includes objects, sites, knowledge and literary or artistic creation of that people which may be created or rediscovered in the future based upon their heritage.

13. The heritage of indigenous peoples includes all moveable cultural property as defined by the relevant conventions of UNESCO; all kinds of literary and artistic creation such as music, dance, song, ceremonies, symbols and designs, narratives and poetry and all forms of documentation of and by indigenous peoples; all kinds of scientific, agricultural, technical, medicinal, biodiversity-related and ecological knowledge, including innovations based upon that knowledge, cultigens, remedies, medicines and the use of flora and fauna; human remains; immoveable cultural property such as sacred sites of cultural, natural and historical significance and burials.

14. Every element of an indigenous peoples' heritage has owners, which may be the whole people, a particular family or clan, an association or community, or individuals, who have been specially taught or initiated to be such custodians. The owners of heritage must be determined in accordance with indigenous peoples' own customs, laws and practices.

Transmission of heritage

15. Indigenous peoples' heritage should continue to be transmitted, preferably through indigenous languages, and learned in the forms traditionally used and rules and practices for the culturally appropriate transmission of this heritage and dissemination of its use should be formally recognized and incorporated in the national legal system.

16. Governments, international organizations and private institutions should:

(a) support the development of educational, research, and training centres which are controlled by indigenous communities, and strengthen these communities' capacity to document, protect, teach, and apply all aspects of their heritage;

(b) ensure that the use of traditional languages in education, arts and the mass media is respected and, to the extent possible, promoted and strengthened;

(c) support the development of regional and global networks for the exchange of information and experience among indigenous peoples in the fields of science, culture, education and the arts, including support for systems of electronic information and multi-media communication;

(d) provide the necessary financial resources and institutional support to ensure that every indigenous child has the opportunity to know, develop and exercise the manifestation of his/her heritage, especially to achieve full fluency and literacy in his/her own language, as well as an official language.

Recovery and restitution of heritage

17. Governments, international organizations and private institutions should assist indigenous peoples and communities in recovering control and possession of their moveable cultural property and other heritage, including from across international borders, through adequate agreements and/or appropriate domestic governmental action including if necessary the creation of adequate institutions and mechanisms.

18. In co-operation with indigenous peoples, UNESCO should facilitate the mediation of the recovery of moveable cultural property from across international borders, at the request of the traditional owners of the property concerned.

19. Human remains and associated funerary objects and documentation must be returned to their descendants in a culturally appropriate manner, as determined by the indigenous peoples concerned. Documentation may be retained, or otherwise used only in such form and manner as may be agreed upon with the peoples concerned.

20. Moveable cultural property should be returned wherever possible to its traditional owners, particularly if shown to be of significant cultural, religious or historical value to them. Moveable cultural property should only be retained by universities, museums, private institutions or individuals in accordance with the terms of a recorded agreement with the traditional owners for the sharing of the custody and interpretation of the property.

21. Under no circumstances should human remains or any other sacred elements of an indigenous peoples' heritage be publicly displayed, except in a manner deemed appropriate by the peoples concerned.

22. In the case of objects or other elements of heritage which were removed or recorded in the past, the traditional owners of which can no longer be identified precisely, the traditional owners are presumed to be the indigenous people associated with the territory from which these objects were removed or recordings were made.

National legislation and programmes

23. National laws for the protection of indigenous peoples' heritage should:

(a) be adopted following consultations with the peoples concerned, in particular the traditional owners and teachers of religious, sacred and spiritual knowledge, and, wherever possible, should have the informed consent of the peoples concerned;

(b) guarantee that indigenous peoples can obtain prompt, effective and affordable judicial or administrative action in their own languages to prevent, punish and obtain full restitution and just compensation for the acquisition, documentation or use of their heritage without proper authorization of the traditional owners;

(c) deny to any person or corporation the right to obtain patent, copyright or other legal protection for any element of indigenous peoples' heritage without adequate documentation of the free and informed consent of the traditional owners to an arrangement for the sharing of ownership, control, use and benefits;

(d) ensure the labelling, correct attribution and legal protection of indigenous peoples' artistic, literary and cultural works whenever they are offered for public display or sale.

24. In the event of a dispute over the custody or use of any element of an indigenous peoples' heritage, judicial and administrative bodies should be guided by the advice of indigenous elders who are recognized by the indigenous communities or peoples concerned as having specific knowledge of traditional laws.

25. Governments should take immediate steps, in co-operation with the indigenous peoples concerned, to identify sacred and ceremonial sites, including burials, healing places, and traditional places of teaching, and to protect them from unauthorized entry, use, destruction or deterioration.

Researchers and scholarly institutions

26. Any person, organization or group of organizations whatsoever legal or factual form, aim or activity (profit/non-profit; public/private; local/national/regional or international) must refrain from any act, whatsoever its nature, having as its purpose or effect the use or exploitation of any part of indigenous peoples' heritage whatsoever the means or forms given to this act.

27. All researchers and scholarly institutions within their competences should take steps to provide indigenous peoples and communities with comprehensive inventories of the cultural property, and documentation of indigenous peoples' heritage, which they may have in their custody.

28. Researchers and scholarly institutions should return all elements of indigenous peoples' heritage to the traditional owners upon demand, or obtain formal agreements with the traditional owners for the shared custody, use and interpretation of their heritage.

29. Researchers and scholarly institutions should decline any offers for the donation or sale of elements of indigenous peoples' heritage, without first contacting the peoples or communities directly concerned and ascertaining the wishes of the traditional owners.

30. Researchers and scholarly institutions must refrain from engaging in any study of previously undescribed species or cultivated varieties of plants, animals or micro-organisms, or naturally occurring pharmaceuticals, without first obtaining satisfactory documentation that the specimens were acquired with the consent of the traditional owners.

31. Researchers must not publish information obtained from indigenous peoples or the results of research conducted on flora, fauna, microbes or materials discovered through the assistance of indigenous peoples, without identifying the traditional owners and obtaining their consent to citation or publication and provide compensation when a commercial benefit is generated from such information.

32. No research or research application concerning the human genome should prevail over respect for the human rights, fundamental freedoms and human dignity of indigenous individuals and peoples.

33. Researchers and scholarly institutions should make every possible effort to increase indigenous peoples' access to all forms of medical, scientific and technical education, and participation in all research activities which may affect them or be of benefit to them.

34. Professional associations of scientists, engineers and scholars, in collaboration with indigenous peoples, should sponsor seminars and widely disseminate publications to promote ethical conduct in conformity with these guidelines and discipline members who act in contravention.

Business and industry

35. In dealings with indigenous peoples, business and industry should respect the same guidelines as researchers and scholarly institutions.

36. Business and industry should ensure they have a prior, free and informed consent of indigenous peoples when entering into agreements for the rights to discover, record and use previously undescribed species or cultivated varieties of plants, animals or micro-organisms, or naturally occurring pharmaceuticals. Any agreement should ensure that the indigenous peoples concerned continue to be primary beneficiaries of commercial application.

37. Business and industry should refrain from offering incentives to any individuals to claim traditional rights of ownership or leadership within an indigenous community, in violation of their trust within the community and the customs and laws of the indigenous peoples concerned.

38. Business and industry should refrain from employing anyone to acquire and record traditional knowledge or other heritage of indigenous peoples in violation of these guidelines.

39. Business and industry should contribute financially and otherwise to the development of educational and research institutions controlled by indigenous peoples and communities.

40. All forms of tourism based on indigenous peoples' heritage must be restricted to activities which have the formal approval of the peoples and communities concerned, and which are conducted under their supervision and control.

Artists, writers and performers

41. Artists, writers and performers should refrain from incorporating elements of indigenous heritage, particularly those of a sacred character, into their works without the prior, free and informed consent of the traditional owners.

42. Artists, writers and performers should support the full artistic and cultural development of indigenous peoples, and encourage public support for the development and greater recognition of indigenous artists, writers and performers.

43. Artists, writers and performers should contribute, through their individual works and professional organizations, to the greater public understanding and respect for the indigenous heritage associated with the country in which they live as well as with the international community as a whole.

Public information and education

44. The media in all countries should take effective measures to promote understanding of and respect for indigenous peoples' heritage, in particular through special broadcasts and public-service programmes prepared in collaboration with indigenous peoples.

45. The media should respect the privacy of indigenous peoples, in particular concerning traditional religious, cultural and ceremonial activities, and refrain from exploiting or sensationalizing indigenous peoples' heritage.

46. The media should actively assist indigenous peoples in exposing any activities, public or private, which destroy or degrade indigenous peoples' heritage.

47. Governments must ensure that school curricula and textbooks teach understanding and respect for indigenous peoples' heritage and history and recognize the contribution of indigenous peoples to creativity and cultural diversity.

International organizations

48. The Secretary-General and the governing bodies of the competent specialized agencies should ensure that the task of coordinating international co-operation in this field is entrusted to appropriate organs and specialized agencies of the United Nations, with adequate means of implementation.

49. In co-operation with indigenous peoples, the United Nations should bring these principles and guidelines to the attention of all Member States through, *inter alia*, international, regional and national seminars and publications, with a view to promoting the strengthening of national legislation and international conventions in this field.

50. The United Nations should publish and circulate to all parties concerned (Governments, international organizations, indigenous peoples and non-governmental organizations) a comprehensive annual report, based upon information from all available sources, including indigenous peoples themselves, on the problems experienced and solutions adopted in the protection of indigenous peoples' heritage in all countries.

51. Indigenous peoples and their representative organizations should enjoy direct access to, and participate in, all intergovernmental discussions and negotiations in the field of intellectual property rights, to share their views on the measures needed to protect their heritage through international law.

52. In collaboration with indigenous peoples and Governments concerned, the United Nations should develop a confidential list of sacred and ceremonial sites that require special measures for their protection and conservation, and provide financial and technical assistance to indigenous peoples for these purposes.

53. In collaboration with indigenous peoples and Governments concerned, the United Nations should establish a trust fund with a mandate to act as a global agent for the recovery of compensation for the unconsented or inappropriate use of indigenous peoples' heritage, and to assist indigenous peoples in developing the institutional capacity to defend their own heritage.

54. United Nations operational agencies, as well as the international financial institutions and regional and bilateral development assistance programmes, should give priority to providing financial and technical support to indigenous communities for capacity-building and exchanges of experience focused on local control of research and education.

55. The United Nations should consider as a matter of urgent priority the drafting of a convention for the protection of the heritage of indigenous peoples.

Appendix X

World Conference Against Racism, Racial Discrimination, Xenophobia and Related Intolerance, Programme of Action

Agenda item 9, adopted 8 Sept. 2001 in Durban, South Africa
UN Doc. A/Conf.189/5 (2001) (edited).

I. Sources, Causes, Forms and Contemporary Manifestations of Racism, Racial Discrimination, Xenophobia and Related Intolerance

Recognizing the urgent need to translate the objectives of the Declaration into a practical and workable Programme of Action, the World Conference against Racism, Racial Discrimination, Xenophobia and Related Intolerance:

1. *Urge*s States in their national efforts, and in co-operation with other States, regional and international organizations and financial institutions, to promote the use of public and private investment in consultation with the affected communities in order to eradicate poverty, particularly in those areas in which victims of racism, racial discrimination, xenophobia and related intolerance predominantly live;

[...]

Indigenous peoples

15. *Urges* States:

(a) To adopt or continue to apply, in concert with them, constitutional, administrative, legislative, judicial and all necessary measures to promote, protect and ensure the enjoyment by indigenous peoples of their rights, as well as to guarantee them the exercise of their human rights and fundamental freedoms on the basis of equality, non-discrimination and full and free participation in all areas of society, in particular in matters affecting or concerning their interests;

(b) To promote better knowledge of and respect for indigenous cultures and heritage; and welcomes measures already taken by States in these respects;

16. *Urges* States to work with indigenous peoples to stimulate their access to economic activities and increase their level of employment, where appropriate, through the establishment, acquisition or expansion by indigenous peoples of enterprises, and the implementation of measures such as training, the provision of technical assistance and credit facilities;

17. *Urges* States to work with indigenous peoples to establish and implement programmes that provide access to training and services that could benefit the development of their communities;

18. *Requests* States to adopt public policies and give impetus to programmes on behalf of and in concert with indigenous women and girls, with a view to promoting their civil, political, economic, social and cultural rights; to putting an end to their situation of disadvantage for reasons of gender and ethnicity; to dealing with urgent problems affecting them in regard to education, their physical and mental health, economic life and in the matter of violence against them, including domestic violence; and to eliminating the situation of

aggravated discrimination suffered by indigenous women and girls on multiple grounds of racism and gender discrimination;

19. *Recommends* that States examine, in conformity with relevant international human rights instruments, norms and standards, their Constitutions, laws, legal systems and policies in order to identify and eradicate racism, racial discrimination, xenophobia and related intolerance towards indigenous peoples and individuals, whether implicit, explicit or inherent;

20. *Calls upon* concerned States to honour and respect their treaties and agreements with indigenous peoples and to accord them due recognition and observance;

21. *Calls upon* States to give full and appropriate consideration to the recommendations produced by indigenous peoples in their own forums on the World Conference;

22. *Requests* States:

(a) To develop and, where they already exist, support institutional mechanisms to promote the accomplishment of the objectives and measures relating to indigenous peoples agreed in this Plan of Action;

(b) To promote in concert with indigenous organizations, local authorities and non-governmental organizations, actions aimed at overcoming racism, racial discrimination, xenophobia and related intolerance against indigenous peoples and to make regular assessments of the progress achieved in this regard;

(c) To promote understanding among society at large of the importance of special measures to overcome disadvantages faced by indigenous peoples;

(d) To consult indigenous representatives in the process of decision-making concerning policies and measures that directly affect them;

23. *Calls upon* States to recognize the particular challenges faced by indigenous peoples and individuals living in urban environments and urges States to implement effective strategies to combat the racism, racial discrimination, xenophobia and related intolerance they encounter, paying particular attention to opportunities for their continued practice of their traditional, cultural, linguistic and spiritual ways of life;

[...]

50. *Urges* States to incorporate a gender perspective in all programmes of action against racism, racial discrimination, xenophobia and related intolerance and to consider the burden of such discrimination which falls particularly on indigenous women, African women, Asian women, women of African descent, women of Asian descent, women migrants and women from other disadvantaged groups, ensuring their access to the resources of production on an equal footing with men, as a means of promoting their participation in the economic and productive development of their communities;

[...]

118. *Urges* States, where appropriate working with other relevant bodies, to commit financial resources to anti-racism education and to media campaigns promoting the values of acceptance, tolerance, diversity and respect for the cultures of all indigenous peoples living

within their national borders. In particular, States should promote an accurate understanding of the histories and cultures of indigenous peoples;

[...]

125. *Urges* States to adopt and implement laws that prohibit discrimination on the basis of race, colour, descent or national or ethnic origin at all levels of education; remove barriers and ensure equal access to quality education that maximizes opportunities for employment in today's job markets; establish and implement methods to measure and track improvement in disadvantaged youths' education performance; support efforts to ensure safe school environments free from violence and free of harassment on the basis of race, colour, descent or national or ethnic origin; and establish financial assistance programmes designed to enable students, regardless of race, colour, descent or ethnic or national origin, to attend institutions of higher education;

[...]

130. *Urges* States, where appropriate working with other relevant bodies, to commit financial resources to anti-racism education and to media campaigns promoting the values of acceptance, tolerance, diversity and respect for the cultures of all indigenous peoples living within their borders. In particular, States should promote an accurate understanding of the histories and cultures of indigenous peoples;

131. *Urges* States, if appropriate in co-operation with relevant organization including youth organizations, to support and implement public formal and non-formal education programmes designed to promote respect for cultural diversity;

[...]

V. Strategies to Achieve Full and Effective Equality, Including International Co-operation and Enhancement of the United Nations and other International Mechanisms in Combating Racism, Racial Discrimination, Xenophobia and Related Intolerance and Follow-Up

[...]

Indigenous peoples

203. *Recommends* that the United Nations Secretary-General conduct an evaluation of the results of the International Decade of the World's Indigenous People (1995-2004) and make recommendations concerning how to mark the end of this Decade, including an appropriate follow-up;

204. *Requests* States to ensure adequate funding for the establishment of an operational framework and a firm basis for the future development of the Permanent Forum on Indigenous Issues within the United Nations system;

205. *Urges* States to co-operate with the work of the Special Rapporteur on the situation of human rights and fundamental freedoms of indigenous people and requests the Secretary-General and the High Commissioner for Human Rights to ensure that the Special Rapporteur is provided with all the necessary human, technical and financial resources to fulfil his/her responsibilities;

206. *Calls* upon States to conclude negotiations on and approve as soon as possible the text of the draft declaration on the rights of indigenous peoples, under discussion by the working group of the Commission on Human Rights to elaborate a draft declaration, in accordance with Commission resolution 1995/32;

207. *Urges* States, in the light of the relationship between racism, racial discrimination, xenophobia and related intolerance and poverty, marginality and social exclusion of peoples and individuals at both the national and international levels, to enhance their policies and measures to reduce income and wealth inequalities and to take appropriate steps, individually and through international co-operation, to promote and protect economic, social and cultural rights on a non-discriminatory basis;

208. *Urges* States and international financial and development institutions to mitigate any negative effects of globalization by examining *inter alia* how their policies and practices affect national populations in general and indigenous peoples in particular; by ensuring that their policies and practices contribute to the eradication of racism through the participation of national populations and, in particular, indigenous peoples in development projects; by further democratizing international financial institutions; and by consulting with indigenous peoples on any matter that may affect their physical, spiritual or cultural integrity;

209. *Invites* financial and development institutions and the operational programmes and specialized agencies of the United Nations, in accordance with their regular budgets and the procedures of their governing bodies:

(a) To assign particular priority to and allocate sufficient funding, within their areas of competence, to the improvement of the status of indigenous peoples, with special attention to the needs of these populations in developing countries, including the preparation of specific programmes with a view to achieving the objectives of the International Decade of the World's Indigenous People;

(b) To carry out special projects, through appropriate channels and in collaboration with indigenous peoples, to support their initiatives at the community level and to facilitate the exchange of information and technical know how between indigenous peoples and experts in these areas.

[...]

Index

E

F

G

H

I

J

L

M

V

W

James (Sa'ke'j) Youngblood Henderson, a member of the Chickasaw Nation, is an internationally recognized authority in Indigenous knowledge, heritage, and jurisprudence, constitutional rights, and human rights. He is Research Director at the Native Law Centre of Canada and teaches Aboriginal law at the University of Saskatchewan. He is the author of *Mi'kmaq Concordat*, *Aboriginal Tenure in the Constitution of Canada*, *First Nation Jurisprudences and Aboriginal Rights*, *Treaty Rights in the Constitution of Canada*, and *Protecting Indigenous Knowledge and Heritage*, and has contributed to many other books and journals. He was one of the strategists who created the Indigenous diplomacy network, working through the Four Directions Council, a Non-Governmental Organization (NGO) in the UN system, and and he was a member of the team that drafted many of the critical documents, including the ILO *Convention Concerning Indigenous and Tribal Peoples in Independent Countries* (1991), *Guidelines and Principles for the Protection of Indigenous Heritage* (1994-2001), and the UN *Declaration on the Rights of Indigenous Peoples* (2007). He has been an advisor to the Minister of Foreign Affairs and International Trade (1997-2003) and the UNESCO *Convention of Cultural Diversity*. Since 2000, he has been a member of the Canadian Commission to UNESCO. In 2005 he was named Indigenous Peoples' Counsel in recognition of his achievements. He has also received the National Aboriginal Achievement Award for Law and Justice (2006) and an Honorary Doctorate of Laws, Carlton University (2007).